Big Mama Thornton

D1453778

Big Mama Thornton

The Life and Music

MICHAEL SPÖRKE

McFarland & Company, Inc., Publishers

Jefferson, North Carolina

LIBRARY OF CONGRESS CATALOGUING-IN-PUBLICATION DATA

Spörke, Michael.
    Big Mama Thornton : the life and music / Michael Spörke.
        p.   cm.
    Includes bibliographical references and index.

    ISBN 978-0-7864-7759-3 (softcover : acid free paper) ∞
    ISBN 978-1-4766-1422-9 (ebook)

    1. Thornton, Big Mama.   2. Blues musicians—
United States—Biography.   3. Singers—United States—
Biography.   I. Title.
    ML420.T467S66 2014
    782.421643092—dc23
    [B]   2014026224

BRITISH LIBRARY CATALOGUING DATA ARE AVAILABLE

© 2014 Michael Spörke. All rights reserved

*No part of this book may be reproduced or transmitted in any form
or by any means, electronic or mechanical, including photocopying
or recording, or by any information storage and retrieval system,
without permission in writing from the publisher.*

On the cover: Publicity photograph of Willie Mae "Big Mama"
Thornton (courtesy of the Billy Vera Collection)

Printed in the United States of America

McFarland & Company, Inc., Publishers
    Box 611, Jefferson, North Carolina 28640
        www.mcfarlandpub.com

For my friends from Big Brother & the Holding Company
whose cover of "Ball and Chain"
made me aware of Big Mama Thornton.

For all the great people who helped me in the writing of this book.

For my wife Nele.

Table of Contents

Acknowledgments

I discovered Willie Mae "Big Mama" Thornton in the same way as many other music lovers: through her song "Ball and Chain" as sung by Janis Joplin with Big Brother & the Holding Company. At that time I was writing the biography of Big Brother & the Holding Company, *Living with the Myth of Janis Joplin*. Janis Joplin's admiration for Big Mama Thornton made me curious about the woman and her music. I started to research the rich universe of the blues and followed the paths of Big Mama Thornton from the mid–twenties to the mid–eighties.

The search for witnesses, especially from the early years of Big Mama Thornton's life, proved to be very difficult. The research for this book was sometimes a race against time. Some of the people who I had the great luck to talk with over the years have since died. Those interviews remain a great treasure in my heart, whether it was with the almost hundred-years-old Big Walter Price talking about his childhood working in the fields, or Ron Thompson spontaneously starting to sing a piece of "Ball and Chain" in the middle of our talk, or the great Jimmy McCracklin looking back with me to his earlier years. I feel blessed, and I'm very grateful that I was able to interview so many companions of Big Mama Thornton. I wish to thank the following friends, colleagues and fans of Big Mama Thornton for their willingness to give me interviews, to share important documents, or to otherwise assist me in my research: Gordon Adamson, Mary Katherine Aldin, Peter Albin, Queen E. Ali, Sam Andrew, Peter Andrews, James Anthony, Mac Arnold, Lee Ashford, Pamela Banks, Wilbur Bascomb, Roy Book Binder, Ed Bland, Debbie Bond, Jeneve R. Brooks, Bobby Brown, Texas Johnny Brown, Tommy Brown, Toney Burkhart, Dave Camp, Ed Cassidy, Richard Chalk, Jeannie Cheatham, Raoul J. Cita, Al Copley, James Cotton, Linette and Jimmy McCracklin, Sailor Chris, Chas McDevitt, Steve Ditzell, Nat Dove, Billy Dunn, Michael Erlewine, Merell Fankhauser, Kim Field, Bob

Acknowledgments

Finch, Graidy Gaines, Peter Gallagher, Garry George, Anthony Geraci, Nelson Giles, Earl Gilliam, Terry Gould, I.J. Gosey, Beverly Robin Green, James Gurley, Chet Helms, David Hoerl, John Lee Hooker, Jr., Milton Hopkins, Chris Huston, Bruce Iglauer, Nathaniel William Johnson, Lloyd Jones, Julius Karpen, Lanny Kasner, Doug McKechnie, John Kilgore, Plume Latraverse, Donal Leace, Eric S. LeBlanc, Don Lee, Paul Lenart, Douglas MacLeod, Mark Lessman, Michael Liberty, Robert Lowery, Peter Malick, Tom Mazzolini, Sandy Morris, Jim Moore, Scotty Moore, Charlie Musselwhite, Lil' Ray Neal, Dan Papaila, Bernie Pearl, Carroll Peery, Ben "King" Perkoff, Michael Pickett, Big Walter Price, Tom Principato, Fritz Rau, Jan van Raay, Robert Ross, J.B. Ross, Terry "Big T" DeRouen, Audrey Anne Rouley, Jay Russio, Phoebe Schneble, Wendy Schumer, Jeannie and Jimmy Scott, Bill Sheffield, Michael Shurtz, Karen Mroczkowski-Del Signore, Eddie Stout, Ronnie Stewart, Chris Strachwitz, Robert Taylor, Ron Thompson, Virgil Thrasher, Teeny Tucker, Christine Valenza, Dave Walker, Derrick "Big" Walker, Michael "Mudcat" Ward, Paul Winer, Karen Wilborn, Steve Wise, Roger Wood, Gilman Young, Perry Yeldham, and Carlos Zialcita.

I'm also very grateful for all the help from the following photographers and archivists who have made their photographs and collections available for this book: David G. Berger for the Milton J. Hinton Photographic Collection, Willa Davis, Mush Emmons, Jonathan Ezekiel, John "Hoppy" Hopkins, the Jazzland Archives Vienna, Plume Latraverse, Paul Lenart, Gerhard Lenz, Erik Lindahl, Roberto Polillo, Tom Principato, Jan van Raay, Lawrence Robbins, Terry "Big T" DeRouen, Big Mama Thornton Family Estate, Jon Sievert, Billy Vera, and Val Wilmer.

Last but not least I'm very grateful for the help of Sam Andrew of Big Brother & the Holding Company editing this English-language version of the manuscript. As his band always gave credit to Big Mama Thornton for writing "Ball and Chain," I find this to be another great way to honor her. So thank you very much, Sam!

Preface

"You ain't nothing but a Hound Dog." With these words, shouted into the microphone, she will always be remembered: Willie Mae Thornton, better known as Big Mama Thornton. Her story exemplifies the life and work of many blues musicians and is characterized by the ups and downs of an artist's career.

She was a performer from the heart or, as the legendary Jimmy McCracklin told me, she was "one hell of an entertainer."[1] But what's most commonly told about her are countless rumors about her life and stories about her being a difficult person. One of those rumors has become a common assumption of writers when it comes to Big Mama Thornton: It's said that she was a lesbian. This rumor was one of the first things that many people told me when I interviewed them about Big Mama Thornton, but I was unable to locate any material documenting this rumor. Other rumors say that she shot a man and that she danced naked at one point in her life to make a living. Nothing of this is true, but it fits perfectly with a picture of a cranky, heavy drinking, unpredictable, somehow dangerous and difficult person, which is how she was often described in her lifetime and how she is still described today in liner notes and other sources. These descriptions, in my opinion, are rooted mainly "in men's discomfort with an assertive black woman, present an image that has been incorporated into the historical record."[2] But the rumors and unilateral descriptions don't tell the whole truth about Big Mama Thornton.

Big Mama Thornton definitely was a strong personality. "I always had self-respect. I was responsible for looking after myself because I was on my own. And I always held my head high," she said.[3] And it was without a doubt necessary to be strong in order to survive in the harsh winds of the music business. Big Mama Thornton, in her best years, was so strong that she sometimes picked up a large standing stage microphone in one hand, singing through the microphone while holding the stand airborne and pointing its large iron bottom at the audience. But she was by no means the hardcore woman that many want to see in her. Sure, her masculine, sometimes intimidating appearance and her alcohol addiction are important aspects of her personal history. But behind this sometimes rough exterior was a very sensitive and humorous woman. Big Mama Thornton herself said that many people were just drawing a picture of her as rude and dangerous because they were jealous about a woman who is successful in show business:

> They lied on me, said I would "fight the promoters." I never did fight the promoters. All I ever did was ask them for my money. Pay me and there won't be no hard feelings. They always have been jealous of me because when I hit that stage, I perform. I give you entertainment. I don't go out on stage trying to look pretty. I was born pretty. Just get out there and perform. I get out there and crack a few jokes and sing my song and people love it. That's why they were jealous of me, because the people were giving me recognition and they didn't get the recognition I had, because I was unique.[4]

For the people who really did know her, Big Mama Thornton was above all "a wonderfully sensitive and caring singer and she had a heart of gold," as Chris Strachwitz described her.[5]

Though Big Mama Thornton's early career was still circumscribed by the narrow parameters of performing and recording African American music for an African American audience, she managed to get a wider audience over the years in her home country and in Europe. Big Mama Thornton was celebrated by adoring fans on tours through Europe and was one of the stars of the American blues revival. Too often she had to make do with low-paying club performances. But whenever she seemed about to fall into oblivion, she started again, and proved her uniqueness. Without much education, but with an insatiable love for music, she managed to grow from the poor girl from Alabama to the esteemed, world-renowned artist. She lived, as her fellow musician Nat Dove put it, the way she wanted to.

Big Mama Thornton never became a big star and did not leave a large repertoire as Muddy Waters or Howlin' Wolf did. But her influence on other musicians is still tremendous. She sang the megahit "Hound Dog" before the major record labels began to copy or cover successful R&B songs for the predominantly white pop market and Elvis Presley made a worldwide hit with the song. And Big Mama Thornton wrote "Ball and Chain," the song that catapulted Janis Joplin with Big Brother & the Holding Company at the Monterey Pop Festival to sudden fame. "The cross-racial exchanges that Big Mama Thornton and others had been involved in during the 1950s and 1960s made this integrated blues-rock scene and sound possible. By the early 1970s young white fans and musicians played and identified with the blues that Thornton and the other blues revival musicians had taught them," Maureen Mahon points out correctly.[6]

Big Mama Thornton could sing in the energetic style of a great blues vocalist, or, as she said herself, "I can sing louder than any mike … and I don't want no mike louder than me!"[7] She could also perform heart-wrenching ballads. With her vocal range and her multi-instrumental skills, she is one of the greatest blues musicians ever, or, as legendary rhythm and blues guitarist and master keyboardist Ron Thompson puts it: "She was certainly a big person. She was somebody that you knew was in the room, when she was there. She was a very good person, but she was no joke. She was one of the originals. She is in that group of people I believe like Muddy Waters, Howlin' Wolf, Lightnin' Hopkins and then Big Mama Thornton, you know. She could sing her ass off. It was intense what she was doing. She was like the real deal."[8]

Considering all of this, I was deeply astonished that no comprehensive biography of Big Mama Thornton existed until today. The present work fills that void.

The book traces the path of a young priest's daughter, Willie Mae Thornton from Alabama, as she became Big Mama Thornton and rose to a place in the pantheon on the blues Olympus. The story begins with her first musical attempts and her first engagement in the Atlanta-based Hot Harlem Revue as a young girl of fourteen. Next follows her journey to the Mecca of Texas Blues, Houston. We dive into the world of dance clubs and the Chitlin' Circuit with Gatemouth Brown, B.B. King, Junior Parker, Johnny Ace, and Johnny Otis, as well as the story of Big Mama Thornton's biggest hit, "Hound Dog."

Following the slowdown of the blues music industry in the early sixties Big Mama Thornton next made her way to California, she struggled to survive; she then celebrated a grandiose musical comeback after an acclaimed European tour. In the course of the blues revival and the hippie movement, Big Mama Thornton met Janis Joplin and Big Brother & the Holding Company, whose cover of "Ball and Chain" popularized Big Mama Thornton with a new, young white audience.

With the end of the sixties, Big Mama Thornton again proved her perseverance. Despite the declining interest in the old-school blues, she still found herself to be a sought-after performer in the U.S. and in Europe. And even if her hard way of life and her excessive alcohol abuse took its toll, Big Mama Thornton performed and recorded until her untimely death.

While there are dozens of books about Elvis Presley and Janis Joplin, this book is an attempt to tell Big Mama Thornton's story for the first time. It's a tribute to the more than four-decades career of a remarkable, self-confident, dominant, sensitive and highly musical personality. I hope that readers will enjoy this book and will turn on their record and CD players to listen to Big Mama Thornton's music.

1

The Early Years of Willie Mae "Big Mama" Thornton

In American society before 1920, blues and jazz were only recorded by white musicians. Black people were, with very few exceptions, prevented from recording because of racism. By 1920, black musicians such as Mamie Smith, Ethel Waters and others could finally start to record their own music. Mamie Smith's song "Crazy Blues" of 1920 was the first successful recording from a black blues singer. In 1923, Bessie Smith, probably the most famous blues belter at that time, received her first recording contract and began her short but very successful recording career. She recorded about 160 discs until 1931, when Columbia Records did not extend her contract. "The Empress of the Blues" died tragically in 1933.

The American society at this time was characterized by economic recession, domestic unrest, prejudice against immigrants from Southern Europe, hatred for Communists and an increase in racism. The Ku Klux Klan was particularly strong in this period. In the Midwest and Southeast, for example, the KKK had millions of members. Only a year before a new electrical recording technology was introduced and Blind Lemon Jefferson, who would become the dominant blues figure of the late 1920s and the first star of the folk blues, would make his first recordings, a black girl was born into this troubled time in Ariton, a small town in Dale County near Montgomery, Alabama, on December 11, 1926. The girl was named Binnie Willie Mae Thornton. Most sources say that she was born in Montgomery, but her certificate of birth clearly lists Ariton as her birthplace. She might have later named Montgomery as her birthplace because it would have been more recognizable to people outside of Alabama than Ariton.[1] Alabama was a land of large cotton plantations. Montgomery itself became famous as the first capital of the Confederacy, and although the first battle of the Civil War was at Fort Sumter in South Carolina, Montgomery was the seat of Jefferson Davis, president of the Southern States.

Willie Mae grew up as a daughter of George W. Thornton, 51, a Baptist minister, and his wife Mattie Haynes, 32, who was a housewife. When she was born, Willie Mae had five siblings, three brothers, Judge, 3, C. W., 7, and George W. Jr., 9, and two sisters, Gussie, 14, and Roxie, 16.[2] Two years after Willie Mae Thornton was born her parents gave birth to another child, a boy called E.W., who died directly after his birth. By the time Willie Mae was four years old, her family moved to Troy City, Pike County, Alabama. Their mother sang Christian songs with passion in the church choir. "We went to church a lot and I sang there sometimes but not especially often," said Willie Mae Thornton about her childhood.[3]

Very early she developed a feature that would later earn her the famous nickname "Big Mama," but only earned her mockery and spite from her classmates in those days: she was very tall. Willie Mae went to a one-room schoolhouse together with her half-sister Mattie Fields. Mattie and Willie Mae had the same father but grew up in separate households. The kids teased and tormented Willie Mae and pulled her long black hair. Willie Mae hunched over and tried to be as small as the other kids, but with no success. Her half-sister needed to defend her against the classmates. Besides those normal childhood problems, the times were hard when Willie Mae was young. The Wall Street Crash on so-called Black Thursday, October 24, 1929, signaled the beginning of the Great Depression in the United States. Amid widespread economic ruin, the hard life of black America became even worse.

Willie Mae's mother was very sick and so the young girl had to take care of her and couldn't go to school on a regular basis. But she found very early her musical destiny. She taught herself how to play the harmonica when she was just eight years old by watching her older brother Calliope or C.W. Thornton, later known as "Harp" Thornton. Not that her brother would have taught her to play the harmonica; she had to use the old harmonicas he threw in the trash.

In 1939, Willie Mae, now thirteen years old, was only in third grade when her mother died in a Montgomery sanatorium of tuberculosis, and now Willie Mae had to find a job to support her family. She left school and never really learned how to read and write. Willie Mae moved in the house of relatives in Barbour County Alabama, and found herself a job washing and cleaning spittoons in the local tavern. One night the tavern's regular vocalist got drunk so Willie Mae convinced the tavern owner that she could do the job. She never looked back after that.

Willie Mae Thornton recalls those first steps into the music business in an interview with Ralph Gleason: "I like my own old down home singing, with the feeling. I learned to sing blues by myself. The first blues I ever heard was Bessie Smith, Memphis Minnie and Big Maceo. My singing comes from experience, my own experience, my own feeling. I got my own feelings for everything. I never had no one to teach me nothing. I never went to school for music or nothing. I stayed home to take care of my mother who was sick. I taught myself to sing and to blow harmonica and even to play drums by watching other people. I can't read music but I know where I'm singing! If I hear a blues I like, I try to sing it in my own way. It's always best to have something of your own. I don't sing like nobody but myself."[4] This method of learning was, of course, not very unusual in those days, or even now. Many of the blues musicians just learned to play by watching other people. And ten years later Big Mama Thornton adds to her explanation about her music: "Back in them yesteryears when I was comin' up, listening to Bessie Smith and all, they sung from their heart and soul and expressed themselves. That's why when I do a song by Jimmy Reed or somebody, I have my own way of singing it. Because I don't want to be Jimmy Reed, I want to be me. I like to put myself into whatever I'm doin' so I can feel it."[5]

At the time when Eddie Durham recorded the first music featuring the electric guitar, the modern instrument that would help to transform the sound of the blues, Willie Mae was about 14 years old. Her chance to leave her difficult life in Alabama and go on her own way came in 1940 when Sammy Green's Hot Harlem Revue, with the comedian Snake Anthony, played at the Pekin Theatre in Montgomery. The theatre organized a singing audition and Willie Mae took part. The impulse to do this came probably from Diamond Teeth Mary. The singer, whose real name was Mary Smith McClain, was born on August 27, 1902. Better known as "Walking Mary" and later "Diamond Teeth Mary," she was the half-sister of Bessie Smith (Smith's mother was one of Mary's four stepmothers). At the age of thirteen, young McClain couldn't stand the beatings any longer and left

Ad for the grand opening of the Bronze Peacock Club in Houston, Texas, opened by Don Robey on February 18, 1946 (author's collection).

home to join the circus disguised as a boy in her brother's clothes. It was Mary's own skills as an acrobat and singer that enabled her to survive. McClain spent the 1920s and 1930s performing in a variety of medicine and minstrel shows. She traveled in troupes like Irwin C. Miller's Brown Skin Models, the Davis S. Bell Medicine Show and for eleven years as part of the infamous Rabbit Foot Minstrels. During the 1940s, McClain had diamonds removed from a bracelet and set into her upper and lower front teeth, creating a dazzling stage effect. The diamonds earned McClain her nickname. Diamond Teeth Mary was performing with the Hot Harlem Revue and years later she remembered how she had met Willie Mae Thornton during those days when Willie Mae was working on a garbage truck. Diamond Teeth Mary heard Willie Mae singing when the garbage truck went by, took her off the garbage truck and told her about the singing contest for Sammy Greens Hot Harlem Revue. This story was confirmed by Big Mama Thornton shortly before she died when Diamond Teeth Mary visited Gerde's Folk City in 11 West Fourth Street at the corner of Mercer Street in Greenwich Village with Peter Gallagher, Diamond Teeth Mary's manager, while Big Mama was doing a set. "I took Diamond Teeth Mary to the club one night when Big Mama Thornton was performing," says Peter Gallagher, "and Big Mama was there with Odetta. Big Mama was in a wheelchair. When you walk in the club, you have to walk right by the front of the stage. Big Mama Thornton looked out and she saw Mary. She stopped in the middle of a song and started crying. Mary got on stage and Big Mama announced to the crowd, 'This is Walking Mary Smith, she pulled me off a garbage truck.'"[6]

In fact, the fourteen-year-old girl won first prize in the contest and since Sammy Green was looking for a singer, Willie Mae Thornton didn't think too long about it, took this chance and began traveling with Sammy Green's Hot Harlem Revue. What may appear today as a desperate act of a teenage girl was not particularly uncommon in the Deep South before World War II. While parents wanted their kids to work at home or in the fields, you had to leave home to make your own way.

The revue that Diamond Teeth Mary and the young Willie Mae Thornton sang in was based in Atlanta where Sammy Green owned a few big whorehouses and rooming houses on Decatur Street. Green was described by contemporaries as a short man of about five feet and three inches, very light-skinned, and of a slender build with very straight hair. He looked more Chinese than like a black person. Sammy Green had started his business with selling popcorn and candy and later he sold rooms per hour to the prostitutes on Decatur Street. When he enlarged his horizons, he formed the Hot Harlem Revue. Sammy even bought a bus with big letters on the side that read "SAMMY GREEN HOT HARLEM REVUE." When Thornton joined it, The Hot Harlem Revue consisted of comics, girls in line and eighteen musicians. With about fifty people, they played mainly theatres. "We played Birmingham every Monday and Tuesday, Montgomery on Wednesday, and Macon on Thursday, then back to Atlanta for Friday and Saturday," remembers Billy Wright,[7] who danced with the revue when Thornton was a member. The troupe traveled on two buses and one truck around the area in Alabama and Georgia, according to Leon Long, who was doing the booking for the Sammy Green Hot Harlem Revue. Thornton shared the stage during those years with people like Little Richard and Chuck Willis and was billed as the "New Bessie Smith."

The place on Decatur Street where black people could have their own live shows was the 81 Bailey Theatre. "Snake Anthony was the MC there and it was the place, where, until the 1940s, almost every black star started a career. Bessie Smith had spent several years working there during the 1920s. Snake was a comedian and he was really something. Chuck Willis was part of the show, and so were Tommy Brown, the Austell Adams Orchestra, Zella Mayes and Helen Thompson. We would play Birmingham every Thursday, and be back in Atlanta every Friday, at Bailey's 81 Theater, on Decatur Street," recalls Little Richard. "With the exception of the band members, Snake himself, and the comedian, everybody on his show was a sissy."[8] "Snake" Anthony often shared the bill with Sammy Green's Hot Harlem Revue at the 81 Bailey Theatre. For the next few years, Willie Mae toured with this outfit in the Southern states. She remembers the first tour: "We played in Atlanta, Birmingham, back home in Montgomery, Columbus, South Carolina, Florida. We played all over the South. When the War began, we played especially in theatres in Texas."[9]

Willie Mae established herself quickly in the show and learned things she would need her whole life. She sang, danced, and played harmonica and drums. She even performed comedy in the revue and said many years later: "I still use a little bit of that now."[10] The singer Jimmy Scott, who first rose to national prominence as "Little Jimmy Scott" in the Lionel Hampton Band when he sang lead on the late 1940s hit "Everybody's Somebody's Fool," recorded in December 1949, and which became a top ten R&B hit in 1950, remembers performing with Willie Mae Thornton in those years. "I performed with her everywhere in the middle South in the 1940s when I was touring with Caldonia's Revue (Estelle Young). We sang a number together."[11] And Atlanta was really a kick-off place. "If you didn't go over here it wasn't with much chance that you will make in New York. So we had to perform and play good. But if you made in Atlanta, you could go to

New York,"[12] recalls Atlanta-based blues singer Tommy Brown, who achieved the most success in the early 1950s, particularly on records with the Griffin Brothers.

But to make a living from music was not an easy task. And so Willie Mae needed some work besides music because, as Tommy Brown notes, "in those days we didn't make much money with music. They didn't play our music on the air because they said it was dirty music. We couldn't get into white clubs. On Saturday night the white clubs closed at 12 o'clock. But the black clubs stayed open until 4 o'clock, because that was the only time black people could go out. But if you didn't get into the club before midnight, you couldn't get into the black club, because the white people where in there. So they [the white people] could come to our club but we couldn't come to theirs." he says. Tommy Brown will never forget how he first met Willie Mae Thornton in front of the 81 Bailey Theatre while she was working in her second job: "I was a teenager and had a band playing a show there at the 81 in a show with a guy named Snake Anthony and in front of the theatre Willie Mae Thornton had a shoe shine stand. And she was shining shoes there. That was the way she was making a living at that time. She was big and wore overalls like man." That still wasn't always enough, but even though she kept coming home to her family in Alabama once in a while, she never came back constantly and managed the hard way of life on her own. "I had a hard way to go when I come up. Sometimes had to go to somebody's back door and ask for bread and something cool to drink. Sometimes they said no. I just kept on walking. I just made myself happy. People didn't know I was worried a lot of times. I always kept a smile on my face. I always be round friends, buy drinks, laugh. But they didn't know what was going through my mind. A lot of times, man, I didn't have nothing to eat. They didn't know it. I was smiling. Didn't have nowhere to stay. They didn't know that. I slept in all-night restaurants and barrooms. Course it don't make no difference now. It's all the past. Anyway, I couldn't express what I went through. It don't make no sense to people today,"[13] Big Mama Thornton recalls.

If that wasn't hard enough for a young girl, Willie Mae became pregnant about this time and had a son. She kept the son with her on the road and tried to be a good mother, but the authorities took her boy away from her. Willie Mae Thornton would only rarely talk about that later, but it must have left a big hole in her heart.

2

Hound Dog—The Peacock Years and Johnny Otis

After a 1948 show in Houston the now–22-year-old Willie Mae Thornton left the Hot Harlem Revue because of financial irregularities and decided to stayed in Texas. The blues music scene had changed a lot since the years of Bessie Smith and Mamie Smith. Arthur "Big Boy" Crudup had recorded "That's All Right." Within a decade, Elvis Presley would record the song for his debut. In 1947, T-Bone Walker had played electric guitar on his standard recording "Call it Stormy Monday" and Muddy Waters made his first Chicago recordings, beginning his tenure as the dominant figure in the Chicago blues and a key link between the Mississippi Delta and the urban styles.

Just shortly after Thornton arrived in Houston, Jerry Wexler, an editor at *Billboard* magazine, substitutes the term "rhythm and blues" for the older "race records." And Houston was the Mecca for the music now called rhythm and blues. "In those days you could walk in just about any club, hear live music and have fun," remembers Houston's guitar legend and studio musician for Houston's Duke/Peacock Records, Texas Johnny Brown, who toured with Bobby "Blue" Bland and Junior Parker in the 1950s and 1960s as guitarist and bandleader.[1] The people appreciated the music and they loved the blues. But there were only a few women who stepped out and tried to make it in the music world. Willie Mae Thornton was one of them.

In 1950, Willie Mae Thornton finally made her first record with two songs called "All Right Baby" and "Bad Luck Got My Man," for the tiny E&W label on Houston's Dallas Avenue. She didn't use her own name this time. The disc appeared with the title *The Harlem Stars*. In 1950, she also came to the notice of a tenor sax man and vocalist called Joe "Papoose" Fritz and he hired her as a singer for fifty dollars a night in his band at the

Eldorado Ballroom in Houston. As described in the *Handbook of Texas Music*, the Eldorado Ballroom was "this venue, owned and operated by African Americans" that occupied the entire second floor of the Eldorado Building, located (across from historic Emancipation Park) in the southwest quadrant of the intersection of Elgin and Dowling Street in the Third Ward from Houston, home to the city's largest and most diverse black population.[2] It was a big nightclub in the third ward in town. In fact, it was *the* club in those days and had a great reputation even outside of Houston, as Texas Johnny Brown recalls: "I remember we used to travel from place to place where people were never been out of their town before. And if they found out that we are from Houston, they asked us, 'Hey, have you ever been to the Eldorado.' Everybody did know about the Eldorado Ballroom."[3]

From the late 1930s till the early 1970s, the Eldorado was the venue of choice for upscale blues and jazz performances featuring touring stars and local talents, or in the words of Milton Hopkins, a cousin of Sam "Lightnin'" Hopkins, who would after years with the Upsetters and other acts join the B.B. King tour band in the seventies as B.B.'s rhythm guitar player: "The Eldorado Ballroom of course was a big club, with big dance floor and when you got a chance to play in the Eldorado Ballroom, you hit the big time. Being able to play the Eldorado Ballroom was one of the goals for most young up and coming musicians in Houston."[4] B.B. King, James Brown, Bobby "Blue" Bland—just about everybody came there. If you didn't play there you just were nobody.

Willie Mae Thornton, on her way to becoming one of those big names, played at the Eldorado Ballroom with the house band lead by I. H. "Ike" Smalley, a saxophone player who was part of the house band for the Eldorado Ballroom for eight years. Later, she played also with Pluma Davis and would soon meet many of the great blues people in those days. "Yes, Gatemouth Brown was very well known then. He recorded on the Peacock Label. I had the chance to meet Louis Jordan who also came to town. Big Joe Turner was there too and also Fats Domino was in Houston when 'They Call Me the Fat Man' came out,"[5] she recalled later. During this time she would meet people like Big Joe Turner and others that she would stay in touch with and play with over her whole career.

Willie Mae played in Houston, sometimes together with her older Brother C.W. "Harp" Thornton on drums and with Earl Gilliam on piano different gigs in town with blues and some rock 'n' roll. It was at this time that Don Robey, owner of Peacock Records, heard Willie Mae at the Eldorado Ballroom and signed her to an exclusive five-year contract and had her play in his Bronze Peacock Club. As Joe "Papoose" Fritz puts it: "She soon joined my band as a vocalist—everybody had to have a female vocalist in those days. I paid her $50 a night until Don Robey stole her away from me."[6]

Don Robey was the personal manager of guitarist and singer Clarence Gatemouth Brown who came from Orange, Texas. T. Bone Walker had found Gatemouth Brown in San Antonio and T. Bone Walker was not doing very well physically, so he brought in Gatemouth Brown to sub for him. Brown was quite a character. He could shoot a rat he saw out of the car while driving fast.

Gatemouth Brown was in Houston, managed by Don Robey, but since there were no booking agencies interested in Brown, Evelyn Johnson, who worked with Don Robey, applied for a booking license to the American Federation of Musician and created the Buffalo Booking Agency. Through that agency, Johnson could book Brown in Texas and also soon in Arkansas, Louisiana, Mississippi and by 1951 even for a series of shows in California. The role of Johnson was not appreciated enough in the view of many who knew her. For B. B. King she was "one of the greatest women of her time."[7] She managed to watch over the interests of the artist as well as Don Robey's interests and what was best for his business. So, in Brown's words "she made Robey,"[8] but in a way Brown made Robey too. Because of Brown, Don Robey and Evelyn Johnson founded Peacock Records, and because of Brown they both founded the Buffalo Booking Agency. Since neither Brown nor the agency could attract large audiences, they created a route of small clubs and venues. Later musicians and agents would only refer to Buffalo Booking Agency venues as the "chitlin circuit." The result was a market area that eventually included not only Texas but Arkansas, Louisiana, Mississippi, Alabama and Georgia. When the artist roster grew, Peacock artists could also be booked in St. Louis, Kansas City and Chicago.

Don Robey himself was "a fast talking business man," as Texas Johnny Brown says. By his own admission Don Robey was a gambler, a risk taker, an entrepreneur. His club had a better show than the Eldorado or Club Matinee because he had the stage right out in the middle of the floor, and you sat around it like it was ringside at a fight.

Tommy Brown remembers Don Robey: "I talked with him once. He wanted to record me but I didn't like his attitude. So I wouldn't record with him. He would come in with his briefcase full of money and that was supposed to impress you. And then he would sign you up. They never paid you. He never did that to me, because I didn't allow him to."[9] Don Robey was a businessman. Milton Hopkins adds, "If you had to do business with Don Robey and you didn't know your business, you will get hurt. And that happened to a lot of people. Don Robey was a good guy, but he was a very sharp businessman. He looked for opportunities to better his condition."

In the blues music business, Robey was without a doubt a giant. Grady Gaines, famed for his band The Upsetters and his work with Little Richard, says: "I got nothing but good to say about Don Robey. I wish we had a Don Robey in Houston right now. As long as you took care of your business with him, you didn't have a problem with him."[10]

Willie Mae's association with Robey must have been a very stormy one, as Little Richard, who worked for Peacock at the same time, remembers, "Robey was known for beating people up. He would beat everybody up, but Big Mama Thornton. He was scared of her, and she was built like a big bull."[11] If that's really true or not we'll never know, but Willie Mae Thornton had already developed a reputation for heavy drinking and masculine behavior. Evelyn Johnson of the Booking Agency considered her a "female thug. She was very blunt, and she used a lot of bad language. She wore khaki pants, shirts all the time. Part of it was her overall mental thing. Part of it was her exposure, and it was just her. And she was very prone to say 'I ain't wearing that.' And finally it was just a matter of going to some of the stores where I shopped. She said, 'Look here boss lady, I ain't going in there.' So we went to other stores, places where we could get bigger clothes. We bought her a lace dress, fixed her whole luggage up, and hired a woman to travel with her to dress her, you know. The woman got involved with one of the musicians and they didn't get along, and all. She fired the woman because she didn't want to do this."[12]

Willie Mae's habit of dressing like a man produced the rumor that she may have been a lesbian. It is a rumor that followed her through her whole life and that is still often part of stories about her. But in fact other than this has been told as a rumor over and over again, there is no evident proof for this. As Johnny Otis says: "I could never get a handle on Willie Mae sexually and that's not a judgment. If you're homosexual or whatever, it's nobody's damn business what you do in bed.... All I can honestly say is that she was a good, intelligent person. I personally never saw her with any men, but on the other hand, I never saw her with any woman either." And Jimmy Moore, Big Mama Thornton's former manager in the sixties, agrees with that and says: "I hear people say, that she was gay, but I never saw any indication. In the matter of fact I used to bring ladies backstage to get her autographs and I had to argue with her, because she said: 'I don't want to talk to them. They just want to make fun of me.'"

Besides playing at Don Robey's Bronze Peacock, Willie Mae toured the so-called Chitlin' Circuit and she and Marie Adams became the female heavyweights at Peacock Records. But at this point Don Robey could not already know this, so Willie Mae Thornton was some kind of a new project for him, without knowing if she would have any success.

Willie Mae Thornton did her first record at Peacock in the beginning of January 1951, at Bill Holford's ACA Studio, where most of the Peacock recording sessions took place. Accompanied by the Joe Scott Orchestra, Willie Mae Thornton recorded the single "I'm All Fed Up/Partnership Blues." Joe Scott was the A&R man for Peacock Records and according to Texas Johnny Brown "a wonderful writer and arranger." One of the people who played in Joe Scotts Orchestra during those first recordings with Willie Mae Thornton was bass player I.J. Gosey, who was born on January 25, 1937, in a small East Texas town called Newton. He was playing with a group called Arthur Boatwright and the Joy Boys, and Joe Scott needed a bass player. He had heard Gosey, liked him and gave him the recording job. The ACA was a nice little studio and they worked all day and night, recorded right there. After Robey was satisfied with the recording, Holford always mastered the finished tapes and did send masters to New Jersey, Indiana and California manufactures. The records were then shipped to distributors around the country.

Since *Billboard* did not review this first single of Willie Mae Thornton, Robey announced its availability himself as an example of new Blues and Boogie in a *Billboard* display of Peacock releases. The third song of this first session in January 1951, "Mischievous Boogie," appeared in the summer of 1952. Even though *Billboard* hailed this one as worthy of attention, it too failed in the charts.

It seems that Robey had more important things to do than to promote Thornton. Peacock was on the way to expand outside of the South and Southwest and new distributors in Los Angeles, New Orleans and Cincin-

Big Mama Thornton playing baseball with Johnny Otis (left) and Andrew Matthew from the Johnny Otis Orchestra (courtesy Billy Vera Collection).

nati were added for Peacock Records. Those busy times may be the reason why Thornton's next recording did not take place until December 1951, when she, accompanied by the Bill Harvey Band, recorded the songs "No Jody For Me" and "Let Your Tears Fall Baby" as a further Peacock single. This time the record was reviewed in *Billboard*. About "Let Your Tears Fall Baby" they wrote: "Jump Blues gets a good shouting vocal from Thornton, plus solid background." And "No Jody For Me" was featured: "Chanter socks over the lyrics on this better-than-average blues. Band gives good support."[13] But none of the four *Billboard* reviewers scored either of the sides higher than 74 (Good) so again commercial success was denied. This was certainly not the reception Don Robey had hoped for. Even though the song was a hit around Houston, the music didn't really bring her enough income at the time and Willie Mae Thornton started again shining shoes, like she did in Atlanta years before. And Thornton kept on going with her music and worked with Roy Milton, Joe Ligon and others.

But change was in the air, not just in Houston but everywhere. The beat of Jackie Brenstons record *Rocket 88* presaged rock 'n' roll. Alan Fred started his radio show where he featured Muddy Waters, Howlin' Wolf and popularized the term rock 'n' roll. Willie Mae became part of a two-week show at the Bronze Peacock Club. With her were Billy Wright with Marie Adams and Jimmy McCracklin and the Blues Blasters as the headliners. Jimmy McCracklin, born James David Walker on August 13, 1921, became a famous pianist, vocalist, and songwriter. His style contained West Coast blues, Jump blues, and R&B. Over a career that spanned seven decades, he said he had written almost a thousand songs and had recorded hundreds of them. McCracklin recorded over thirty albums, and earned four gold records. For many, he is probably the most important musician to come out of the Bay Area in the post–World War II years. He recorded a debut single for Globe Records, "Miss Mattie Left Me," in 1945, and recorded "Street Loafin' Woman" in 1946. McCracklin recorded for a number of labels in Los Angeles and Oakland, prior to joining Modern Records in 1949–1950. In 1946, he formed his group called Jimmy McCracklin and his Blues Blasters with guitarist Lafayette Thomas. "When I first met her, we were both working for Peacock Records. She played a show

Publicity photo of Willie Mae Thornton while she performed with the Johnny Otis Band. This was shortly before she got her name "Big Mama Thornton" (courtesy Billy Vera Collection).

together with my band. We played in Houston, Texas, at the Peacock Club," Jimmy McCracklin says. "We worked together in Texas with my band. She worked with my band on so many jobs. My name was just as big as her name. We both were on the same show. By working with me we become friends."[14] The friendship between Jimmy McCracklin and Willie Mae Thornton was to become very important for Willie Mae a few years later. Meanwhile, Willie Mae's "Let Your Tears Fall Baby" proved to be a solid commercial hit. In 1951, she recorded the "Cotton Picking Blues" and "Everytime I Think of You" with the Bill Harvey Orchestra. Again, she didn't have the chance to prove her ability to play a great harmonica. In fact she never recorded her harmonica playing while she was in Houston for Peacock Records, because "all they wanted was for me to just sing,"[15] as she recalled thirty years later.

Then, in early 1952, Willie Mae Thornton, now 25-years-old, made a very meaningful acquaintance: Johnny Otis came to Houston with his Rhythm & Blues Caravan. Johnny Otis and his traveling musical revue was known in black communities all over the country and was one of the last great rhythm and blues touring bands in the 1950s. Johnny Otis was a singer, musician, composer, arranger, band leader, talent scout, disc jockey, record producer, television show host, artist, author, journalist, minister, and impresario. A seminal influence on American R&B and rock 'n' roll, Otis discovered artists such as Little Esther, Jackie Wilson, Little Willie John and Hank Ballard. Known as the original "King of Rock 'n' Roll," he is commonly referred to as the "Godfather of Rhythm and Blues." Otis is now probably best known for "Willie and the Hand Jive," a top 10-pop hit in 1958. With the new agreement between Robey and Otis, Otis was now able to have influence into a great pool of talents from the Houston area. Perhaps because Don Robey could not find a way to launch Willie Mae Thornton's career with the blues shouting style she had brought with her to Peacock, Robey seized the opportunity to audition Thornton along with several others of his artists to Otis, who was mostly impressed by Marie Adams and Thornton. Otis negotiated a deal with Robey in which he would take some of Robey's artists on tour with the revue and that he would also record them in Los Angeles and give the finished masters to Don Robey. The deal included taking along Thornton for recording sessions and touring, so she went on tour with Otis's band. This turned out to be an extraordinarily successful strategy. In fact, Thornton became known outside of Texas while playing outside of the south for the first time as part of Otis's Rhythm & Blues Caravan and impressed critics and audiences throughout the country. The *Chicago Defender* reported that Thornton "stopped the show in the Tacoma, Oakland and Richmond auditoriums, as well as in Stockton, Sacramento, Bakersfield and the Elks Auditorium in Los Angeles." In San Diego, the local newspaper reported that "they called out the fire department to cool her off!"[16] *Cash Box* noted her as the "show-stopper" of the Johnny Otis Revue.[17] Between the shows Otis had established a special kind of entertainment for his orchestra. He and others played baseball in between shows, and Thornton proved to be especially enthusiastic about the game. Otis did built a baseball team that regularly competed with other teams of musicians. Sometimes, when the Johnny Otis Orchestra was in Los Angeles, Otis held games on Wednesday nights at the South Park in Los Angeles that were attended by about one thousand people watching the teams.[18]

While Willie Mae was on tour, "Everytime I Think of You" from the Bill Harvey session of 1952, along with the earlier recorded "Mischievous Boogie," came out as her third Peacock single. Meanwhile, Willie Mae Thornton was designated by Don Robey as the house rocker and show stopper at Peacock Records.

On August 13, 1952, Johnny Otis and his Orchestra recorded several songs with Willie Mae at Radio Recorder Studio on Santa Monica Boulevard in Los Angeles. Pete Lewis was on guitar, James Von Streeter and Fred Ford played horns, and Devonia Williams played keys.

In the following October, Willie Mae Thornton toured with Johnny Otis on the West Coast and they prepared a Texas tour over the holidays. While Thornton made her mark as a star performer in Johnny Otis's show, Johnny Ace established himself as national recording star. His "My Song" climbed on the way to the top position in the R&B charts. Ace's success made the Duke Label and Johnny Ace famous and made Don Robey a major player in the independent R&B business. Robey was now in a much better position to positioning his Peacock artists for national attention. If Robey had to settle for occasional *Billboard* record reviews, his label now got, after Johnny Ace's success, more reception, and by the end of 1952, Robey was assured *Billboard* reviews for his artists on Duke or Peacock.

From November 28 until December 5, 1952, the Johnny Otis Orchestra with Little Esther, Mel Walker and Willie Mae Thornton played at the Apollo Theatre in New York's Harlem. It was Thornton's first appearance

ANNUAL HOLIDAY OPENING

BRONZE PEACOCK CLUB

DEC. 24 THRU JAN. 1st

BIGGEST And BEST
FLOOR SHOW EVER
IN HOUSTON

Featuring

★ **EDGAR BLANCHARD**
and his great orchestra, his guitar and vocals.

★ **ALONZO STEWARY**
Sensational Drummer and Vocalist

★ **WILLE MAE** (Big Mama) **THORNTON**
Direct from The Apollo Theatre New York City

★ **HAROLD CONNER**
Great Crooner - The Wonder boy from Cincinati, Ohio

★ **THE ORIGINAL CALDONIA**
Comediene and Contortinist

★ **THE BRONZE CHANDU**
Greatest Magician & Tap Dancer Living

★ **WINNIE THE WIGGLER**
World's Greatest Hig Tosser-Dances on her Head

COME EARLY—NO RESERVATIONS
ADM. $1.50 AT DOOR

Ad for a show at the Bronze Peacock Club in Houston, Texas, December 24–January 1, 1952. Willie Mae Thornton had just come back from her successful appearance at the Apollo Theatre in New York City, where was nicknamed "Big Mama" (author's collection).

Big Mama Thornton performing with the Johnny Otis Orchestra in 1952 (courtesy Billy Vera Collection).

at the Apollo. She had been on the road as a musician for over ten years now, but she had no hit single to present to the audience so she sang her version of Billy Ward and the Dominos, "Have Mercy Baby" during her appearance at the Apollo. Here they minted a nickname for her after the audience applauded so much that they had to pull the curtain down to

Johnny Otis, Big Mama Thornton and Don Robey posing for the camera after Big Mama Thornton's great success with "Hound Dog" (courtesy Billy Vera Collection).

move on with the show. From then on, Otis placed her last on the bill because he thought they would never get on to the rest of the show if she opened. "I played opposite Little Esther at the Johnny Otis Show in 1952, and I didn't have no record and I was singing The Dominos' song 'Have Mercy, Mercy, Baby,' and I stole the show! We played the Apollo in New York and that's where they made their mistake. They put me on first. I wasn't out there to put no one off stage. I was out there to get known and I did! I stopped the show. They had to put the curtain down. Little Esther never got on that first show. That's when they put my name in lights and Mr. Frank Shiffman, the manager, came backstage hollerin' to Johnny Otis and poking me in the arms with his fingers (it was sore for a week). 'You said you had a star and you got a star! You got to put her on to close the show!'"[19] Willie Mae Thornton said to Ralph Gleason of the *San Francisco Chronicle*. The next night Thornton not only closed the show but she saw

23

her name in lights as the star of the show for the first time. From that day on, she was called Big Mama Thornton. She knew exactly what she wanted and what she did not want, as Johnny Otis later recalled: since her clothing style didn't really fit those venues Otis persuaded her to wear a gown. But Thornton wasn't too easy to persuade. "She came on stage, kicked up her legs and there were those Texas boots," Otis recalled later.[20] Otis was also the one who asked Big Mama Thornton for the first time to play the harmonica on stage, after he had discovered her ability to play the instrument: "I was touring with Johnny Otis during the '50s," she said in a *New York Times* interview, "and I blowed the harmonica one night and shook him up. 'Why didn't you tell me you could play that thing?' I said, 'Well, you didn't ask me. All you want me to is stand up and sing.'"[21]

After the great success at the Apollo Theatre, Big Mama Thornton opened a show at the Bronze Peacock Club in Houston and was now also celebrated in her home base in Houston, Texas. At year's end "Everytime I Think of You" charts well in Atlanta and Florida, and Don Robey was rewarded for his decision to stick with Big Mama Thornton since her next released single became a huge hit; in fact it was the biggest hit that Don Robey's Peacock Records ever released.

One of the songs that Big Mama Thornton recorded on August 13, 1952, with Johnny Otis and his Orchestra while they were in Los Angeles was "Hound Dog," which became Willie Mae Thornton's signature hit, written by Jerry Leiber and Mike Stoller. Leiber (April 25, 1933–August 22, 2011) and Stoller (born March 13, 1933) were American songwriting and record-producing partners. Stoller was the composer and Leiber the lyricist. They would go on to write many amazing songs. Their most famous songs include "Jailhouse Rock," "Don't," "Kansas City," "Stand By Me" (with Ben E. King), and "On Broadway" (with Barry Mann and Cynthia Weil). Leiber and Stoller wrote "Hound Dog" especially for Big Mama. "The afternoon we saw her, Johnny Otis told us to come down to his garage in the back of his house, where he used to rehearse. He wanted us to listen to his people and see if we could write some tunes for them. We saw Big Mama and she knocked me cold. She looked like the biggest, bad-ass, saltiest chick you would ever see. And she was mean, a 'lady bear' as they used to call 'em. She must have been 350 pounds and she had all these scars all over her face. I had to write a song for her that basically said 'Go fuck yourself' but how do you do it without actually saying it? And how to do it telling a story? I couldn't just have a song full of expletives," Stoller says. "She was a wonderful blues singer with a great moaning style, but it was as much her appearance as her blues style that influenced the writing of 'Hound Dog' and the idea that we wanted her to growl it, which she rejected at first, her thing was 'Don't tell me how to sing no song.'"[22] After watching and hearing Thornton, Jerry Leiber and Mike Stoller went home and composed, in about fifteen minutes, the song that would make her famous. Jerry Leiber recalled: "'Hound Dog' was the first record we produced, although unofficially Johnny Otis had played drums at the rehearsal, he had the snare turned off and was playing some old southern, Latin-sounding kind of beat. On the actual recording date, he had his road drummer playing because Johnny was supposed to be running the session for Don Robey of Peacock Records. It wasn't happening so Jerry [Leiber] said, 'Johnny, get on the drums, the way you were,' and then Johnny said, 'Who's gonna run the session?' and we said, 'We will.' Jerry went into the booth and directed from there. I stayed on the floor and worked with the musicians. There were only two takes and both of them were good, but the second was better than the first."[23] So, in fact, Johnny Otis was the one who played drums on the original recording of "Hound Dog."

Willie Mae Thornton singing is what makes this song so special. Her voice is "intimate, improvisatory and unadorned by heavy effects. Its sits front and center of the mix." Pete Lewis on guitar "uses a series of restrained 'fill-in' lines relying on bend 'bluesy' notes in the call and response pattern trading measures with Thornton's full and throaty singing. Thornton both pushes and pulls the beat, cleverly singing around the downbeats by anticipating or following the first beat of a measure and hitting the downbeat at different points of the verse each time, creating a subtle and constant tension between the vocal lines and the band so often characteristic of interwar and late–1940s blues," describes Charles Fairchild. [24]

"Leiber and Stoller brought me the song, 'Hound Dog,'" Johnny Otis recalls of the time he produced Willie Mae Thornton's recording of what was to become an R&B, and then rock 'n' roll, classic. "Parts of it weren't really acceptable. I didn't like that reference to chicken and watermelon, said, 'Let's get that crap out of there' … This came out and was a big smash, and everything was all right. I had half the publishing rights and one third of the song-writing."[25]

In January 1953, "Hound Dog" and "Nightmare" are released as Peacock single #1612, recorded with the Johnny Otis Band. "Hound Dog" takes off immediately and begins to look like a national hit. Big Mama Thornton still toured the country with the Johnny Otis revue. On some occasions Jimmy Witherspoon was headlining, a friend that Big Mama Thornton was in touch with her whole life. Thornton recalled later how she learned her record was in circulation while she was on her way to a performance with the Johnny Otis Orchestra during this tour in Dayton, Ohio. "I was going to the theater and I just turned the radio on in the car and the man said, 'Here's a record that's going nationwide: 'Hound Dog,' by Willie Mae Thornton.' I said, 'That's me!' [*laughs*] I hadn't heard the record in so long. So when we get to the theater they was blasting it. You could hear it from the theater, from the loudspeaker. They were just playing 'Hound Dog' all over the theater. So I goes up in the operating room, I say, 'Do you mind playing that again?' 'Cause I hadn't heard the record in so long I forgot the words myself. So I stood there while he was playing it, listening to it. So that evening I sang it on the show, and everybody went for it. 'Hound Dog' just took off like a jet."[26]

The rawness of the sound, combined with the sexuality of the lyrics, made the song a smash hit on the black charts, where the song climbed right away to number one, and stayed there for seven weeks. Big Mama Thornton's "race record," which never had a chance on the pop charts, nevertheless sold, according to Don Robey, between 500,000 and 750,000 copies.

The song made Big Mama Thornton famous in the national blues community and established Peacock Records as a major independent label in the black secular music scene. Peacock had three new pressing plants running full blast to keep up with the demand for Big Mama Thornton's record. In *Billboard* Don Robey screamed in a Peacock ad, "This is a HIT, HIT, HIT."[27] And a week later, the song was a "new record to watch" at *Billboard*, and the reviewer wrote, "This is a wild slicing loaded with excitement. Willie Mae Thornton hands it a sock reading, selling the tune powerfully, while the ork swings the rhumba blues with a pulsating beat that builds all the way. Thrush's vocal is outstanding, and the backing is infectious. This one is mighty potent and could bust through quickly. A solid effort for the boxes."[28] *Cash Box* made the song its "Rhythm 'n' Blues Sleeper of the Week" and noted, "Willie Mae Thornton gives a frenzied performance" and described Thornton as a singer who was "easy when she should be easy,

Big Mama Thornton performing as supporting act for Johnny Ace in Texas in 1953 (courtesy Billy Vera Collection).

and riving when she has to band it home." Overall, there was according to *Billboard*, "just enough of the spiritual feel to stir up the emotions and raise the blood pressure."[29] *Down Beat* called the song "one of the biggest rhythm and blues records of all time."[30]

Thornton's recording of "Hound Dog," and the acquisition of Johnny Ace and the Duke Records, would change Don Robey's operations from a regional to a national one. With Robey's acquiring of the Memphis record label Duke and the artists who came with it, Robey created a great synthesis—Houston and Memphis. For example, the Bobby "Blue" Bland was from Memphis but his band leader was Joe Scott from Houston. Spurred on by the success of gospel records, Thornton's "Hound Dog" and Johnny Ace's records, Peacock and Duke Records' moved now into a new modern headquarters on Erastus Street in Houston.

With the chart success of "Hound Dog," Thornton was added to the new Peacock Blues Consolidated Package Show, which featured Johnny Ace, Junior Parker and Bobby "Blue" Bland, or in Thornton's own words: "Anyway, in 1953, when 'Hound Dog' broke loose for me, that's when I met Johnny Ace. I worked on his show up to 1954."[31] Through packages, the Buffalo Booking Agency could book acts that weren't famous at the time. So if you wanted to book Johnny Ace, you had to book Bobby "Blue" Bland, Big Mama Thornton or others in the package too. Don Robey was responsible for putting a road band together for the package, and he and Evelyn Johnson also selected road managers to be responsible for decisions while the package was on tour. Part of the touring band in this package was a young guitarist named Milton Hopkins who had just agreed to work for Robey, after he had asked him to join the tour band. "I was in front of my mom's and dad's house and I was wondering what a white fellow was doing coming to my house that day. He got out of his car and introduced himself, said he is Don Robey and he owns Duke/Peacock Records and he was looking for Milton Hopkins. After I told him that I was who he was looking for he ask me if I would be interested in going on the road with a band. I didn't know whether to say yes or no. My instinct told me to say yes. So I told him yes and he started to tell me who I was working with, how much money I make and those kinds of things. And that's how that started," Milton Hopkins remembers his first meeting with Robey. Also part of the Johnny Ace/Big Mama Thornton Revue was the young bass player Curtis Tillman. Tillman would stay until 1955 with the band. But he met Thornton again in the sixties and stayed with her band for many years and even recorded with her.

In April, "Hound Dog" was, according to *Cashbox* magazine, the nation's top-selling blues record and ranked first in sales in New York, Chicago, New Orleans, San Francisco, Newark, Memphis, Dallas, Cincinnati, Los Angeles and St. Louis. Rufus Thomas recorded an answer song to "Hound Dog" called "Bear Cat" on Sun Records (#181) which was common in the field of rhythm and blues. Big Mama Thornton's success with "Hound Dog" even generated not just one but six answer songs in 1953, but Rufus Thomas's version was the most successful one. By April 18 "Hound Dog" was number one in the R&B records sales and "Bear Cat" was number ten. Don Robey had positioned Big Mama Thornton's song as the original and had warned dealers, distributors and operators to beware of imitations but "Bear Cat" continued to climb the charts and reach the number three position. Robey sued Sun Records successfully and was awarded 2 percent of all "Bear Cat" profit plus court costs. By midsummer, it was obvious that "Hound Dog" would be the biggest seller in the history of Peacock Records. And according to the *Billboard* tabulations, Robey's Peacock and Duke labels accounted for number two in R&B record national sales with "Hound Dog" and three of the ten positions for juke-box plays with "Hound Dog" at number three, Earl Forest's "Whoopin' and Hollerin'" at number eight and Johnny Ace's "Cross My Heart" at number nine.

In August, Thornton appeared with Johnny Ace and his band at the Shrine Auditorium in Los Angeles at the Fourth Annual Rhythm & Blues Jubilee, and they both got ready for a big coast to coast tour during the fall. Big Mama Thornton played now mostly in front of big audiences numbering 18 to 80 thousand. The audience was mostly black but all big venues had a section set aside for white people, as Milton Hopkins remembers. "We had a lot of them. Things weren't progressive and we knew that there was white who liked what we did and loved it. And they would come out and see us. We all grew to understand that. We were not allowed to meet them and couldn't give anybody any autographs. The police was watching to make sure that the black and the white didn't get together," observes Hopkins.

In late September after the incredible run of "Hound Dog," Big Mama Thornton had her second signature tune with the release of "They Call Me Big Mama" with the flip side "Cotton Picking Blues" (Peacock #1621). These songs were also recorded in a session on August 13, 1952, with the Johnny Otis Band featuring Don Johnson on trumpet, George Washington on trombone, James Von Streeter on tenor sax, Fred Ford on baritone sax, Devonia Williams on piano, Pete Lewis on guitar, Albert Winston on bass, Leard Bell on drums, and Johnny Otis on vibes and drums. But "They Call Me Big Mama" was not as great a success as "Hound Dog," and *Billboard* said: "A fair side, with good instrumental support. Okay follow-up to 'Hound Dog.'" And about "Cotton Picking Blues" they wrote that it is "a much more primitive, moody type of blues, with long piano interlude."[32]

Big Mama Thornton was on the top of the R&B record charts for about six months and never reached that success again but even if her other Peacock records would not penetrate the charts on a national or regional level, she was still a successful touring performer and box-office attraction as Johnny Ace's opening act. Appearing with Ace clearly enlarged her audience since she alone was not anymore a headliner. But that is not very surprising. Not many women R&B recording stars in those days could compete with the male acts, whether in public appearance or in record sales. The reason is easy to explain: The women were the ones who bought records and they wanted to hear the male acts singing.

In late October, Thornton and Johnny Ace were set to appear at New York's Apollo Theater in their first eastern show. They were joined by Little Junior Parker & His Blue Flames and the Harptones on the tour, and in addition to the Apollo they played at the Howard Theater in Washington and the Royal Theater in Baltimore. On Thanksgiving night in Houston, B.B. King joined the Ace-Thornton-Parker show and at the end of the year, Peacock released Big Mama Thornton's next single "The Big Change" and "I Ain't No Fool Either" (#1626).

On December 5, 1953, the new record from Johnny Ace called *Yes Baby* was released (Duke #118) with "Saving My Love For You" on the flipside. *Billboard* raved, "Ace proves on this side that he can sell a rhythm tune as well as a ballad. He really comes thru with a powerful rendition on this jump effort, while the combo and an unbilled singer swings out behind him. This side, too, has more than a chance to make it."[33] The unbilled singer mentioned here was none other than Big Mama Thornton. Whether Don Robey thought it prudent not to tarnish the upscale image of Duke Records with a lowdown blues singer like Thornton, or whether he thought Thornton's vocals were merely backup vocals or an additional instrument and unworthy to be mentioned, we will never know. But, just a year later the live performance of this song as a duet between Johnny Ace and Thornton would become famous as the last public performance of Ace.

Big Mama Thornton began touring the Southeast in 1954 with Johnny Ace and the orchestra of drummer C.C. Pinkston. They played one-nighters in the Alabama-Georgia area throughout January and February. In March, Big Mama Thornton and Ace did a week at Pep's Musical Bar in Philadelphia backed by the Johnny Board Band. Then they played a series of one-nighters in Michigan and Ohio, followed by a week at the Apollo Theatre in New York beginning April 23. According to the *R&B Beat* and the *Rhythm and Blues Notes*, this second appearance by Johnny Ace, and Big Mama Thornton's fourth appearance at the Apollo, was a "smashing package" with Big Mama Thornton being "Peacock's belting lady killer of the blues."[34] The "reigning king and Queen of Blues," as the *New York Age Defender* called them, had a great triumph.[35] *Variety* wrote in a review: "Miss Thornton and Ace split the vocalistics with support from a driving seven-man combo/four rhythm, two reed and a brass. Femme is a heavy rhythm & blues thrush while Ace is a mellow crooner. The contrast is effective and sustains interest and excitement all the way. Miss Thornton blasts her disk fave, 'Hound Dog,' 'Let Your Tears Fall' and 'For You My Love,' with the kind of gusto that keeps the aud rocking. Ave, a new disk fave in the r&b field, wins with 'The Clock,' 'Follow the Rules' and 'Saving My Love.'"[36]

It was Johnny Ace's greatest success at the Apollo, and his last one, too. Big Mama Thornton would come back to this place, where she got her nickname and stopped the show for the first time, later again in the following years. The ensemble was to travel to Ohio and the Midwest. The same month, Thornton's new single "I Smell A Rat" and "I've Searched The World Over" are released (Peacock #1632). Thornton was now always advertised with her song "Hound Dog" and added were actual recordings like "I Ain't No Fool Either" and Johnny Ace was called the piano wizard and vocalist.

In June, "I Smell A Rat" sells well and brings in big box office on the road in the Carolinas where the Ace/Thornton package toured one-nighters. *Billboard* even speculated that the song "could be one of the strongest records of the season," but in fact it failed.[37] In July, Big Mama Thornton and Johnny Ace returned to Houston for what would be Ace's next and sadly last recording session. The rest of July, Thornton and Ace were touring through Texas, Louisiana, and New Mexico.

In August, as Thornton toured the Southwest, Peacock Records released "Stop Hopping On Me" and "Story Of My Blues" (# 1642). By September, "Stop Hopping On Me" was selling well in Memphis and St. Louis. Then, in October, Peacock released Big Mama Thornton's next single "Rock a Bye Baby" and "Walking Blues" (#1647) and added to the Ace-Thornton package for a West Coast swing were Memphis Slim and Faye Adams. The musicians enjoyed the touring as band member Milton Hopkins remembers: "We worked close to two years, I think. We didn't have a hard time. Johnny was a very jovial type person, he liked to talk and have fun and Willie Mae was basically the same. They drank a little alcohol, they would get high. But they were always able to do their job and there was no hardship. And I treasure the time that I was with them." Johnny Ace and Willie Mae didn't play every night together, but they did play three, four nights a week together. "Just like we were locals but we were traveling too. We were travelling different towns all over the nation. We were jumping everywhere," Hopkins says.

Despite the fun they had on tour, segregation was always a problem in those days, as Hopkins recalls." We played the smaller venues, like a larger club, where there were no white people. There was no restaurant or hotel where black people could stay. Houston, Dallas, Fort Worth, Memphis, Mobile, Atlanta, these were the only places that had accommodations for black people. Other than that, when we went to small towns, people really boarded us in their private homes if we had to stay overnight. Only most of the large cities had some kind of accommodations for black folks." Even promoting the show wasn't easy in those circumstances, and black radio stations were the main source of word of mouth advertisement and "sometimes two, three days before the concert they would mount some big speakers on automobiles and ride through the neighborhood announcing the coming of a concert. And that's the way they did it," Hopkins says.

Big Mama Thornton, Johnny Ace and all other traveling blues musicians were also facing routine dangers that all performers face. B.B. King, for instance, survived automobile accidents, dancehall fires, shootings and so on. Liquor was an essential part of the scene, and drug use was also not uncommon. For Thornton's touring partner Johnny Ace, the danger resulted from his love for pistols.

Ace had bought a pistol in Florida, a state that has the shape of a pistol, and he treated his new pistol like a toy, as the bandleader Johnny Board remembers. "He and I were the only ones who could drive his car and when we stopped on the road sometimes to relieve ourselves in a field, he would take out the gun and shoot in the air like a child with a cap pistol," Board says.[38] Hopkins describes the tour life then as being a kind of playground for Johnny Ace. "He loved to wrestle and horse-ass, and play around. He was always jolly and full of pep and energy. He loved to drink gin and he liked women. Johnny's idea of fun was driving his car 900 miles an hour, pistol in hand, shooting out the zeros on the speed-limit signs," says Hopkins.[39] But while others, like Gatemouth Brown, could handle this kind of dangerous play, without anything happening, Ace was soon to be taking is last shot.

Christmas was a normal work day for the band, so they played on Christmas Eve 1954 in Port Arthur, Texas, the birthplace, incidentally of Janis Joplin. After the show, Johnny Ace left the club to meet his girlfriend, Olivia Gibbs, in Houston. He invited the band, including Big Mama Thornton, to a Christmas meal at his girlfriend's. When they arrived at Gibb's place in Houston, Ace started playing Russian roulette with an unloaded gun. The next day he would repeat his dangerous play again. Ace and Thornton played December 25 at the City Auditorium in Houston for a "Negro Christmas" dance. Ace and Thornton had finished the first set, as they always did, with a duet of Ace's hit 'Yes, Baby.'" Big Mama Thornton opened the show and Johnny Ace was the feature. "Finally they did the duet, and they would close together and that was very fascinating and people went wild over it," Evelyn Johnson remembers.[40]

During intermission between 11:00 and 11:15 p.m., Johnny Ace went backstage in the dressing room, playing with his gun and drinking vodka. At least five people were in the dressing room, according to different witnesses, including Johnny Ace's girlfriend Olivia Gibb, her friend Mary Carter and Big Mama Thornton. The most complete account of what happened then is the deposition given to authorities by Big Mama Thornton at 12:40 a.m. on December 26, 1954. Her exact words were: "We arrived at the City Auditorium at around 7:20 p.m. and the dance started about eight o'clock. I did not sing until about nine o'clock when I sing five numbers. The band played two more numbers. I then went to the dressing room to change clothes, but I got busy signing autographs and I did not get to change clothes. Johnny Ace came to the dressing room and he signed some autographs. He started to leave out the door when some people stopped to talk to him. About that time, Olivia, Johnny Ace's girlfriend walked up and Johnny and Olivia came into the dressing room. Johnny sit on a dresser in the dressing room and Olivia sit on his lap. Shortly after he sit down, two more people who were in the dressing room, Mary Carter and Joe Hamilton, began running around. I looked over at Johnny and noticed he had a pistol in his hand. It was a pistol he bought somewhere in Florida. It was a .22 cal. revolver. Johnny was pointing this pistol at Mary Carter and Joe Hamilton. He was kind of waving it around. I asked Johnny to let me see the gun. He gave it to me and when I turned the chamber a .22 cal. Bullet fell out in my hand. Johnny told me to put it back in where it wouldn't fall out. I put it back and gave it to him. I told him not to snap it to nobody. After he got the pistol back, Johnny pointed the pistol at Mary Carter and pulled the trigger. It snapped. Olivia was still sitting on his lap. I told Johnny again not to snap the pistol at anybody. Johnny then put the pistol to Olivia's head and pulled the trigger. It snapped. Johnny said, 'I'll show you that it won't shoot.' He held the pistol up and looked at it first and then put it to his head. I started towards the door and heard the pistol go off. I turned around and saw Johnny falling to the floor. I saw that he was shot and I run on stage and told the people in the band about it. I stayed there until the officers arrived." When Johnny Ace realized he was going to die, "that kinky hair of his shot straight out," remembers Big Mama Thornton.[41]

What was the attraction for Johnny Ace to play with pistols? Whatever it was, in the end it killed him. There are a few rumors about Johnny Ace's death but all other versions of that moment vary only a little and corroborate Thornton's version. So there is no reason to doubt what Big Mama Thornton said about Johnny Ace's last minutes. The live performance of "Yes Baby" sung by Thornton and Ace on December 26, 1954 at Houston's City Auditorium would now and for all time be Ace's last performance. Thornton had lost a long-time colleague and friend, and she showed her respect for Ace by being one of the honorary pallbearers at his funeral.

With the death of Johnny Ace, a hero for many people and other musicians, was gone. One of those musicians who admired Ace's work wanted to see him perform on this day in Houston. But he came too late. His name was Elvis Presley. Presley's guitar player, Scotty Moore, remembers: "We knew that Johnny Ace was working that week in Houston and hoped that there would be a show we could see. As it happened, he was dead before we arrived, but Elvis and I went to the venue where Johnny Ace had died and were shown the dressing room where it happened."[42]

After a long time touring, Big Mama Thornton now recorded new songs for Peacock Records, trying to make another hit and to find herself a new way without Johnny Ace. In March of 1955, "Laugh Laugh Laugh" and "The Fish" (Peacock #1650) came out, and later in the year Thornton recorded "How Come" and "Tarzan And The Dignified Monkey" with Elroy Peace on vocal (#1654). Another song that she recorded in that time, called "You don't move me no more," never got released until a CD came out in 1986 from Ace Records. The song is interesting since it features a young guitarist named Roy Gaines, brother of Grady Gaines, with a stunning guitar break. But none of these records had a big impact in the charts.

Big Mama Thornton now played the clubs on her own and also toured often with Junior Parker and Bobby "Blue" Bland, as Texas Johnny Brown recalls, who was part of Parker's and Bland's backing band. Thornton's work with Peacock Records came slowly to an end, but she was still a live attraction and toured again with the Johnny Otis Show, from coast to coast.

One time, they had to break a show with Thornton in Houston up into three shows because too many people came. In early 1956, Thornton performed at the Club Matinee in Houston at the show hosted by DJ King Bee. King Bee had a show there every Tuesday night. "She was telling jokes, since she was a comedian at one time. The first note she sang was just hair-raising. She had a very dynamic effect on me," Texas-born piano player Nat Dove recalls of seeing her then at the Club Matinee for the first time.[43]

By 1956, the rock 'n' roll age was universal, and, as Elvis Presley recorded "Hound Dog" to international acclaim, Peacock rereleased Big Mama Thornton's original version (Peacock #1612). The Presley record spurred a number of lawsuits over publishing rights. When Presley made "Hound Dog" a mega hit, Leiber and Stoller admitted they had assigned Otis one third of the mechanical rights on record sales, but they claimed they owned all of the composer's rights. Although Johnny Otis recalled that Leiber and Stoller gave him a one-third share of the writers' credit on the song, in the end Otis lost his publishing and songwriting rights, as he recalls. "They sued me in court. They won; they beat me out of it. I could have sent my kids to college, like they sent theirs," Otis said. "But, oh well, if I dwell on that I get quite unhappy, so we try to move on."[44] Although the Presley version of the song was not inspired directly by Big Mama Thornton, he had of course known of her first release of the song. Scotty Moore owns the original 78 recording of "Hound Dog" that was owned by Elvis. Moore received the record as part of the collection of records that Elvis brought to him in Nashville in 1968 to copy in his studio.

Big Mama Thornton's whole career at Peacock Records started to unraveled after Johnny Ace "decided he didn't want to be in the world no more; I guess that's what he decided, cause he blew his brain out,"[45] as Thornton later puts it, but life had to go on for her. Thornton was now seen as one who has departed from the rock/pop mainstream, and so her affiliation with Peacock Records ended. Maybe Robey refused to renew her recording contract or, as Thornton would put it, she quit recording with Peacock because the label cheated her.

3

Unlucky Girl—From Texas to California

Big Mama Thornton left Houston in 1956 and set off with Gatemouth Brown on a tour of the West Coast. Thornton now had to deal with a changing musical surrounding. First there was the rock 'n' roll age. The time for the old blues was slowing down, and many blues artists in general were barely recognized in the U.S. By contrast, the interest in the blues had grown in Europe.

Before 1940 the real blues made almost no impact upon Europe. But with war's end and a rising pan–European impetus to move on, the arts in general underwent a renaissance, of which jazz and, as a result, the blues, became a part. Many blues artists took their chance to perform in Europe in the late forties. The first one was blues pianist Sam Price, who sat down in a Paris studio in February 1948 and cut six boogie solos, thus becoming the first blues musician to record outside the U.S. The following spring Leadbelly, in his only European appearance, played several under-attended but warmly received concerts in the same city; a young Alexis Korner made the pilgrimage from London and it spurred him into becoming a busy blues pilgrim in Britain. In June 1950, Josh White recorded the first guitar blues made outside the U.S. He went on to London to broadcast for the BBC and to Milan where he recorded. The biggest single impact, however, was the appearance of Big Bill Broonzy in 1951. Between his premiere expedition and his final 1957 tour, he returned every year except 1954, played concerts in London, Nottingham, Brighton and Edinburgh; in Paris and elsewhere in France; in Brussels, Antwerp, Copenhagen, Milan and Madrid; appeared on French radio, British and Italian television; was filmed in Brussels; saw his somewhat fanciful but entertaining autobiography published; and had many European-made records issued aimed at his new European audience.

In 1958 Chris Barber brought Brownie McGhee and Sonny Terry to England, including an appearance on British television. That year also witnessed Muddy Waters' first controversial British appearance, again engineered by Barber. Within an emerging fanbase that valued the acoustic guitar as the premiere blues instrument, Muddy's amplification startled and dismayed many, but it also riveted others. In time, Jack Dupree, Memphis Slim, Roosevelt Sykes, Little Brother Montgomery and Speckled Red all appeared in England, as did Chicago harmonica player James Cotton.

By the time Big Mama Thornton went on her own in California, the traditional jazz-inspired Skiffle craze, a music steeped in the blues, was the starting point of several British acts that would later be part of the British Invasion. The most successful Skiffle musician, Lonnie Donegan, who is credited with singlehandedly popularizing Skiffle in Britain, had two top–20 U.S. pre-invasion hits in 1956. Donegan was a huge influence on just about every band that made it big in the 1960s.

One of the first blues-influenced British Skiffle bands who played in the U.S. was the Chas McDevitt Skiffle Group. The group had a hit with the song "Freight Train" and appeared on *The Ed Sullivan Show* in July 1957. As a young man Chas McDevitt got in touch with the American singer, guitarist, songwriter, actor, and civil rights activist Josh White. "I first heard Josh White on a series broadcast on the BBC in about 1950. He had his records released on Decca over here and no doubt the radio broadcasts were as a result of this. It was about this time I began writing to him. As with other youngsters my only contact to this music was via records and the radio." McDevitt recalls the time when he had the chance to finally see his icons perform: "As soon as visiting musicians came over and defied the Musicians Union ban, I went to as many live shows as possible; Big Bill Broonzy, Lonnie Johnson, T Bone Walker. I would see the occasional Blues singer like Big Joe Turner and Brownie McGhee as well as Jimmy Rushing. When in New York for our appearance on *The Ed Sullivan Show* in July 1957, I caught the Alan Freed Summer Festival at the Paramount and this featured Joe Turner, Screamin' Jay Hawkins, Chuck Berry, Sam The Man Taylor, The Moonglows, The Cadillacs, Ruth Brown, La Verne Baker, etc., etc."[1] Many British bands would follow the Chas McDevitt Skiffle Group and bring the blues back to the American audience.

But for now Big Mama Thornton could not see this coming. She settled in the Bay Area, where she mostly played local blues clubs. An old friend from the Peacock years, Jimmy McCracklin, helped her to settle. Thornton toured, with McCracklin and his band as the headliner. Jimmy had several big songs out at that time. One song called "I Just Got To Know" was recorded for his own Art-Tone label in Oakland. Later, the record made no. 2 on the R&B chart. Thornton would be advertised, in the tour package with McCracklin, as the "Hound Dog Gal."[2]

In fact, Thornton stayed with McCracklin and his wife for a long time because "she had no peoples out here," as McCracklin remembers. "I brought her with me from Texas to California. She wanted to get away from Texas because she wasn't doing too well. She was working but she wasn't making any money. She wanted to try California. I did the best that I could to help her. She lived with me in my house in Richmond, California, for five years in the late fifties before she left and lived on her own in California. But I wouldn't take care of her. She took care for herself. She went her way and got her jobs and I went my way. But she was often booked on the same shows. I was my chief and she was her chief." But, later, when Big Mama Thornton lived on her own, they always stayed in touch. "I met her so often because she lived right in San Francisco right across the bridge. And she was working with the new guy that was managing her," McCracklin remembers.

Thornton also never lost contact with Johnny Otis, and they remained close friends until Thornton died. And Thornton was a very good friend to have. If necessary she even defended Otis. Otis recalls, for instance, that one night at a dance in Florida, a drunk came out of the crowd and slapped him in the face. Thornton picked up the drunk, threw him across the floor and told him: "Don't nobody mess with my buddy!"[3] On February 9, 1957, she joined up again with her old friend and his band. She was part of a two-day show in San Francisco and Oakland where Johnny Otis presented his rock 'n' roll concert—a show featuring forty top recording artists, including Julie Stevens, The Youngsters, Mel Williams, Don and Dewey, Little Arthur Mathews, The Premiers, Arthur Jee Mays, Marie Adams and The Three Tons of Joy, Little Julian Herrera, Jackie Kelso and Abe Moore.

After she had left Houston, the single "Just Like a Dog" and "My Man Called Me" (Peacock #1681) was released as her last production for Robey's Peacock Label and "Hound Dog" had a spurt of airplay during the summer of 1958 which lead to another rerelease of the original by Peacock Records. But that didn't mean that Thornton would earn a lot of money. As Jimmy

McCracklin says about the situation in the late fifties: "In those days nobody was making big money, like they make now. She was just playing the kind of clubs that I was playing. What we call the Chitlin clubs, the small clubs. The white people were running the clubs and you just had to play along with it. That's all we could do. That was it." For Thornton, that meant that she played at many California clubs such as the Basin Street West in San Francisco, the Rhumboogie and the Gateway in Oakland and the Beach-comber Club in Santa Cruz. Living in Oakland, Thornton played mostly with a small band that included Pete Lewis on guitar, Piney Clark, and Baby Calloway on piano. She traveled in an old car and had her drum set in the back of the car. There was Big Mama Thornton, a major star on the R&B circuit only a few years ago, but light years away from the white entertainment scene at that point.

This was the time when Chris Strachwitz of Arhoolie Records first saw her performing at the small Beachcomber Club in Santa Cruz after someone recommended that he should go to her performance. The club was right on the Boardwalk right across from the beach, frequented by sailors and other young people. Thornton played drums, she had her name on the drums and she sang and played the harmonica, which she always put in a glass full of water in order to keep the instrument wet. Sometimes Thornton played harp with one hand and drums with the other. Strachwitz tried to record her, but time had not yet come for this chance. Pete Lewis was drinking a whole lot, so Thornton could not get him to play right. Pete finally just quit. Big Mama didn't have anyone to play guitar after Pete Lewis quit so Robert Lowery, who had settled in Santa Cruz in 1957, took over the guitar for a month. They even played outside Santa Cruz sometimes, with a repertoire that included also a few numbers by Jimmy Reed.

Not only rock 'n' roll but also folk music had become increasingly popular. "This folk music revival in the later 1950s and early 1960s was just that, a revival, an attempt to revive a music that most felt was already deeply embedded in the past. The revival started out looking back and, for the most part, stayed that way for many years. We sought to revive and find our future in past songs rather than writing our own songs for the future," Michael Erlewin says, and adds: "Although some blues was included in many of the early folk festivals, it was almost exclusively of the acoustic 'folk-blues' variety, more of an add-on than a featured style at folk festivals like the one in Newport, Rhode Island. It was the 'folk' in folk-blues that was what most people came to hear, not the blues. The 'blues' was just a feeling that the folk-blues held for many of us and was not recognized as the genre it is today, at least by folkies like me. Until the late '60s, modern, electric, citified blues were almost exclusively the province of black Americans, made available on black record labels or served up in hundreds of small clubs and bars across the land. White Americans didn't go there. The most famous festival for that new music is probably the Newport Folk Festival which was established in 1959 by George Wein with a lineup of the Kingston Trio, Odetta, Sonny Terry and Brownie McGhee, and Pete Seeger."[4]

Meanwhile, Big Mama Thornton met Carroll Peery in Los Angeles. Peery ran the kitchen and bar of L.A.'s famous blues club, Ash Grove, for many years and was the manager for the Chambers Brothers, a soul-music group, best known for its 1968 hit, the 11-minute song "Time Has Come Today." Peery was very impressed with what Thornton did know about the blues and what the blues was for. Peery told her that he liked her performance and that she could be quite a successful act in the future. Of course, Thornton was very happy to hear this not knowing that Peery was correct with his vision. Though they didn't immediately start working together, Peery would later help Thornton to find her way back in the business.

Also in 1959, a 15-year-old boy named Billy Dunn was introduced to Thornton by her regular guitar player at that time, Jimmie Mamou. The first time Billy Dunn played with Thornton was the Beachcomber Club in Santa Cruz. They played together for about five years in the summer when the boardwalk was open. In the wintertime, they stopped playing there. Their song list at this time consisted of mostly blues covers, like the Lowell Fulson song "Reconsider Baby" or "My Little Boy Was A Country Boy" and "Mother in Law," and a few of Thornton's songs like "Hound Dog," plus some rock 'n' roll. Thornton lived in the Eddy Hotel and Motel on Eddy Street in San Francisco at the time. She had a room that was her home base, where she kept her things when she was on the road.

After Big Mama Thornton, Jimmie Mamou and Billy Dunn played for a while in Santa Cruz, they also got some gigs in Russell City in the year 1961. Russell City was a little town of African-Americans who migrated to California from the Deep South. It was one of the proving grounds for many blues musicians. Russell City, an unincorporated area of Hayward, California, was about twelve minutes from the city of Oakland, this community of modest houses and small farms along the bay is now gone.

During its heyday, Russell City was a down-home community, known for its clubs with dirt floors, bootleg electricity and a steady stream of musicians playing a unique style of Delta blues. Russell City was part of the county, with a county sheriff rather than a police force. It was a very tough town. If you played in Russell and you couldn't play, then you better get out. But Big Mama could play, so they went to the Russell City Country Club and played two or three times on Friday and Saturday nights. The Russell City Country Club was a little country nightclub. There were cows and the smell was in the air. One time, Thornton and Billy Dunn had a fight there on the bandstand. Dunn went to jail, and Thornton tried to help him, so they took her too. Thornton was on probation for having a couple of fights in Santa Cruz before this happened. So she and Dunn got in jail and stayed in jail for a couple hours. When they got out they were fast friends again. Thornton would cook for him in his mother's house, something she liked to do a lot. They met Jimmy Reed in his hotel and jammed with Billy Dunn playing the piano, Reed playing harp and guitar, and Big Mama Thornton playing harp and singing. But after the fight on stage, the Russell City Country Club soon fired Thornton; when she was also fired from the Beachcomber Club in Santa Cruz, Billy Dunn and Jimmy Mamou stayed at the club on their own.

A little time after Carroll Peery had met Thornton for the first time, he became a partner in a nightclub called The Cabale in Berkeley. Thornton had called him for some work in the club and soon they became friends because she trusted him. There were all kinds of managers that wanted to grab her and for a person that cannot write and read properly it's an easy thing to get cheated. So she asked Peery for some help. He suggested a manager for her and introduced them. But it didn't work out. While Thornton was still struggling finding gigs, there were the first signs in the air that this may change. Muddy Waters had just played the Newport Jazz Festival with great success. His live recording from the festival was Grammy-nominated, and it became a blues commerce center. The proceedings were filmed by the United States Information Service, and Chess records issued *Muddy Waters at Newport*, quickly released on Nixa in the UK. The impact was enormous, and it became an iconic album, deeply impressing young lads like Eric Clapton and Mick Jagger.

Beginning in June 1960, Paul and Valerie Oliver, armed with a BBC tape recorder and a decent camera, accompanied part of the way by Strachwitz, spent the summer traveling in the U.S. and recording blues artists for what would become both the book and record *Conversation with the Blues*, as well as the foundations of Arhoolie Records. Seen now as a major milestone in blues history, this three-month expedition netted performances by over 50 artists, from Roosevelt Sykes and Otis Spann through Black Ace and Lightning Hopkins to J. B. Lenoir and beyond.

Returning to Britain, Paul Oliver prepared the material into three radio shows broadcast by the BBC, and in November 1960 Chris Strachwitz launched Arhoolie Records with an LP by Mance Lipscomb, recorded that summer. Within the same time frame German writer Joachim Berendt and American photographer William Claxton also toured the U.S. They were looking for jazz of all persuasions as well as blues and gospel.

All this happened in the beginning without any direct consequences for Big Mama Thornton's career. The black blues audience had aged, as the artist had. The next generation of black youth identified themselves more with the burgeoning soul sound. Blues music was stigmatized as their parents' music. Thornton only played small clubs and, like many of her contemporary blues colleagues, struggled to make a living.

Nineteen sixty-one would bring Big Mama Thornton her next chances to record. Thornton recorded her first 45's since leaving Peacock Records for the Bay-Tone Label in Oakland owned by Bradley Taylor. Taylor recorded, between 1958 and 1963, both obscure and better-known artists. Among his recording artists Thornton was the most well-known. Her song recorded for the label included "You Did Me Wrong" and "Big Mama's Blues" (Bay-Tone #107). *Billboard* mentioned her single in the May 15, 1961, issue and highlights that "Willie Mae Thornton returns to the world of recording with this shouting reading of standard blues effort. Her vitality could help it get spins."[5] Despite the good critical notice, the single was no success. Thornton also recorded another song for Taylor's Bay-Tone label that would soon be her second signature hit, "Ball and Chain." Bay-Tone Records didn't have the sense to release the song, but had her sign an agreement that caused her trouble when she planned to release the song a few years later. The same year, Thornton also recorded for Bob Geddins on his Irma Label. Geddins was a San Francisco Bay Area-based R&B musician and record producer. Geddins was also called the "Godfather of Oakland Blues," founded and owned numerous small independent record labels, including Art-Tone, Big Town or Irma. Geddins produced acts including

Lowell Fulson, Jimmy McCracklin, Johnny Fuller, Sugar Pie DeSanto and Etta James, but never made the big business. In fact, he had to change his studios often since he never could pay the rent. And Big Mama Thornton's recording for his label, the single "Big Mama's Coming Home" / "Don't Talk Back" (Irma 13X), wasn't a big hit either.

4

"I'm Feeling Alright"

The first attempts of Chris Strachwitz to record Big Mama Thornton with Gatemouth Brown and his band failed. But he would not give up on the plan to record her. There is a strange rumor that Thornton sang and danced at that time in an obscure group called the Cherry Sisters in order to make a living. But other than the fact that this is mentioned in some places and in one liner note, there is no proof for this.

A big change for the better came in 1964. At the time, Thornton performed often at the Savoy Hotel in Richmond. "I had my office in the California Hotel in L.A., which was a very popular hotel for black entertainers at that time. There was a local singer, Bob Jeffries who knew both of us. He kept telling me about this woman that was working in Richmond at the Savoy that could really sing," Jimmy Moore remembers. "And Bill said, 'But I don't think she knows the business, and you are a manager.' He said, 'I think if you guys got together you could really do something.' So I said, 'Ok,' and he would tell me what room she was in. She was living at the hotel at that time. And every day he would ask me: 'Did you call her?' and I said, 'No I didn't get around to it.' There was a Chinese restaurant in the hotel, and I was having coffee one day and he was telling me again, 'You know really I wish she was here,' and at that moment she walked through the door and he said, 'There she is now.' And he said to her, 'This is the guy I've been telling you about' so we had a little chat. I went over to the jazz workshop to see Cannonball Adderly. At the break we were talking, and I said to him, 'You know I was talking to this blues singer Big Mama Thornton. I'm thinking about signing her.' And he said, 'Sign her tomorrow man.' So I took his advice and when I came back, I signed her."[1] Jimmy Moore, owner of Jasman Records, created in 1959, had already produced Joan Adams and The Veshells, a female vocal trio. With Moore as her manager, the big festivals and shows came back into Big Mama Thornton's life and

Four Chicago bluesmen backstage somewhere in the English Midlands during a blues tour around 1964. From left: Muddy Waters and Otis Spann jam with Sonny Terry and Brownie McGee in between sets (© John "Hoppy" Hopkins).

she could benefit from the growing interest in her music. "When I signed her she was working as support for $25 a night. I was talking to Ralph Gleason and I mentioned to him that I had signed her. And he mentioned it to Jimmy Lyons, who was the producer of the Monterey Jazz Festival. Jimmy Lyons called me and Big Mama did that first festival show in 1964."

Besides Big Mama Thornton, the Monterey Jazz Festival featured some of the greatest jazz and blues musicians at that time, such as the Duke Ellington Orchestra, the Dizzy Gillespie Quintet and the Miles Davis Quintet with Wayne Shorter, Herbie Hancock, Ron Carter and Tony Williams, Gerry Mulligan, the Thelonious Monk Quartet, Lou Rawls, Joe Williams, Woody Herman and the Art Farmer Quartet. But it was Big Mama Thornton who was the big hit at the festival. According to William Minor in his book Monterey Jazz Festival Forty Legendary Years, Thornton "would become a Festival favorite." He adds: "Yet the Monterey audience recognized her for what she was: the real thing, an authentic blues singer. On "Hound Dog" her voice remained playful even while wailing, growling, wagging her

46

tail, barking, bitching—all at the same time."[2] And Ralph Gleason wrote that Thornton was "pound for pound the best woman blues singer alive today."[3] In fact, Thornton would play the festival again to great success in 1966 and 1968.

Following her appearances at the festival, Thornton did some local shows and clubs around her home area. She had moved to Los Angeles and she began to get serious about things, and seemed to be fine. She played at the Jazz Workshop in Boston with Muddy Waters, a double show with Miles Davis, and another one with Louie Jordan. "Miles asked Big Mama to do some tune on her harmonica and he said, 'Man I wish I could play harmonica like that,'" remembers Jimmy Moore.

On February 26, 1965, Thornton played the Santa Monica Civic Center in Los Angeles with Chuck Berry and Skip James and others. On February 27, Thornton was one of the performers at the blues festival in the Berkeley Community Centre. The concert was headlined by Chuck Berry and Big

Howling Wolf (center) with Sunnyland Slim (piano), Hubert Sumlin (guitar) and Willie Dixon (upright bass) at the 3rd American Folk Blues Festival Tour 1964 in England (© John "Hoppy" Hopkins).

Mama Thornton was announced as the "Hit of the Monterey Jazz Festival." Other performers were the Chambers Brothers and Fred McDowell.

Then the big chance for Big Mama Thornton came with a call from Germany, where Horst Lippmann and Fritz Rau had organized the American Folk Blues Festival since 1962. These festivals were tours through Europe with groups of black blues artists thankful to get some work. The festival continued almost annually until 1972, and then after an eight-year hiatus the festival again took place in 1980 until its final performance in 1985.

The idea for the American Folk Blues Festival came from the German jazz publicist Joachim-Ernst Berendt after his U.S. trip in 1960, and promoters Horst Lippmann and Fritz Rau brought his idea to fruition. Lippmann, who was a great jazz fan, was aware of the fact that blues had been a strong element of African American music since the 1920s. John Lewis, the pianist with the Modern Jazz Quartet, gave Lippmann and Rau the suggestion about blues music. The quartet toured Europe in 1957, and Lewis told them about the kingdom of the blues that was not even well-known in the U.S. Lippmann and Rau were jazz promoters and had just finished a tour with Cannonball Adderly, who had played with Miles Davis. Cannonball gave them the address of Dixon, the influential blues composer and bassist from Chicago, and from 1958 on Lippmann and Rau experimented with getting Willie Dixon over to Europe. Finally, in 1962, they were able to present the first real blues program in Europe. In that first program were Memphis Slim, T-Bone Walker, Shakey Jake, Willie Dixon, Helen Humes, Sonny Terry, Brownie McGhee, John Lee Hooker and drummer Armand "Jump" Jackson. Dixon was so warmly received in Europe that he thought all of his blues friends should come over and play in the European countries. The American Folk Blues Festival won a completely new audience, namely young people who saw that rock 'n' roll came from the blues. As a result Horst Lippmann went to America's ghettos to find, with the help of Willie Dixon, good blues singers who were not known outside of their little area and brought them every year to perform in Europe. Dixon was a pivotal figure in the European breakthrough of blues. By contacting Dixon they were given access to the blues culture of the southern United States. In the course of the next years, over a hundred blues artists performed at the American Folk Blues Festival, many of them several times.

While white America for the most part did not even know this music existed until the late sixties, Europe had been in love with American black music after World War II, especially blues and jazz, and it quickly became a more hospitable home for blues artists than America. Now, with the American Folk Blues Festival, for the very first time, a wide range of marginalized and often too long forgotten American blues musicians played in Europe's biggest concert halls.

The impact of the American Folk Blues Festival was remarkable for the American blues musicians. It arrived just in time for a generational shift that brought an entire new audience to the blues. Thanks to the festivals, Europe heard such blues greats as T-Bone Walker, Memphis Slim, Willie Dixon, Sonny Terry, Brownie McGhee, John Lee Hooker and Big Mama Thornton. In a very real sense, Europe was privileged to hear the more modern, electric, city blues well before the general (white) public in America knew anything about it. While renowned blues legends like Muddy Waters, Howlin' Wolf or Big Mama Thornton found it hard to get a job outside of their hometown bars and the Chitlin' Circuit, these players were treated like royalty in Europe, and they played to large audiences in big concert halls.

"Today we realize that these tours of Europe by many of the best, authentic blues personalities, signaled the start of a worldwide appreciation for and fascination with the blues, one of the most appealing and unique of American musical folk traditions," notes Chris Strachwitz.[4]

When the festival started, its impact was most visible in England. In England there were only a few blues bands, like Alexis Corners Blues Incorporated or the Rolling Stones. It was hard for them to get access to original blues records, so the Festival Package was, along with the effort of Chris Barber, one of the first chances for blues fans to hear this music live in concert. During the very first American Folk Blues Festival in 1962 the young Keith Richards and Mick Jagger visited the show at the Free Trade Hall in Manchester to see Sonny Terry, Brownie McGhee, John Lee Hooker, Muddy Waters and others. Led Zeppelin singer Robert Plant recalls seeing to Bukka White, Son House, Sonny Terry and Brownie McGhee for the first time at Birmingham Town Hall between 1963 and 1966, during the American Folk Blues Festival. He says: "When I met Sonny Terry, I had to help him guide the rubber stamp he used to autograph albums."[5] One of the first songs the young Robert Plant sang was Muddy Waters' "Got my Mojo Working."

Those groups were, after hearing their idols in Europe through the

American Folk Blues Festival, busy recording covers of blues classics and pointing out the source—the artists who originally wrote and recorded them. So it was the British bands that showed white Americans how to play the blues. When Willie Dixon and Muddy Waters came to England as part of the festival they met the young British blues musicians and left tapes for them.

The first album of the Rolling Stones from April 1964 contained tunes like Jimmy Reed's "Honest I Do" Willie Dixon's "I Just Want to Make Love to You," "I'm a King Bee," plus songs by Chuck Berry and Rufus Thomas. A month later Muddy Waters told the *Melody Maker* about the Rolling Stones: "They're my boys. I like their version of 'I Just Want to Make Love to You.' They fade it out just like we did. One more trip and they'll have it. Believe me, I'll come back one more time and then I won't need to come back no more."[6] He was absolutely right with his vision. With the first album they called the attention of the young white audiences in the U.S. to the delights and profundity of the blues.

Chris Huston from the British band The Undertakers, one of those bands belonging to the so-called British Invasion, recalls the impact of the blues on his music: "The first blues recordings that I can ever remember hearing were those of Huddie 'Leadbelly' Ledbetter and Sonny Terry and Brownie McGhee. This would have been in the late fifties. To me they were, at the time, something to do with, and a part of, the folk music that seemed to be popular in the mid to late fifties, and which was a music that I was not particularly attracted to. But Leadbelly and Sonny Terry and Brownie McGhee were different. How different, and what that difference was, I only saw as the color of their skin and the soulful way they sang, although I could never have expressed it that way, back then. Of course, they were singing the blues. But I was introduced to the blues under the auspices of folk music, and knowing no difference, accepted that. It was only a few years later, in the early 1960s, that I found and heard blues music for real. We, The Undertakers, were starting to get popular and were going down to London and the South of England to play shows. While in London we would go to the various record stores there and were exposed to a range of music choices that were not available in Liverpool, at that time. There were also the street markets, where there would be people selling vinyl albums, some new and some used. I got my first albums from the street markets. As might be expected after all this time, I cannot remember the exact order in which I bought those early albums, but they included such artists as Ray Charles, Lowell Fulson, John Lee Hooker, Bobby "Blue" Bland, James Brown, Otis Spann, Howlin' Wolf, Lightnin' Hopkins and Lonnie Johnson. To be truthful, I did not know what I was listening to when I played those early blues records. I had no musical sophistication, nor the knowledge that would go with it. I just knew that something very special was going on. I was mesmerized by it and 'sucked it up.'"[7]

In 1964 Lippmann and Rau wanted to have Lightnin' Hopkins on the American Folk Blues Festival tour. That's when they got in touch with Chris Strachwitz. During the tour Strachwitz told the Germans about Big Mama Thornton and her appearances at the Monterey Jazz Festival, because he knew that Rau and Lippmann were looking for a female blues voice. They always wanted a woman singer on the program. In 1964, they had Sugar Pie De Santo in the program. But now they had booked Big Mama Thornton.

5

Big Mama Thornton's First European Tour

Chris Strachwitz still had Big Mama Thornton's contact information after he had met her in Los Angeles some time before. So he went on to arrange everything, and in September 1965 he, Jimmy Moore and Big Mama Thornton flew over to Germany where the American Folk Blues Festival of 1965 began on September 27, 1965. The fact that Thornton was going on tour through Europe already gave her good press in her home country. So the *Oakland Tribune* wrote that she "may not be the most widely known or the greatest artist in her field (though one of the best) there is no question she is biggest."[1]

The European tour started with a TV show that was filmed from September 27–30 in Baden-Baden/Germany. Lippmann and Rau had organized a television production, *Jazz Heard and Seen with Joachim Ernst Berendt*, that included Thornton. The video from that production is a great example of Thornton's appearance during that time and can be seen on the DVD collection *American Folk Blues Festival.*

The first live show took place on October 1 in Bern, Switzerland, followed by appearances in Switzerland (Lausanne, Zürich, Luzern, Basel, Genf), Germany (Mannheim, Bremen, Hamburg, Berlin, Düsseldorf, Iserlohn, Munich, Frankfurt), Denmark (Copenhagen), Sweden (Stockholm), England (London, Manchester, Newcastle, Glasgow, Birmingham, Bristol), Belgium (Brussels), Netherlands (Amsterdam, The Hague), Ireland (Belfast, Dublin), France (Strasbourg, Paris) and Spain (Barcelona). In addition to Big Mama Thornton, the lineup for the American Folk Blues Festival in 1965 consisted of J. B. Lenoir, Buddy Guy, Eddie Boyd, Lonesome Jimmy, Lee Robinson, Fred Below, John Lee Hooker, Roosevelt Sykes, Big Walter, Shaky Horton, Fred McDowell and Dr. Ross.

CITY HALL,

Northumberland Road, Newcastle upon Tyne, 1.

SATURDAY, 16th OCTOBER, 1965
at 7.30 p.m.

NATIONAL JAZZ FEDERATION

presents

4th AMERICAN
FOLK - BLUES FESTIVAL

F 74

BALCONY 6/–   SEAT

Booking Agents: A. E. Cook, Limited, 5-6, Saville Place Newcastle upon Tyne, (Tel. 22901).

This Portion to be retained.

Philips Printers Ltd., Newcastle upon Tyne

Ticket for the 4th American Folk Blues Festival show on October 16, 1965, in Newcastle upon Tyne, England (author's collection).

Big Mama was always put on at the end of each show. She was the highlight. And she had a good band behind her. Thornton knew this was her big chance for a comeback and she gave it all she got. In Paris only one concert was scheduled, but bowing to public demand, there was another show presented on midnight. Both shows were sold out and Thornton got, according to *Billboard*, "storming applause."[2]

In London, they presented the Festival Concert in the Royal Albert Hall three times in succession. Lippmann and Rau brought the blues to all these beautiful halls. In Zurich, for example, they played in the concert hall and not simply in a nightclub. The artists stayed in gorgeous hotels and for many of them it was a culture shock to be suddenly in Europe playing in lovely concert halls.

From left: Shakey Horton, Big Mama Thornton, J.B. Lenore, and Dr. Ross performing at the 4th American Folk Blues Festival at the Fairfield Hall in Croyton, England, on October 11, 1965 (© Val Wilmer).

The musicians were deeply moved by the enthusiasm and even the love of the public. They felt the appreciation and for many of these artists, it was difficult to find their way in these new surroundings. For instance, Sonny Boy Williams was a bull in a china shop and he did some damage to a bathroom in a good hotel. The festival crew was almost thrown out of that place. Or Shakey Jake Harris, a young harmonica player from Chicago, who gave his harp to Brian Jones from the Rolling Stones: the police arrested Shakey because he wanted to take a girl to his room. In those days the hotel regulations in Germany were quite strict and the doorman wouldn't let the woman enter. Shakey pulled out his knife. He didn't hurt anyone but they called the police anyway. The next morning they woke up Fritz Rau. He went to the chief of police and was able to free Shakey. The police chief happened to be on the board of several folk music clubs. Rau told him about the blues and Shakey played the blues for him, and the chief was knocked out, so the tour could be continued with Shakey.

As Jimmy Moore remembers, the atmosphere was great and the European audience enjoyed the shows very much: "Fritz Rau and Horst Lippman, they were nice people. I really enjoyed that. I bought along a tape recorder for rehearsal purposes. The first reception was so great, I made a tape to send it to Ralph Gleason and interviewed some people. I interviewed everybody that was on the bill. And the conversation was, 'Why do you think the reception is so much greater than back home,' and of course they all gave their opinion. The American Folk Blues Festival was really

Big Mama Thornton performing at the 4th American Folk Blues Festival at the Fairfield Hall in Croyton, England, on October 11, 1965 (© Val Wilmer).

something. The first night we played in Baden-Baden. We were all so amazed at the size and the type of audience that we played. Big Mama wore cowboy boots, jeans and a big hat. She was big and tough. There was complete silence during the performance and then afterwards standing ovations. And the first night after she did about three or four numbers the audience was so moved when they gave her a big bouquet of roses. She cried. She cried onstage. I couldn't believe it. When we started to tour, lots of little things happened. It was quite an experience for both of us. The type of hall that we played in and the audience was so attentive, well dressed. What really got us: you could hear a pin drop while she sang, awesome. I have to credit the Europeans with really listening to the blues with respect. It really opened my eyes to the blues. Like Fred McDowell or Eddie Boyd, I didn't even know who they were until that tour." Jimmy Moore recalls a story that proves Big Mama Thornton wasn't blind to her rights, although she must have been overwhelmed by the success she had: "I recall one night we all did a recording after the show and were trying to get Big Mama out early so she could get some rest. It was like two o'clock in the morning because we had had the recording to do. We were trying to get Big Mama Thornton to finish so she could get some rest. I was just nervous, everybody was nervous. They were trying hard to get the recording correct and finally they had it correct. They paid me as usual. So I was standing outside and I remember it was cold. There was a cab waiting, I had the door open and so she comes out and stops. And that time she was very huge. I had my back to her and could feel her breath. And she says 'Where is my money. I want my money. You didn't sing did you?' And I said 'I have it as usual, what are you talking about.' She was really mad and upset. But we finally got in the car and took off."[3]

Tour member Buddy Guy remembers the tour and Big Mama Thornton's professionalism very well: "During one of those concerts when I was playing 'Hound Dog' behind her, her teeth fell out. I didn't know what she'd do. Well, sir, she just bent down, picked up her teeth, and put 'em back in her mouth without missing a lick. She kept on singing, and holy shit, that woman could sing!"[4]

In her hometown paper, this festival tour soon got a lot of recognition. The *Oakland Tribune* wrote about the tour, recognizing that it provides a new perspective for all members of the American Folk Blues Festival.

During the festival, Thornton also got the chance to finally produce an album for Chris Strachwitz's Arhoolie Records. "I had finally realized what an amazing versatile singer Big Mama was when I heard her jamming with only Fred McDowell's eerie slide guitar backing her improvised lyrics in a hotel room," Strachwitz recalls.[5] *Big Mama in Europe* was recorded on October 20, 1965, at the Wessex Studio in London and released on Arhoolie F1028. "Just about every musician on the tour wanted to back her but Buddy Guy had an all-star band from Chicago and was the official backup band at the nightly concerts. For the recording the All Stars all came to the studio and Fred McDowell contributed the right taste of country blues magic."[6] The backing band for Big Mama Thornton included Buddy Guy (guitar), Eddie Boyd (piano or organ), Walter "Shakey" Horton (harmonica) and

Fred Below (drums) and Jimmy Lee Robinson (bass). All musicians were members of the year's American Folk Blues Festival and had been backing Thornton at concerts earlier on the tour in Germany. Besides tunes that Big Mama wrote on her own, like "Swing It On Home" or "Down Home Shakedown," the band also recorded a new version of "Hound Dog" and the Willie Dixon song "Little Red Rooster" plus a song called "Unlucky Girl" that was given to her by Jack Dupree whom she met along the festival route. The CD version of that recording also contains an interview session between Big Mama Thornton and Chris Strachwitz. It's one of the very few audio interviews with Thornton that still exists.

"I never enjoyed myself more in my old homeland than during these tours with musicians loved and admired. It was an amazing experiment— not only getting to know the artists and their cultures better—but seeing the enthusiastic reception given them by audiences all over Europe," German-born Chris Strachwitz says.[7] This feeling can also be read too through the lines of the article by David Illingworth in the *English Jazz Journal* from November 1965, reviewing the show at the Fairfield Hall, Croyton, England, October 11, 1965: "Sitting down saying 'I'm gone do the best I can,' McDowell played some wonderful bottleneck guitar and sang the slow blues with moving simplicity, head nodding from side to side.... All too soon Fred McDowell was gone, but Big Mama Thornton was no anti-climax. Her voice was a big surprise to me, being far less rough than on the records I have heard. On her first number particularly, a medium swinger "Further Up The Road," she showed a great feeling for light and shade.... "The Right Time" (Ray Charles version) followed, and then Mama's famous Hound Dog—a fine stomping piece, with Guy Wailing on guitar. The show ended with a mass instrumental rave; Lenore, Shakey Horton, Dr. Ross and Mama Thornton all playing harmonicas, Sykes and Eddie Boyd duetting at the piano, and a good old Fred McDowell doing a little buck dance."[8]

The European fans had little or no knowledge about black culture and didn't even know the language but the blues musicians were treated like stars. And most of them had never experienced something like this before in their home country. So it was for Big Mama Thornton. Her success in Europe was incredible. Thornton would, for the rest of her life, always tell friends and family that she felt great in Europe since they didn't treat her like second class, but like someone with a very special talent. "She was so celebrated. The first time she encountered anything like that was at the Monterey Jazz Festival. She was a huge hit. And then in Europe people adored her. They brought flowers up to her. She was totally amazed by it. But in a way it was also very difficult to be back in the U.S. then," Jimmy Moore says.

6

Back Home

While Big Mama Thornton toured successfully through Europe, times had changed at home. Only a little before this time, American blues music was a dead art in its own country. During the mid- and late 1960s, all that changed. Now slightly after the British Invasion, which spawned such bands as the Sir Douglas Quintet and the Beau Brummels, the late summer and early fall of 1965 saw the emerging dancehall scene in San Francisco and the arrival of bands like the Jefferson Airplane, Quicksilver Messenger Service and the Grateful Dead.

In 1964 the Haight Ashbury district of San Francisco showed no signs of being the birthplace of a movement that would cause such a furor throughout the United States and around the world. The Haight was a quiet, blue-collar neighborhood where students, professors, workers, and immigrants lived. There was one coffeehouse on Hayes Street, really nearer in spirit to the University of San Francisco's drama department than to anything that would happen later in Haight. This was the Blue Unicorn founded by Sheila McCafferty and Jackson DeGovia, two actors from the University.

There were secondhand shops on Divisadero Street where artists went to buy their clothes, and there was Mike Ferguson's Magic Theatre For Madmen Only, a title borrowed from Hermann Hesse. The dress code for the newly emerging generation became an eclectic mixture of Edwardian and Cowboy. The hip district in the San Francisco of 1960–1964 was North Beach where the "beatniks" (*San Francisco Chronicle* writer Herb Caen coined the term) discussed politics, played folk music, listened to jazz, and where people like Allen Ginsberg, Michael McClure, Jack Kerouac, Gary Snyder, Neal Cassidy and a whole generation from the 1950s drank wine, traded stories and came to terms with their "beat" condition.

While visiting natives of the Amazon, Ginsberg learned about hallucinogens. He joined the Great Being, as he called it. Golden insects appeared to him, he heard the noises of the jungle animals, and he felt great empathy with the Amazon peoples, especially the four who had taken the drugs with him. Ginsberg took some of these potions back to New York for further experimentation. His interest in consciousness expanding drugs ultimately brought him into contact with Timothy Leary, who had made a similar trip to the southern lands, in this case Mexico. The Mazatec people of Mexico used psilocybin mushrooms in their religious ceremonies. In August of 1960, Timothy Leary went to Guernavaca and ingested the mushrooms.

At Harvard, Leary met Richard Alpert with whom he was to write many papers, articles and books on consciousness-expanding drugs. Harvard University became alarmed at the messianic and psychedelic zeal of Leary and Alpert, and the men were set free from academia in 1963: to change the world through the use of psychotropic drugs and to make this new spiritual medicine available for everyone. Ginsberg, Kerouac, and other influential members of the beat generation were in sympathy with Leary's and Alpert's mission and they became the Johnny Appleseeds of a new era.

Thus, Leary and Alpert (later known as Ram Dass) began a sort of drug propaganda campaign. They traveled, beginning in 1964, from one college to another reporting on the effects of the new drugs and raving about their splendid psychedelic adventures. For many of their listeners their talk was an enchanted window that looked out to a new human behavior, where a positive new life and true self-knowledge were possible. Thus, the new drug LSD had come into its own and the psychedelic culture had begun. LSD is an abbreviation for lysergic acid diethylamide, and it was known colloquially as acid. Several groups were formed for the purpose of testing, toasting and tasting the effects of LSD. The central figure in this experimental period was Ken Kesey, celebrated author of *One Flew Over The Cuckoo's Nest*, who, with his Merry Pranksters, toured the country in a wildly colored bus called Further and spread the word about acid. The "Acid Tests" propagated the (still legal) use of LSD because they were a vivid musical, social, artistic example of the possibilities of the drug. Kesey began his acquaintance with LSD and the CIA at Stanford University, but now he moved out into society with a group of pioneers, beautiful, creative, adventurous young people in the vanguard of their time. The CIA wanted to use LSD as a chemical weapon. Kesey's family wanted to use LSD as a love drug.

Psychotropic drugs were only one aspect of this new age, and not the most important aspect either. A whole generation became positive in outlook, hopeful for the future. This was quite a change from the Beat era which was rather one of despair and cynicism. The counterculture that formed in San Francisco from 1965 to 1970 was a world of color, growth, enthusiasm and a feeling that with just a little bit of luck, the world could change. Womens' rights, civil rights, gay rights, the rights of people less fortunate than the majority began to be considered seriously. There was a new feeling of empathy and a hope that there just might be a chance to solve some real problems, the main problem being the war in Vietnam. If you take LSD, it becomes difficult to think of killing another creature, especially for such a questionable goal as empire building.

"Can You Pass the Acid Test?" was the question asked by the circle around Ken Kesey and the successful celebrant was ordained into the Holy Communion, the select circle, of the new movement. The first Acid Test was held in a house in La Honda near Santa Cruz, California, where the Merry Pranksters congregated. There were film clips and a light show flickering on the walls, the Warlocks (later renamed the Grateful Dead) played. The Beat generation's search for new adventures and lifestyles evolved into a political change in American society.

John F. Kennedy, a Democrat, had been in the White House and his courageous spirit raised the expectations of young people. President Kennedy promoted and emphasized a new national worth in his campaign speeches, recognizing the idealism and the rights of the individual. He called for everyone to contribute personally to the common good. He wanted a break with the past, a New Frontier, which would signal, among other things, a new commitment to eliminating social injustices and the building of a positive new relationship with other countries in the world.

Young people accepted Kennedy's invitation to develop their personal initiative and to begin to correct such obvious social injustices as racism, which was daily becoming more explosive and dangerous to a free society. The highpoint in the new emphasis on racial equality was the August 1963 Washington protest march of 250,000 people of all colors. From the Lincoln Memorial, the participants made heartfelt pleas demanding justice for all, and in conclusion Martin Luther King electrified the crowd with his famous "I have a dream" speech, which sounded like a hymn with a rhythm and beauty that are still enthralling.

The growing civil-rights movement and the revolt against the Vietnam War were important cornerstones for a movement which was meant to create a different social model. Rock musicians, students, artists, beatniks, freaks, adventurers, dreamers and young people in general formed a new cultural scene. This movement, the counterculture, found its expression in music, light shows, drugs, and an alternative lifestyle of thinking and reading about new ideas. All of this was a fertile ground for the psychedelic music. Young people were looking for an outlet, an escape route, from their insecure and threatened position as potential draftees for a war that they saw as misguided at best. The scene in San Francisco and Berkeley seemed to at the time like a desperate chance to party before it all ended. On October 16, 1965, there was an event called "A Tribute To Dr. Strange" at the Longshoreman's Hall. This was the first psychedelic rock concert in the world. The Jefferson Airplane played, as did The Marbles and The Great Society. Many in that Longshoreman's Hall congregation had come straight from the first antiwar demonstration in the Bay Area. Some days later, the light show and the music would be organized for Timothy Leary, who was in prison because of his drug experiments. The first of three shows took place on November 6, 1965, and the enthusiasm was overpowering. The community now got a sense of its own size. Shortly after that the scene in San Francisco expanded. Psychedelic music was the soundtrack for these new adventures. The Beatles' concert in San Francisco in October 1965 signaled a change from the folk music of the Beats to the electric rock music of the Haight Ashbury era.

In Haight Ashbury, the Thelin brothers opened the world's first psychedelic head shop on January 1, 1966, offering books on LSD and other drugs, scented candles, records and San Francisco band posters. Psychedelic drugs were, for the Thelin brothers and an increasing number of their contemporaries, a signpost that would show the way out of this crisis. The Psychedelic Shop quickly became a meeting place for devotees of a new alternative culture. Shortly after the opening of the shop, there was a three-day event, the Trips Festival, which signaled the unofficial debut of the steadily growing psychedelic community. Bands like the Jefferson Airplane, Grateful Dead and Big Brother & the Holding Company would soon rise to fame while playing in places like the Avalon Ballroom, the Fillmore Auditorium or the Matrix. Big Mama Thornton would play with each of these bands many times.

"While within the black community the door was slowly closing on the blues artists (even the artists knew this), another and much wider door for this music was opening onto white America, an open door that would extend the careers for many of these artists and secure their music well into the future," explains Michael Erlewine.[1] That's when the world's millions of rock fans got caught up in the "roots" revival through concerts like the American Folk Blues Festival, because the interest in true, authentic folk music evolved into the interest in true, authentic blues music. Many of the musicians in San Francisco, Los Angeles and New York had been playing folk music and that folk music slowly evolved into a real interest in folk blues. From there it was just a matter of plugging in. The fact that blues was the basis for rock 'n' roll and allowed emotional, fevered solos made it all more alluring. This new development brought B. B. King, Albert King, Big Mama Thornton, Bessie Smith, Mance Lipscomb, Freddie King, Ma Rainey, Skip James, Elizabeth Cotton, Mississippi John Hurt, Muddy Waters and a number of other blues artists out of obscurity and onto the charts, almost at the eleventh hour.

The black American blues artists clearly saw this connection, and Muddy Waters once said at a 1970 concert in London, "If it wasn't for the Stones, none of the white kids in the States would have heard of Muddy Waters, B.B. King or any of 'em. Nobody knew my music in the States until they played it."[2] Thornton, among others, was more than willing to be discovered. She needed the money and appreciated the recognition.

Back home in Los Angeles from her European tour, Thornton recorded the Gershwin song "Summertime" and "Truth Comes To The Light" (#0033/#0034), "Tomcat" (#0039) and "Yes I Cried/Mercy" (#0050) for Sotoplay Records, her first single since 1961. Sotoplay's owner Nate McCoy remembers, "Through George 'Harmonica' Smith, I hooked up with Big Mama Thornton. They was tight, and I was a writer and a lot of people thought I was a good writer. Big Mama said, 'I'll let you write for me.' She was the greatest blues singer ever and I got along with her great. She'd tell people: 'This is my song writer.'"[3] Smith became a longtime friend of Thornton. He himself was a respected blues legend. Besides accompanying artists like Thornton, he made his own records. He also was kind of a father figure for other young harmonica player like Rod Piazza and others.

The same year Thornton also recorded for Kent Records, with the Johnny Talbot Band, "Before Day" and "Me And My Chauffeur" (#424

Kent). Besides singing and playing the harmonica, Thornton also played drums on those songs. "Me And My Chauffeur" or the "Chauffeur Blues," as the song was also called, was originally performed and recorded in 1941 by Memphis Minnie. Jefferson Airplane recorded a version of this song on the *Jefferson Airplane Takes Off* album, with Signe Anderson as the lead vocalist. On April 25, 1966, Thornton made her next recordings. For Galaxy, she recorded "Because It's Love" (749) and "Life Goes On" (746).

While the Muddy Waters Band is playing at the second Berkeley Blues Festival in April 1966, Chris Strachwitz, who was one of the organizers of the festival, took the opportunity to ask Muddy Waters if he would be interested in a recording with Thornton. "It took almost every dollar I had in the bank to make that session come true," Chris Strachwitz recalls.[4] Of course, Muddy was always interested in work for his band, and without any rehearsals Thornton recorded her second album for Arhoolie Records. *Big Mama Thornton Vol. 2: The Queen at Monterey with the Chicago Blues Band* was recorded at the Coast Recorders in San Francisco. The Muddy Waters outfit consisted of Muddy Waters (guitar), Sammy Lawhorn (guitar), James Cotton (harmonica), Otis Spann (piano), Luther Johnson (bass guitar), and Francis Clay (drums). The band had a subtle and sensitive style and could perfectly accompany Big Mama Thornton on songs like "Big Mama's Blues," "I'm Feeling Alright," "Everything Gonna Be Alright," "Big Mama's Bumble Bee Blues," "Looking The World Over," "Big Mama's Shuffle," and "Since I Fell For You," just to name a few.

Besides recording, Thornton continued to play the Bay Area club scene the whole year of 1966. On May 22, Thornton performed at the Both/And Club on Divisadero Street in San Francisco. Thornton now often performed at the Both/And Club, and on September 11, 1966, she even took part in a benefit for the Both/And Club at The Fillmore with Garry Goodrow, Jon Hendricks, Elvin Jones, The Joe Henderson Quartet, Denny Zeitlin Trio, Jefferson Airplane, Great Society, Wildflower and Bill Ham.

Between 1966 and 1969, Thornton was more and more in demand on campuses, in clubs, folk festivals, and rock festivals and would, with great success, play some of the biggest festivals, record new singles and albums and become a regular on the nightclub circuit. On September 17, 1966, Thornton appeared again at the Monterey Jazz Festival on Saturday afternoon in a program titled "Nothing But the Blues" an appendage by Jon Hendricks to his "Evolution of the blues" play. *Billboard*, on October 1, 1966, wrote that it was "Miss Thornton who stole the show from such blues greats as Muddy Waters and Memphis Slim by showing long-haired rockers that the blues means heart and soul."[5] She sang some spirituals like "Steal Away, Old-Time Religion" and "Down By The Riverside" besides her hit *Hound Dog*.

Thornton would from now on also appear regularly at the legendary blues showcase called Ash Grove Club on Melrose Avenue in Los Angeles. The Ash Grove was the place to go in L.A. if you really loved the blues. Owned by Ed Pearl, it had a high standard for performers. At the Ash Grove, Thornton met and played with a couple of later well-known musicians and was always very warmly received. One of the people she met and played with at the Ash Grove was Ed Cassidy, a drummer, who was the house percussionist at that time in the club. Cassidy was instantly recognizable by his shaven head and his fondness for wearing black. Ed played there with his stepson Randy Wolfe, later known as Randy California, and they both would soon form the band Spirit. At the Ash Grove, Big Mama also met Bernie Pearl, the brother of the club owner, Ed Pearl. "I had just returned from a trip back east with Luke 'Long Gone' Miles, when Big Mama Thornton was scheduled to open a run at the Ash Grove. I was primarily an acoustic guitarist, but had been working on my electric guitar playing for about a year. The guitarist who had made the trip from Oakland with her had either been fired or quit on the day of her opening. My brother asked me to come down and audition for her. I did so, playing the half dozen B.B. King licks I had memorized. She hired me on the spot," Pearl says.[6] So Pearl would join Big Mama's band which was then lead by her old friend from the Peacock Record days, Curtis Tillman (bass), along with Nat Dove (piano) and Everett Minor (sax). Pearl would stay with the band from October-November 1966 and play weekend shows at the Ash Grove and several other gigs. One of them was at Soledad Prison. "We played a concert for the inmates at Soledad Prison—quite memorable—and a night (possibly two nights) at the club run by Monterey Jazz Festival Founder, Jimmy Lyons, who also arranged the Soledad gig." Soledad is a maximum-security jail, and Bernie Pearl remembers how he "shuddered when they slammed those big metal gates behind us. Big Mama was swaggering down the corridors once inside, and the men all called to her—she was having a ball. As it turned out, she knew several of the men inside." At this event, Thornton showed her comedic style that she would use all her life on stage. "The men

Jo Jones and Big Mama Thornton at a rehearsal in Carnegie Hall in New York City, preparing for John Hammond's Spirituals to Swing: 30th Anniversary Concert on January 15, 1967 (photograph by Milt Hinton © Milton J. Hinton Photographic Collection).

filed into a very large auditorium (maybe 1,000), the band plays a few tunes and Curtis announces her to wild applause, and she takes the microphone and says, 'Good morning, ladies and gentlemen.' There's dead silence for a second, and then everybody absolutely breaks up in howling laughter," Pearl recalls. The band played with Thornton also on October 8, 1966, at the Pacific Jazz Festival in Costa Mesa, California along with Jon Hendricks, Jimmy Rushing, Shakey Horton, Memphis Slim, Jefferson Airplane, Muddy Waters and the Butterfield Blues Band on the same bill.

From October 14–16, 1966, Big Mama Thornton and her band were on the same bill with The Paul Butterfield Blues Band and Jefferson Airplane for a run of six shows at the Fillmore Auditorium. The Paul Butterfield Blues Band "opened up blues to white players," as Michael Erlewine says. "This racially mixed band playing authentic Chicago blues sent a lightning bolt–like signal to all of us who were just waking up to the blues anyway. Their message was that white players could overcome their fear to play black music, including the blues. The Paul Butterfield Blues Band set the standard and set white musicians on notice that anybody was free to try to play the blues. We were emboldened to try." For scholars of Jefferson Airplane lore, this three-day run has inspired endless discussion, as it encompasses the most critical transition in the group's history: the departure of original female vocalist Signe Anderson, and the emergence of Grace Slick as her replacement.

On November 1, 1966, Thornton and her band were also part of a "giant fund-raiser for California gubernatorial candidate Pat Brown at the Winterland Auditorium in San Francisco," Bernie Pearl recalls. Nat Dove notes that "memorably, Sammy Davis, Jr. was also on the bill. Big Mama tore it up! She blew harp mostly, but would regularly also take a turn at the drums: A great entertainer."[7]

From November 10 until November 20 of that year, Thornton again played the Both/And club in San Francisco, and the *Oakland Tribune* gave a great review: "The flexible, vibrant voice, the blues-infused harmonica, and the ebullient personality of 'Big Mama' Thornton proved their potency last night as the singer overcame the handicap of a ragged accompaniment and charmed the audience at the Both/And Club. Miss Thornton, whose home now is Oakland and who has come to international attention in the last year as the result of concert tours and records, dominated proceedings from the first to last. Her former group of accompanists—and a fine one it was—recently departed, and the quartet presently backing her is not yet in the groove. Additionally, the electric guitar's volume was so high it occasionally wiped out Miss Thornton's voice. Undaunted, the majestic singer carried on without faulting. Her rousing version of 'Watermelon Man' included a down home monologue that was in the great tradition of this humor. From this she sauntered through 'Going Down Slow' an old blues that demonstrated the smoothness of her voice. The audience loved it and Miss Thornton responded with several earthy jokes that she correctly judged would register with her listeners. Before concluding the set she played drums while the drummer turned to the tenor saxophone. This added nothing to the performance. Completely different were Miss Thornton's several solos on harmonica. Her ability to draw horn-like lines from this simple instrument is remarkable. Needless to say, she swings."[8]

Thornton was still looking like a Big Mama in those days. She was, large and in charge, as they say, and funny, energetic, and quite commanding onstage. A real character in the best sense, she was, as Bernie Pearl says, "tough-talking," and he would have hated to have to fight her, but she was also "very congenial and funny: A kind of larger-than-life character and the center of attraction when she entered a room, who could be very charming." When Bernie Pearl left the band because, he "really didn't play well," as he says, he remained friendly with Thornton and stayed in touch with the band members. Thornton's band would change personnel a lot. Only Curtis Tillman and Nat Dove stayed in there the whole time.

7

Ball and Chain

It was in the Both/And club that a historical meeting took place. During one of her performances at the Both/And club, Janis Joplin and members of Big Brother & the Holding Company heard Big Mama Thornton. Joplin greatly admired Thornton for many years. In Thornton's set she played one of the songs that she had recorded for the Baytone Records in 1961: "Ball and Chain." The band heard something in the song and they thought about slowing it down a bit and to change the key. "It was in a club in San Francisco called the Both/And. It was a blues and jazz club. Janis and I went to see Big Mama Thornton when she was playing there and that was the first time that we heard 'Ball and Chain.' She performed 'Ball and Chain' and I said to Janis afterward: 'You know we could rearrange that song.' It was in a major key, kind of an up-tempo thing the way she did it. I said: 'We could put in a minor key and slow it down and make it a heavier song.' We went backstage after the show and talked to Big Mama and that's how we first met her and got 'Ball and Chain.' It was just right after Janis joined the band. And basically that's how this song arrangement came about. It was basically my arrangement to slow it down, change the key and everything," Big Brother & the Holding Company guitar player James Gurley remembers: "We were all into the blues. We played a lot of shows with a lot of those blues guys Albert King, B.B. King, Howlin' Wolf, John Lee Hooker, all those guys. But we always thought that we should do something more with it than just trying to play their songs the way they played them. You want to be creative, you know. I don't want to be a re-creator. I want to be a creator."[1] After Thornton's set at the Both/And Club, Janis Joplin and James Gurley asked her if they could do "Ball and Chain." "OK, take it and sing it," was all she said and then she meticulously wrote them down the lyrics of the song. Thornton allowed the band to perform her song and her manager Jim Moore signed the release for Big Brother & the Holding Co. to do "Ball and Chain."

Thornton was an important musical model for Joplin, the singer of the band, who would just a bit later rise to fame on her own, and one of Janis's signature tunes, of course, would be "Ball and Chain." Joplin called Thornton her mentor and said, "She sings the blues with such heart and soul. I have learned so much from her and only wish I could sing as well as Willie Mae," Joplin's friend Tony Burkhart recalls.[2] Big Mama Thornton and Big Brother & the Holding Company with Janis Joplin would from now on often share the stage over the next years, when Big Mama Thornton opened them and later for Janis Joplin's solo shows on a couple of dates, something Elvis Presley never did. Consequently, in contrast to Elvis, Thornton spoke highly of Joplin, who publicly acknowledged her. Speaking about Joplin in 1972, Thornton said, "I gave her the right and the permission to make 'Ball and Chain.' And she always was my idol before she passed away … and I thank her for helping me. I'll always go along the line with that."[3] And later she adds: "It's all right. It made me money. At least I got paid for it, and I'm still drawing royalties."[4] Thornton would mostly mention Joplin as she introduced the song, calling her "the late and great Janis Joplin" on some occasions.

The music scene wasn't that easy for the original blues people. Even if Big Mama Thornton was greatly respected and loved, it was blues rock that dominated the scene, and the audience for the real deal in clubs like the Ash Grove was considerably smaller. But Thornton was not the person to quit playing because of that. She performed around the bay area in blues and jazz clubs but also in bigger halls with a set list that consisted of songs like her biggest hit "Hound Dog" and "Ball and Chain" and also "Little Red Rooster" and non-blues songs like "Summertime" and "Wade In the Water," waiting for her chance to come. Her chance came with the counterculture and the hippies.

From December 9 to 11, 1966, she played to a sold out Fillmore Auditorium on the same bill as the Grateful Dead and Tim Rose. The Grateful Dead were sole headliners at the Fillmore for the first time on the weekend. They had shared top booking a number of times, and Big Mama Thornton was only starting to get known to white hippies, so there's no question that the Grateful Dead were the principal attraction this weekend, but it was the beginning of what would come later on. The year ended for Thornton with a weekend at the Ash Grove from December 16 to 18, 1966.

Things were going well for Thornton and at one time even Duke

Ellington wanted to work with her, as Jimmy Moore recalls: "Duke Ellington talked to me at the Monterey Festival that he would like to do something with her. He was at Monterey. So when we got back from a tour I said to her 'Duke wanted to call you' she said 'What Duke ?' and I said 'Duke Ellington,' 'The real Duke?' she asked, 'What are you talking about?'"[5] Thornton was for some reason afraid and refused to talk to Ellington, so they didn't do a deal with him.

Thornton began the year 1967 with the Grateful Dead on January 6, 1967, in the Freeborn Hall, UC Davis, and continued with two concerts on January 7 at Jazz '67 on the Berkeley campus. Her shows were very well received and critics celebrated her, as this *Oakland Tribune* article demon-

Connie Pappas (from the Golden Bear Club), Julius Karpen (manager of Big Brother & the Holding Company), Big Mama Thornton and club owner George Papadopoulo backstage at the Golden Bear Club, September, 1967 (author's collection).

Big Mama Thornton with her band in 1968. On the far left is guitar player Terry "Big T" DeRouen (© collection of Terry "Big T" DeRouen).

strates: "Big Mama, who, after years of scuffling finally is gaining widespread recognition as one of the outstanding blues singers of her time … was magnificent Saturday night. She sang two concerts and at each the audience … was wildly enthusiastic. Although a smart blue dress and a new hairdo added an attractive note to her appearance, Miss Thornton's big-framed, heavy-set figure still was as commanding as her voice…. Naturally she climaxed her turn with "Hound Dog" which she had sung long before Elvis Presley was heard of…. She seemed to have a delightful time from first to last, and her listeners left no doubt of their enjoyment. One of these was Gerald Wilson, who has been in jazz since the Jimmy Lunceford days and now is best known for his own big band, from Los Angeles. 'I've never heard her before in person,' Wilson told me before the concert. Afterwards he remarked: 'She's too much. This is a night I'll remember.'"[6]

7. Ball and Chain

Now Big Mama Thornton had the opportunity to play at Carnegie Hall as part of John Hammond's *From Spirituals to Swing: 30th Anniversary concert.* The original *From Spirituals to Swing* was a show of two concerts presented by John Hammond in Carnegie Hall on December 23, 1938, and December 24, 1939. In many ways, these 1938 and 1939 Carnegie Hall concerts ushered in an exciting period of black music for the American public. While great bandleaders like Benny Goodman had been blurring the color line for years, *From Spirituals to Swing* was the first prominent Carnegie Hall production to present African American performers to an integrated audience. Besides the racial and political implications of John Hammond's controversial shows, the producer was able to bring together some of the era's finest talent in jazz, blues, and gospel music. The concerts included performances by Count Basie, Benny Goodman, Big Joe Turner and Pete Johnson, Helen Humes, Meade Lux Lewis, Albert Ammons, Mitchell's Christian Singers, the Golden Gate Quartet, James P. Johnson, Big Bill Broonzy and Sonny Terry.

But at the time Thornton was asked to join this 30th anniversary concert, she had somehow become involved with the boxer Archie Moore, who once was the light heavyweight world champion and who holds the record for the most career knockouts by any boxer. "They were pretty friendly. I had [known] about it but I didn't know how serious it was. I thought that he was some kid that didn't know what he was doing," Jimmy Moore says. But Archie Moore wanted to take over Big Mama Thornton's management. "I tried to talk to her and I said to her: 'This guy is a boxer and he has a manager. He has someone managing him in something that he knows about. How can he manage you when he knows nothing about the music business?' But she could not see it, so she went ahead," Moore recalls.

Despite the trouble between Thornton and Moore, they went to New York to Carnegie Hall where she performed at the *Spirituals to Swing* show together with the Count Basie Orchestra on January 15, 1967. Jimmy Moore remembers that Thornton refused for some reason to play with the young George Benson at the show: "We did a couple of takes and finally she just absolutely refused. She started to get ugly," he says. John Hammond had planned a TV special and a movie with the show. But because of the controversy with Archie Moore about the management for Big Mama, that never happened.

Finally, Moore took over the management for Big Mama in February

1967. Jimmy Moore filed a suit against Archie Moore and Thornton, making clear that he was still her manager. Thornton came to him before the suit and said, "Why don't we go ahead and make some money." But Jimmy Moore wanted to prove to her that he knew what he was doing and that he had a valid contract. Moore won the eventual lawsuit but he never worked with Big Mama again.

Thornton didn't have a lot of luck with her managers throughout her career. One reason may be that she was in some way not made for the business. In contrast to her rough behavior and masculine mode of dress, Thornton was a sweet person. And it is a rare artist who can understand and deal equally with people who only think about money; that wasn't different for Thornton. "She used to love to hang on the corner with a fellow at a liquor store. She was just a regular country girl. I remember once we did a job and I gave her a share, which was about 900 dollars. And the next day she walks up the street and I stayed in the lobby. She got all this money sticking in her pockets. And I said, 'What are you doing. You can't walk around like that with all that money.' So I took her to Wells Fargo and opened an account for her. It didn't last too long. I don't think the people that managed her after me, had cared at all. The other thing is it was kind of difficult to get her to understand about saving, cause she just wasn't used to it. Basically she was naive about a lot of stuff. That's why Archie Moore really is a guy that messed up. She was getting confused," Jimmy Moore says.

Moore says, looking back: "I think she realized the mistake and she started to drink heavily. I would occasionally see her again and say 'hi' to her. She really realized that she had made a mistake. Of course I made a mistake myself. I should have just put it behind me and just have dropped my pride. She was very sensitive because of her size. She was basically a nice person but very insecure outside of music and being onstage. She was sensitive that she thought she should know more about how to handle herself. She was shy. What I regret is not so much the money but the music that could have made. John Hammond called her the 'greatest living blues singer' at that time. Given the opportunity she could have done anything musically."

But with poor management by Archie Moore, Thornton came into some business trouble. On March 18 she was scheduled to play the UCLA "Chamber Jazz" but the show was postponed to April 22, because of booking complications resulting from the problems between Thornton and Jimmy Moore. Nevertheless, Thornton continued to play and record the whole year of 1967. In April, Thornton performed at the Bear's Lair of the Student Union in Berkeley and on April 8 she played the Jazz Festival 1967 at the Berkeley Hearst Greek Theatre on the UC campus. While performing in Berkeley at the Greek Theatre, Thornton accidentally helped out two young fellows who had no ticket for the show. The young boys had been discovered by security and ran around the back of the amphitheater through a big bed of ivy. Suddenly they found themselves down into a room that had no ceiling: it was the backstage dressing room. Sitting by herself in that dressing room was Big Mama Thornton. After the boys explained to her that they were being chased by security guards, Thornton didn't make any trouble but helped them out. She ushered the boys from her dressing room to the wing of the stage. There she looked out for a place for them to stay out of sight so they could enjoy the show.

At the end of the month, on April 28 and 29, Thornton played the California Hall in San Francisco with Big Brother & the Holding Company plus The Weeds and a light show by Aurora Glory Alice on the same bill.

On May 9, Thornton began a week's engagement at the Jazz Workshop backed by a group that included saxophonist Jules Broussard, pianist Nat Dove, guitarist Jay Hodge, drummer Linton Jacquet and George Smith, harmonica. On May 12, Thornton was, along with Quicksilver Messenger Service, the Bobby Hutcherson-Harold Land Quintet, the Majesties from East Palo Alto and special guest performer Mike Bloomfield, part of the "Pops Festival" organized by students at the College of San Mateo, California. Prior to the event the *Times of San Mateo* wrote about Thornton: "Standing ovations are nothing rare to Big Mama Thornton, the mammoth R&B singer who shares the bill with Quicksilver. Big Mama, who stands an even 6 feet tall and weighs '300' pounds combines her singing talents with a wild harmonica to produce an effect which has stamped her as one of the most dynamic and exciting performers in the blues-field."[7] From September 19–24, 1967, Thornton had daily shows at the Golden Bear Club, Huntington Beach, California, along with Big Brother & the Holding Company. Here she and Janis Joplin met again, and Thornton, according to Big Brother & the Holding Company's manager Julius Karpen, warned Joplin that her drug and alcohol abuse would possibly destroy her voice.

After the recording with the Muddy Waters Band in April 1966, Thornton and Muddy played together more often, and his manager at the time, Bob Messinger, helped Thornton to get more gigs. She played with Muddy's band from coast to coast, as Mac Arnold, who played bass with Muddy Waters from late 1966 until the end of 1967, remembers: "I played coast to coast with Muddy, the whole year of '67. We traveled in automobiles back in those days. And sometimes we traveled from Chicago to California before we had a gig. Travel by automobile was very hard in those days because sometimes there would be a problem and you would be late for a gig. We played in bars in Massachusetts, Maryland, Detroit, Richmond, Florida and that was basically the east coast stuff. On the west coast we played Vancouver, Seattle, San Francisco, Los Angeles and San Diego. That was a really exciting time for me. Big Mama Thornton played with us numerous times around Chicago, Detroit, and Cleveland. She was a really strong person. We were a super team so far. Muddy Waters and Big Mama were very respectful to each other."[8]

Nineteen sixty-seven ended for Big Mama Thornton with an appearance at the New York's Apollo with Odetta, T-Bone Walker, Jimmy Witherspoon, Big Joe Turner and The Chambers Brothers on the bill.

The year 1968 started with shows at the Ash Grove in Los Angeles with Edward Bee Houston on guitar, Curtis Tillman on bass, Everett Minor on tenor sax, Nathaniel Dove on piano, and Gus Wright on the drums. Three of those performances were used on the LP *Ball and Chain* that would be released late that year. Bee Houston would soon leave Thornton's backing band and Terry DeRouen, called Big T, would take over the guitar in her band. "I started playing with Big Mama Thornton after a guitar player she had, named Bee Houston. Big Mama Thornton heard me playing and I think she had a few problems with Bee Houston. Curtis and I would play on and on together and Big Mama would come to one of the gigs that we would play. I was also playing with Pee Wee Crayton. She would come around also to Pee Wee and sit in. She knew me and knew my reputation when she hired me. The guys in that group at that time were the bandleader Curtis Tillman, on drums Gus Right from New Orleans and on piano was Nat Dove and myself on the guitar and Everett Minor. I stayed there for a few years and moved on a little further," Big T recalls.

"We also played the Jazz workshop and the Matrix, The Both/And and the Hungry I, The Original Fillmore Auditorium and the Palace of Fine Arts in San Francisco, the Whisky a Go Go in L.A. and few other things in that area," adds Nat Dove about the time in the late sixties. Thornton took always good care for her band around Curtis Tillman and Dove. "We played the shows in California and we were going to New York to play the Apollo Theatre. On the tour to New York Big Mama Thornton made sure that we went by everybody's hometown for a couple of days before getting into New York," Dove says.

So the year was filled again with big concerts and festivals. On August 3, 1968, Thornton played at the Shrine Exposition Hall, Los Angeles, along with the Jeff Beck Group, Blue Cheer, and Steve Miller Band. On August 30, 1968, she appeared at the Palace of Fine Arts, San Francisco, with Big Brother & the Holding Company, John Stewart and Buffy Ford. On this show Janis Joplin announced that she would leave Big Brother at the end of 1968.

Thornton would now play sometimes with James Cotton after he had left the Muddy Waters Band—for example, on September 2, 1968, at the first Sky River Rock Festival. Among the bands and performers playing at the Sky River Rock Festival were Santana, Country Joe and the Fish, Richard Pryor, Dino Valenti, Byron Pope, It's a Beautiful Day, Peanut Butter Conspiracy, Alice Stuart Thomas, the Youngbloods, New Lost City Ramblers, and local groups such as Juggernaut and Easy Chair. On the last day, the Grateful Dead arrived unscheduled. So it happened that Big Mama Thornton played her show together with James Cotton on mouth harp and Ron "Pigpen" McKernan on organ from the Grateful Dead; one of the Dead's two drummers; and a guitarist from the Dead.

In 1968 Big Brother & the Holding Co. recorded the Big Mama Thornton song "Ball and Chain" on their album *Cheap Thrills*. The album entered the charts on August 31, 1968, stayed in the number one spot for eight weeks and would go gold in three days. This success would bring Thornton even more recognition, and Janis Joplin and Thornton would always show deep respect for each other. Big T says, "I think 'Ball and Chain' give Big Mama Thornton a little more work. We did a show in California in a big old warehouse and Janis Joplin was on that show. I remember the police was trying to stop the playing. And they did a big searching for drugs. And all they found backstage was an empty bottle of hundred proof Old Grand Dad Whiskey. And that was Big Mama's drink. So we laughed about that."[9] At that show, Joplin brought Thornton on stage and introduced her as the songwriter to "Ball and Chain." Then they sang it together.

Ad for a show at the Ash Grove in Hollywood in 1968 (author's collection).

From September 13–15, 1968, Thornton played the Avalon Ballroom featuring George "Harmonica" Smith on harmonica with the British blues legend John Mayall on the same bill, followed by her third appearance at the Monterey Jazz Festival in the same month. Smith and his Southside Blues Band, including Rod Piazza and Buddy Reed, were now very often Thornton's backing band.

7. Ball and Chain

In October she played two shows in Torrance, California. A show on October 18, 1968, with the Grateful Dead on the same bill was followed by a show on October 19, 1968, with the Cleveland Wrecking Company. November 6–10, 1968 saw her at the Whisky a Go Go with Taj Mahal. Then, following the success of Janis Joplin with "Ball and Chain," Arhoolie Records now released a new album with the same title. The *Ball and Chain* LP by Arhoolie records contains three songs from a 1968 session recorded on January 25, 1968, in Hollywood, with Edward "Bee" Houston on guitar, Curtis Tillman on bass, Everett Minor on tenor sax, Nathaniel Dove on piano, and Gus Wright on the drums along with titles by *Lightning Hopkins* and *Larry Williams*.

From November 22 to the 24, 1968, Thornton played at Mandrake's on 1048 University Avenue in Berkeley.

Thornton was still in heavy demand along the country and her regular appearances continued in 1969. Thornton started the year with an eleven-day appearance at The Hungry I in Ghirardelli Square in San Francisco.

Big Mama Thornton and T-Bone Walker performing at the Ann Arbor Blues Festival in 1969 (© Willa Davis).

She played two times Sunday through Thursday and three times on Friday and Saturday. February 12–14, Thornton played at the Keystone Korner Club in North Beach, San Francisco, and continued directly on February 14 until February 16, 1969, with It's a Beautiful Day and Country Weather at the Avalon Ballroom in San Francisco. Those shows were followed by a show in Austin with New Atlantis on March 21, 1969, at the Vulcan Gas Company. From April 15 to 20, she performed at the Boston Tea Party with Ten Years After and Albert King. From April 28 to May 4, she performed at the Ungano's Club in New York City. On May 21, she was part of the First Generation Blues Festival organized by Will Ashwood Kavana. The festival was a series of ten concerts at the Electric Circus on St. Marks Place in Greenwich Village, New York, from May 7 through June 25, 1969. The fes-

Thornton and Walker performing at the Ann Arbor Blues Festival in 1969 (© Willa Davis).

tival featured artists such as Lowell Fulson, Arthur Crudup, John Lee Hooker, Bukka White, Muddy Waters, Willie Dixon and Son House, to name just a few. Thornton was part of the festival lineup on May 21 together with Jesse Fuller.

In the summer 1969, the festival season started again with great success for her with appearances at the biggest festivals of the season. On June 29 she played the Denver Pop Festival and on July 4, 1969, the Saugatuck Pop Festival in Michigan with Procol Harum, Muddy Waters, John Lee Hooker, Bob Seeger, The Crazy World of Arthur Brown, The Stooges and many others. On July 18,

Thornton at the Ann Arbor Blues Festival in 1969 (© Willa Davis).

1969, Thornton played Newport Folk Festival in front of 6,000 people as blues guitarist Roy Book Binder recalls: "It was 1969 ... Newport Folk Festival ... a great one for sure. The blues was well represented, with Son House, the Muddy Waters Blues Band and the Jim Kweskin Jug Band, featuring special guest, Sippie Wallace! She belted out what was surely one of the festival highlights. The crowd went wild!" Binder says.[10] "Wearing a mustard-colored beret, a checked shirt, and a pair of baggy green trousers, Miss Thornton was a commanding figure on stage as she sang out her blues lyrics in a robust voice and played a strident mouth-harp, accompanied by her enthusiastic four-piece Hound Dog Band."[11] The band Thornton played the Newport Festival with consisted of Samuel Lawhorn (guitar), Pinetop

Perkins (piano), Curtis Tillman (bass) and Eddie Horton (drums). Thornton starts the set at the festival with "Mother In Law," a nod to Junior Parker, one of Thornton's major influences. She is featured here on vocal and harmonica. "Her approach to her songs, as she explained in introducing one called 'Mother in Law' is 'I just do it like I feel it.' Her feeling included some hip-swinging dance steps, off-hand remarks and interjections and a lot of hard-driving harmonica playing," as the *New York Times* noted.[12] The song is followed by "Rock Me Baby" with an excellent piano work from Perkins and a guitar solo from Lawton. Thornton spontanevously encourages Lawton to extend the solo even further than usual. Then came "Ball and Chain," which Thornton announced with the words: "And I'm the one that wrote a little record that Janis had a big ball with. We call it 'Ball and Chain.' I am going to sing it for you." The Newport audience was going nuts about her performance. Then Thornton declared that "this is the record I made Elvis Presley rich on," and starts with "Hound Dog." Then they closed with "Swing It On Home." In the middle of the song, Thornton takes over on drums, and while her solo is sloppy and eventually dissolves completely, she is no doubt having a lot of fun on stage and the crowd responds in kind. With the audience howling to keep it going, the group does just that, vamping on the song for an additional four minutes while Thornton struts around the stage whipping the Newport audience into a frenzy. *Billboard* wrote: "Big Mama Thornton was the big attraction of the evening."[13] Backstage at the festival, Thornton took good care of the different musical acts. "Big Mama had her Cadillac in the parking lot backstage, and she cooked for the black acts and sold them soul food," said Bob Messinger, who had booked her for the festival. "She had a butane stove. I didn't pay much attention to it because I had booked her on the job and I didn't want to be associated with it. George Wein [American jazz promoter and producer who has been called the most important non-player in jazz history is the founder of the Newport Jazz Festival], who always demanded quiet backstage and decorum, never said a word."[14]

The next month Thornton was one of the headliners for the last day of another great festival, the Ann Arbor Blues Festival, on August 1–3, 1969. Held two weeks before the famous Woodstock Festival, it focused on big-city, electric blues and included most of the great electric blues players of that time. The Ann Arbor Blues Festival brought together the who's who in blues music at that time: Roosevelt Sykes, Fred McDowell, J.B. Hutto &

the Hawks, Jimmy Dawkins, Junior Wells and B.B. King on the first day; Sleepy John Estes, Luther Allison, Clifton Chenier, Otis Rush, Howlin' Wolf and Muddy Waters on the second day; and Arthur "Big Boy" Crudup, Jimmy "Fast Fingers" Dawkins, Roosevelt Sykes, Luther Allison & the Blue Ebulae, Big Joe Williams, Magic Sam, Freddie King, Sam Lay, T-Bone Walker, Son House, Charlie Musselwhite, Freddy Roulette, Lightnin' Hopkins, and James Cotton on the last day. In those summer days, in August of 1969, "a music legacy was born," as Michael Erlewine puts it. "Several thousand blues lovers gathered in a small athletic field called Fuller Flats near the North Campus of the University of Michigan (a spot along the Huron River in Ann Arbor, Michigan) to witness the first 'Ann Arbor Blues Festival,'" he says.[15] This festival was the first

Thornton performing at the Ann Arbor Blues Festival in 1969 (© Willa Davis).

electric blues festival of its kind in North America and the organizers saw themselves in the tradition of the American Folk and Blues festival in Europe. "When we look back at the roster of performers at those first two Ann Arbor Blues Festivals, it is hard to imagine that all of this great talent managed to converge at one place and time," Michael Erlewine says, and adds, "Can you imagine? There was my dad, the controller of a small Michigan college sitting on folding chairs with blues great Roosevelt Sykes, the two of them leaning back up against a chain-link fence, swapping stories, and having beers all afternoon. They just liked each other and were having a ball. That's the way it was all around—one big getting-to-know-one-another party. It was special."

In this very special surrounding Big Mama Thornton explained on August 3, 1969, to one of the festival organizers, Michael Erlewine, her view of jazz and the new rock 'n' Roll as well as her own music: "Jazz? I don't understand it in the first place. It don't have no ending. Here he is up there blowin' and maybe he blow till he get tired, then he just stop. What about rock 'n' roll? Some folks say: 'It's nothin' but a hopped-up, fast-up blues.' That's all it is. I like to let my audience be close to me, you know what I mean? And I want them to feel that they are close to me, anyway, because I want to be close to them, because I want to express myself to let them know what I do and how I do it. And if they can do it, good luck to 'em, is all I can say."[16]

Because you could not buy alcohol on Sundays, Thornton had brought her own stuff with her, recalls photographer Willa Davis: "I recall one funny scene with Big Mama and a group of young blues fans back stage. They were all standing around her station wagon (she drove to the event herself), they were talking and laughing when one of the guys noticed that she had a case of whiskey in the back of her car. Remember, this was Sunday in Michigan and you could not buy alcohol in stores on Sunday during that time. He got all excited and asked her if she would sell him a bottle. She told him, 'Hell no! I'm no fool, I knew Michigan was dry on Sunday—what's wrong with you. That's my private stash, and don't sell it to nobody.' She said this with laughter in her voice—but she didn't sell him any. He just laughed and said he was just joking with her—but she knew better."[17] The atmosphere during the festival was just fantastic, in front of the audience and backstage where the musicians eat and drank, gambled and had fun. One time, Thornton was making jokes with Howlin' Wolf saying: "'Wolf, I' tell you what: I'll pay you cash money right now if you let me have Hubert [guitar player Hubert Sumlin, of Howlin' Wolf's band].' Wolf laughed, pointed at Evelyn Sumlin, and said: 'Don't ask me for Hubert. There his wife is. You have to ask her.' Thornton laughed and said, 'You just don't want to give me Hubert. I could really, really use Hubert.' He said: 'I could use him too, so I'm keeping him.'"[18]

7. Ball and Chain

From August 15 to 17, 1969, Woodstock marked the high point of the hippie era. The same month, Big Mama Thornton performed at the Sky River Rock Festival II on August 30 with Muddy Waters, It's a Beautiful Day, Sunshine Company, Grateful Dead, Santana, The New Riders of the Purple Sage, Anonymous Artists of America, Blues Image, Cleanliness & Godliness Skiffle Band, Collectors, Congress of Wonders, Country Weather, Dr. Humbead's New Tranquility String Band, Frumious Bandersnatch, The Flying Burrito Brothers, Kaleidoscope, Magic Sam, Mother Earth, Mother Tuckers, The New Lost City Ramblers, New York Rock & Roll Ensemble, James Taylor, and Elsie Weinberg. The same day, blues giant Willie Dixon assembled a few of his best friends and hosted a Labor Day Weekend Festival in Grant Park on Saturday, August 30, 1969, and Thornton performed there too.

In September, she appeared with Muddy Waters at The Plugged Nickel in Chicago, and in October 1969, she played a few times with Sunnyland Slim, vocals, piano; Shakey Jake, harmonica, and herself on drums at the Ash Grove. She also performed with her old friend George Smith. Big Mama Thornton and George "Harmonica" Smith played October 16–18 at the Thee Experience in Los Angeles, California, a new club on the Sunset Strip that was soon known for the concerts featuring the best groups in town. Thornton and Smith were accompanied here by Jay Hodges on tenor sax, J.D. Nichols, a Louisiana native who had already recorded a few singles under his own name, on piano, the great down-home Texas bluesman Bee Houston back on guitar and Flip Graham on bass. One of the shows was recorded by Thornton's new record company, Mercury, and would be released the next year. On the normal song list in these days were blues songs like "Little Red Rooster," "One Black Rat," "Rock Me Baby," "Wade in the Water," "Sweet Little Angel," "Baby Please," "Mojo Workin," "Watermelon Man" and "Don't Need A Doctor." Thornton was obviously comfortable with her backing band and the Los Angeles Times also celebrates her performance: "Then out came Big Mama, wearing a man's shirt and pants and a little blues jockey cap, looking very much like a well–dressed service station attendant. 'I wanna be heard!' she said to her band. 'Turn it down! I wane be heard tonight!' The band turned down, Big Mama honked a few notes on her harmonica, then sang 'I ain't gonna get drunk no more.'" She only sang five songs in her set, "but each one was familiar and well-received. And, as always, Big Mama Thornton was authentic, a quality found infrequently among most young blues practitioners … eight of whom were present as the Bluesberry Jam, sharing the bill with Big Mama."[19] As the shows at the Thee Experience were well received, the recording provided a great example of her possibilities as a live performer in those days. Shortly after the engagement at the Thee Experience on October 21, 1969, Thornton was guest at the TV show *Della*, hosted by singer Della Reese and sidekick Sandy Baron. Probably in the fall of 1969, she performed at the Jazz Workshop in Boston and a then young musician named Peter Malick, who had earlier met Bob Messenger, Muddy Waters' manager, started working for Thornton. "The first gig we did was a week at the Jazz Workshop. She drove east with George Smith and Curtis Tillman, the bass player. They drove in her big Cadillac all the way from Los Angeles for this gig. We also worked in a club called the Colonial Tavern in Toronto. Bob Messinger would book some East Coast-gigs and he called me up and I put together a band. So we worked like a week at Jazz Workshop, we drove up to Toronto and we worked a week at the Colonial Tavern. After that first East Coast experience, she just came to the east by herself and drove that 3,000-mile trip pretty much nonstop. She was quite a character. She was a big drinker and that definitely sort of colored everything. She was often abusive to the band, but for some reason she was always kind to me. Toward the end of a night she could be tough. On each set she got behind the drums and played "Swing On Home Big Mama." Both of those clubs on Sundays used to do a matinee, which was sort of a standard at that time. So you come in and you do three sets from 4 to 7 p.m. And then you come back at nine and do the regular 9 p.m. to 2 a.m. another five sets. Towards the end the night on a Sunday she was like gone. There was no telling what was going to happen. It was a very unpredictable thing. One time up in Toronto, we must have been there for two weeks and she knew up there was this club in Buffalo, New York, which is about two hours' drive from Toronto. Since we had Sunday off in Toronto, she said let's go down to this club in Buffalo, it's a great blues club. So we all piled into her Cadillac and drove down. There was this guy named Jesse James, who had this blues club in Buffalo. So we went down and played. It was like by the end of the first set that we sit in, we got off the stage and there were like literally fifteen, twenty drinks lined up for each of us and everybody wants to buy us a drink. And for her that was like nothing. I don't remember getting back to Toronto, but she drove us back at three in the morning. And we got there. There were certain songs that would be typical and you would know what she was going to come up with. The standard was, we did a couple of instrumentals before we brought her out. And then I think that she used to come up with the 'Mother in Law' blues from Junior Parker. She just did an amazing version. She just sang the crap out of it. The feeling that I remember beside the alcoholic nature of the whole thing was, she was such an awesome talent, an amazing vocalist, had such great style. When she was not totally gone it was just such a joy to be behind her. She is just this thing, you know. She never called out 'Hound Dog,' but she just like going into this 'You ain't nothing but' ... She drags out and drag out and drag out and we be there. It was awesome. None of that stuff was studied. I just feel very pleased to being able to be in her presence. She just brought a totally unique energy, like so many other of that generation of blues artists. It just came from god, it wasn't studied out of book," Malick recalls.[20]

While in Toronto, Thornton did also a TV production on November 5, 1969, taped for music producer David Acomba's *Rock 1* TV special for CBC. She is accompanied here by the local band Whiskey Howl, a Toronto-based Canadian blues band which is notable as being one of the early Canadian bands promoting and developing blues music in Canada. They played their own set in addition to backing up Thornton. The show was broadcast January 11, 1970 on CBC.

At the end of 1969, Thornton made clear that she is more than just a blues singer. With her new record by Mercury Records, with the title *Stronger Than Dirt*, she proved her ability to absorb the modern rock music. She was backed by her own band with Big T DeRouen, Everett Minor, Nat Dove and Curtis Tillman. Her guitar player Big T recalls that he came up with the name of the LP: "I gave her the name of that because there was a commercial on TV. It was advertising some kind of washing powder. I told her about that and she used it for the next title of her album." Nat Dove, who played piano on the record, recalls that they rehearsed a lot for the recording. "Big Mama wanted it to sound as good as possible, but she wanted it to be not so structured. She had some arranges on it too. She wanted to do, what she wanted to do. I wrote the arrangement for 'That Lucky Old Sun.'" *The News* of Van Nuys, California, published a very bad review of the LP headlining "Mama Thornton: 'Dirt' Is a Cop—Out." They wrote: "Mama Thornton. What echoes that name conjures! BIG Mama Thornton. She has a new album out ... a shame. Recorded in North Hollywood (not Chicago or Memphis where it should have been), its arrangements run from fair to cruddy. The playing is a notch lower. It's called *Stronger Than Dirt* and the only reason Mercury released it was to capitalize on the fact that Janis Joplin took much of her styling from Willie Mae Thornton and made a virtuoso display piece out of the latter's 'Ball and Chain.' Don't judge Big Mama by this shuck. There's no better voice around, even though this album reeks of self-conscious image-fulfilling."[21] But other reviews acknowledged that Thornton's effort to find a wider audience "is well worth making," as the *New York Times* did: "Most of Miss Thornton's earlier recordings have been aimed directly at the rhythm & blues market. This time, producer Al Schmitt has another target in mind, and has chosen an appropriately eclectic program. It is Miss Thornton's credit that she finds comfortably personal interpretations of such unfamiliar (for her) material as 'Summertime,' 'That Lucky Old Sun' and Bob Dylan's 'I shall be released,'"[22] and, indeed, the LP brought Big Mama Thornton back onto the *Billboard* charts.

On December 6, 1969, the Altamont Speedway Free Festival took place. The event is best known for having been marred by considerable violence, including one homicide and three accidental deaths and marked, less than four months after Woodstock, the end of the hippie era and de facto conclusion of late–1960s American youth culture. Since this culture had helped to bring back the blues to a new audience, the end of the blues revival was visible on the horizon.

8

The Early Seventies

The year 1970 started for Big Mama Thornton with a week at the Jazz Workshop, the only club on San Francisco's Broadway whose programming was devoted exclusively to jazz, where Thornton ended the holiday hibernation with a show in residence from January 5 to 11 with a backup group—which she, as usual, occasionally joined, on harmonica and drums.

Then her new album was released. Her second album on the Mercury label, *The Way It Is* (Mercury SR 61249), which contained the performance at the Thee Experience in Los Angeles (October 1968), received good reviews in the press, mainly because of her singing. The *Charleston Gazette* wrote on February 28, 1970: "Big Mama isn't ashamed to tell you she learned the blues from listening to Bessie Smith and Memphis Minnie. You don't learn better blues. In this album she liberally demonstrates it with flawless renderings of Willie Dixon, Muddy Waters, Howlin' Wolf material, plus three of her own songs. The last two cuts are exceptional. 'Watermelon Man' is seasoned with Big Mama's own unforgettable harp. Then on 'Don't Need No Doctor,' borne along by Jim Nicholson's piano and Bee Houston's guitar, Big Mama carries into the archives a priceless work of art that is virtually extinct."[1] The *Star News* of Pasadena, California, wrote: "Big Mama Thornton is an old bluester who is 'finally being recognized,' as we are getting used to hearing. On her second Mercury LP *The Way it Is*, she treats a live audience to a uniformly slow, generally dull array of eight songs. Only Big Mama's personality makes the album interesting listening. She is the epitome of 'uppity.' She opens with a harangue against L.A. cops, and manages to thwack Ronald Reagan several times between and during her songs. A combativeness lies just beneath the surface of her music, finally rising in 'Watermelon Man' in which Big Mama engages in a mythic verbal fray with a fruit peddler. She fills spaces between her songs by singing entranced nothings, a spell-like patter which somehow is delightful and ensnaring.

Once on Big Mama's wave length, her music becomes more involving, and in the end, enjoyment overcomes boredom."[2] The song list of the album contains the Willie Dixon classic "Little Red Rooster," the Big Mama Thornton songs "One Black Rat," "Sweet Little Angel," "Watermelon Man," "Don't Need a Doctor," the Muddy Waters songs "Rock Me Baby" and "Baby Please/Got My Mojo Workin'" and the Gospel song "Wade in the Water."

Meanwhile, because of her ongoing success as a live act, Thornton's Peacock recordings where rereleased on Back Beat, a subsidiary of Peacock Records was formed in 1957. The Back Beat LP was called *She's Back—Willie Mae "Big Mama" Thornton* and consisted of the songs "Cotton Picking Blues," "Willie Mae's Blues," "Big Change," "Walking Blues," "Just Can't Help Myself," "Hound Dog," "They Call Me Big Mama," "Tarzan and The Dignified Monkey" and "My Man."

Thornton continued to play in the clubs around the Bay Area. On one of these occasions Carlos Zialcita backed her up with the Chico David Blues Band. Zialcita recalls, "We were performing at a club on Geary Street in San Francisco, called the Celebrity Club. Chico David, who was our bandleader and guitar player, had been the guitar player for Charles Brown. And so he was able through some connections to get in touch with Big Mama Thornton. So when she came to the club most of us were already there, we were already set up. She had a very strong personality. Basically she sat at the bar drinking like a man with the rest of the guys. She was very gracious even though her per-

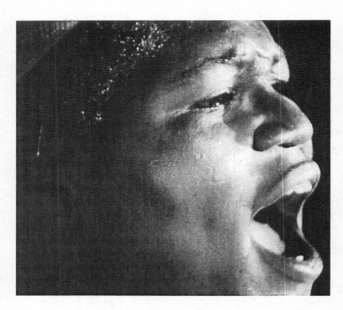

Thornton performing at the Ann Arbor Blues Festival in 1970 (© Lawrence Robbin).

90

sonality was kind of a rough personality. She really liked the Old Granddad liquor. And then she complained that it was only 80 proof and that she wanted to drink the 100 proof. And then they purchased her a bottle and she was very happy. The music was fine. We had studied some Chicago Blues as well as the west coast style blues. So we were able I think to sound pretty well behind Big Mama Thornton. Our bass player in particular had really studied her music and she complimented him."[3]

With this lineup of the Chico David Blues Band, Thornton also played at the University of California in Davis. Boz Scaggs was also on the bill. Zialcita recalls that "Big Mama Thornton of course was a living blues legend and was presented as such. I think it was great, especially, this was the seventies and many people were only hearing about her for the first time because of her connection with Janis Joplin. So we would always do Ball and Chain. She was aware of the popularity of Janis Joplin. I really liked Big Mama Thornton from a personal perspective because she was a devotee of Little Junior Parker. But the way she played Harmonica to me was very reminiscent of Junior Parker who of course is one of my biggest influences. She and I got to play several harmonica duets live in a blues club."

Thornton now toured mostly together with George "Harmonica" Smith. He would always open the show with a few songs and then played together with Thornton. They had a similar arrangement in Atlanta, Georgia, where Thornton's career had started a long time before, from March 27 to April 1, backed up by the Eastside Blues Band at the Twelfth Gate Coffeehouse each night with two shows. The performances were very well attended. Band member Bill Sheffield, guitar and harmonica player from Atlanta, recalls those nights at the Twelfth Gate: "I remember we met George and Mama about an hour before the first show. They were traveling together by car. We opened the show, did about six numbers and then George would join us for several songs." George "Harmonica" Smith must have really impressed the young musician. "I was playing harp at the time and George sort of took me under his wing. He wanted to teach me to make more of a show of it. Walk out through the crowd! He was the most amazing harmonica player I've still ever heard. He soared. I gave up the harmonica shortly thereafter."[4] After the first set, Thornton came on stage. "She was big and round but not really tall. Her attitude made her seem taller. Just her appearance set the crowd a roar! She had for that time a very militant style of dress. Always pants. Never a dress. You couldn't imagine her in one.

And a wool cap that I never saw her without. I think she must have slept in it, a bottle of Old Granddad liquor always close by. We were very nervous. We had never played her songs, only listened to them. She took a pull off the liquor, grabbed the microphone off the stand, looked angrily straight ahead and began. There was no way you couldn't play it right. Her power wouldn't allow it. The point was, it didn't matter how good the band was. She was good enough for all of us. It was so wonderful to hear 'Ball and Chain' sung and not screamed! She could hold a note longer than anyone I've ever heard. A slow blues, it seemed to vary every night, and we would end with a fast shuffle. Mama would sing her way off the stage and George would grab the microphone and start yelling, 'Big Mama Thornton, ladies and gentlemen, Big Mama Thornton!!' She never did more than five or six songs in a show. I think she didn't want to challenge the band any further. But it was always enough. They yelled for more, of course, but no one left dissatisfied. I learned a lot about blues that week. Things that I still use today," Sheffield recalls.

Sometimes, Thornton and Smith would even meet accidentally while they toured separately, as it happened in Jack & Jills Club in Portland, Oregon. "We backed Big Mama for a week at a big room called Jack & Jills in Portland, Oregon. Back in those days it was common to play five nights in one club. Jack & Jills was fantastic! Low ceiling, big stage, with the red curtain in the back, tables to seat a couple hundred people and a nice big dance floor that went right up the middle of the room in front of the bandstand! The week before Big Mama played Jack & Jills, George Smith had played the room. When his gig up north in Bellingham fell through, he came back to Portland and hung out with us and sat in with Big Mama. They both took turns showing off on the drums! Very fun times! She was quite a character. Always sang strong and proud. Only one of her was made and she was great!'" recalled Lloyd Jones,[5] who backed her up with his band Brown Sugar. "I played drums in those days and we had a very powerful guitarist, Jim Mesi, and Harmonica player/ singer by the name of Paul deLay. The bass player, Al Kuzans, was a natural player but quit playing when the band broke up in 1976," Jones adds.

On April 3, Thornton performed at the Berkeley Blues Festival produced by students of U.C. Berkeley. On an evening with great blues performers such as Bukka White, Furry Lewis, Dave Alexander and Robert Pete Williams, it was Thornton's performance that impressed. The *Oakland*

240

The Museum of Modern Art

11 West 53 Street, New York, N.Y. 10019 Tel. 956-6100 Cable: Modernart

No. 86
FOR IMMEDIATE RELEASE

BIG MAMA THORNTON TO APPEAR IN GARDEN

OF MUSEUM OF MODERN ART

The legendary blues and gospel singer BIG MAMA THORNTON will make one of her rare appearances in The Museum of Modern Art's JAZZ IN THE GARDEN series on Thursday, July 22, at 7:30 p.m.

Miss Thornton is best known for her recording of "Hound Dog" prior to Elvis Presley's success with the song, and for her own song "Ball and Chain," later recorded with her permission by Janis Joplin.

She was raised in Montgomery, Alabama and left there to go on the road with Sammy Green's "Hot Harlem Review." She later became known as the Queen of the Blues in Houston, Texas. In 1956, she moved to the West Coast where she still lives, and her concert at the Museum marks the only concert scheduled on the East Coast so far this season.

Big Mama has always been true to herself and what she knows. She has been true to the blues, always singing from her heart. She never sings a song the same way twice because she says "I sings what I feels when I feels it." She never sings pop. She says rock and roll is nothing but the blues speeded up. Her new album, "Saved," will be released on the Warner Brothers label in the next two weeks.

Under the direction of Ed Bland, JAZZ IN THE GARDEN runs for six more Thursday evenings from 7:30 to 9:30 p.m. Admission is $1.00 plus the regular Museum entrance fee ($1.75, members free). Tickets go on sale the Saturday preceding each concert, and are available until concert time. The Garden Restaurant is open for refreshments, and cushions are available for listening comfort. In case of rain, the concert is cancelled.

* *
Additional information and photographs available from Garry George, Press Coordinator, JAZZ IN THE GARDEN, The Museum of Modern Art, 11 West 53 Street, New York 10019. Telephone (212) 956-7298.

Press Release for Thornton's concert during the Jazz in the Garden series at the Museum of Modern Art, New York City, on July 22, 1971 (collection Jan van Raay).

Tribune wrote about the show: "Big Mama's set was notable for the wider use of dynamics and legato she now employs, as well as for her undiminished, joyful shouting segments. The highlight of her act, and of the night, was a strongly moving, extended version of 'Oh Happy Day,' that tore up the house. It seemed this could not be topped but, in an encore, Miss Thornton did it with an up-tempo 'Swingin' on Home' that left even this cantankerous listener cooing."[6] And even the *New York Times* reported about the festival, saying: "Big Mama Thornton closed the show that night and, as is her style, close it she did. Coming on in a plaid cowboy shirt, striped cowboy pants, and buckskin cowboy boots, Big Mama Thornton sang and shouted and sashayed until the crowd was on its feet dancing. 'Are you all happy?' she cried during a long blues version of last spring's gospel hit, 'Happy Day.' When she got a tumultuous 'Yeah' in reply, she shouted back 'I know you are, and you tell your friends to get happy, 'cause it's a happy, happy day, children, and we gotta all stick together.' She wasn't ready, however to leap the generation gap completely."[7] Thornton didn't like at all the habit of

Thornton backstage during the Jazz in the Garden concert at the Museum of Modern Art, New York City, on July 22, 1971 (© Jan van Raay).

smoking pot and so she wasn't shy to tell it her audience: "'Ah know what you're smokin' down there,' she said, 'but we is alcoholics up here, folks, that's why we sweat so much.' After a brief bit on the drums, a tip of her white fur hat, and a final 'May the good Lord take a likin' to ya,' she was gone, twisting all the way off the stage," the *New York Times* closed their concert report.[8] Thornton also may have left a strong impression on Joe Garrett, one of the organizers of the festival, when she proved that she knew what she wanted. Thornton wanted to have her money in cash, right after her set was finished. But since the university didn't allow Garrett to do so, he was in trouble now. The idea of not getting cash right away infuriated Thornton, and with all her size and power, she spun Garrett half way around and blindsided him with a huge roundhouse punch.

On May 2, 1970, Thornton was part of the lineup for B.B. King's first all-blues show in New York's famed Carnegie Hall. And from May 15–16, 1970, Thornton played at the Great Highway in San Francisco with Sandy Bull, Mendelbaum, and Doug McKechnie. Folk musician Sandy Bull played the oud, a pear-shaped stringed instrument commonly used in North African and Middle Eastern music, and Doug McKechnie played a Moog synthesizer—an instrument that was quite new at the time. As McKechnie recalls, "Those were heady times. Sandy Bull was a good friend, I'd never met Big Mama but that night she was warm and friendly. I remember that Big Mama brought the crowd to its feet, deep gospel and blues and soul. Sandy played the oud and was sweet and compelling. I personally play some weird and wild stuff that I was not too thrilled with then, or later. But the high point came for me when Mendelbaum asked me to play with them on their last piece and I did a ramp wave from the depths to the stratosphere that brought the house down. The thing with the Moog was that all the electronics were sensitive to temperature changes. More than a few degrees and everything began to shift, like playing a wet eel, strange and wonderful."[9]

The show at the Great Highway was followed again by a concert at the Jazz Workshop in San Francisco. She was then backed by some new instrumentalists, led by bassist Dale A. Renee, with guitarist Lloyd Howe, tenor Sleepy Carothers, and drummer Ken Kenny.

In August 1970, Thornton appeared in front of more than 8,000 people again at the Ann Arbor Blues Festival. "For this festival, the same concept was followed as with the first: gather together as many of the great blues players, of all styles, as money would allow," says Michael Erlewine.[10] The program for the three-day festival was just as robust as the first festival with Roosevelt Sykes, Bukka White, John Lee Hooker, Howlin' Wolf, Hound Dog Taylor, Albert King, Fred McDowell, Johnny Shines with Sunnyland Slim, Big Joe Turner with T-Bone Walker, Buddy Guy, and Otis Rush, to name just a few. The festival was dedicated to Otis Spann's memory. Many great players had already passed away, starting with the death of Magic Sam in December of 1969. Thornton played Sunday night. The *New York Times* stated that "most of the performers are 'names' only to close followers of blues, and even these fans have never before heard some of the singers and musicians."[11] The 1970 Ann Arbor Blues Festival would be the last. Thornton performed, accompanied by her friend George "Harmonica" Smith, a heart-breaking version of "This Lucky Old Sun" and sang "Ball and Chain."

In October 1970, Thornton performed at the 15th annual Berkeley Folk Festival Open-Air Jubilee Concert, with Pete Seeger, Ewan MacColl, Ramblin' Jack Elliott, Sara Grey, fiddler Earl Collins, and Sam Chatmon. The groups in the concert, all of whom played all-acoustic programs, included Big Brother & the Holding Company, Shane & Co., Joy of Cooking, and the People's International Macedonian Band.

On December 9–16, 1970, she appeared with B.B. King, Junior Parker and Bobby "Blue" Bland at the New York Apollo. The *New York Times* again celebrated Big Mama Thornton's performance. "The hefty woman I saw before, looking much the way Bessie must have is her prime, comes onto the stage. She staggers a little: she is high, or loaded, or just overweight. The audience giggles, sympathetically. She grabs the mike, signals the band, and launches straight into a 12-bar blues. It is fantastic: the power, the authority, sweeps out into that huge cavern of a showplace and gathers up the crowd in a single, warm, joyous clutch. Your heart lifts, people are clapping their hands, a high-voltage charge of energy leaps from fingertip to fingertip around the amphitheater. When, after two choruses, she extracts a mouth harp from her voluminous pink robe and wails tight, beautiful phrased blues into the microphone, that Apollo audience—the toughest in America show business, they say—goes out of its mind. 'Hey!' 'Yeah!' 'Good Gawd Almighty!' 'Play it!' She stops, mumbles something about Janis Joplin and blasts off into 'Ball and Chain,' of course. It is Big Mama Thornton. And she sings her way majestically through the song, ripping off high falsettos, breaks, swoops and shouts with the ears of a virtuoso artist. I realize

Cooperation Funke + Lippmann + Rau				Dienstag **14.** März
10. American Folk Blues Festival u. a. mit Memphis Slim, T-Bone Walker, Big Joe Williams, Big Mama Thronton				**20 Uhr**
1. RANG links				**Musikhalle** **Großer Saal**
DM 10.— Inkl. 5,5 % Mw.-St. sowle Vorverk.- u. Abendkassengeb.	Loge **10**	Platz **17**	Hobusch- Druck	**DM 10.—**

Ticket for the American Folk Blues Festival on March 14, 1972, in Hamburg, Germany (© collection Gerhard Lenz).

just what Janis was after and never got near, what all that straining and posturing and little-girl-with-a-big-voice melodrama was about: it was about what Big Mama Thornton, with apparently no effort and exquisite control, can achieve on any song at all."[12] But the *New York Times* reviewer also clearly writes about the problems Thornton had to fight if her backing band wasn't as good as it should be, one problem she had to deal with too often: "The rhythm is momentous, irresistible, the offbeat as heavy as a … ball and chain. But then something starts to go wrong. The band takes a chorus, but it isn't together and by the time Big Mama starts singing again, even she can't rescue it and the clapping fades."[13] The reviewer than clearly points out what the problem is, saying that if Thornton would have had a proper, skillful management, she would have her own band from the beginning and there would be "half a dozen shrewd heads watching her performance, analyzing and criticizing it, polishing it."[14] But Thornton's problems with her management didn't end and there was no sign that it would lead to a better, more professional management status. The cooperation with Bob Messinger had ended, and somewhere between the end of 1970 and the beginning of 1971, Thornton acquired new management. Link Wyler, a Hollywood actor known from his role in the TV series *Gunsmoke*, took over her management. While she still had good shows and festival offers up to 1970, the offers slowly lessened and the venues became smaller. In 1971, while living in Boston and attending the Berklee School of Music,

Thornton and Big Joe Williams at the American Folk Blues Festival on March 14, 1972, in Bergamo, Italy (© Roberto Polillo).

Thornton, Paul Lenart and T-Bone Walker at the American Folk Blues Festival on March 21, 1972, in Gothenburg, Sweden (© Erik Lindahl).

the guitar player Norman Nardini spent a week playing guitar for Big Mama Thornton and George "Harmonica" Smith at the Jazz Workshop.

Thornton had now signed a contract with Pentagram Records and could finally fulfill one of her biggest dreams. A blues woman and the daughter of a preacher, Thornton loved the blues and what she called the "good singing" of gospel artists like the Dixie Hummingbirds and Mahalia Jackson. That's why she always wanted to record a gospel record. "I've thought about it a great deal, and I'd like very much to do spirituals because I feel that I got the voice. I feel like I got the power. I just feel like I could just do them," Thornton said of her gospel project.[15] And of course Thornton really had the power to sing those gospel songs, and with the album called *Saved* (PE 10005), she achieved her longtime goal. You can hear the gospel

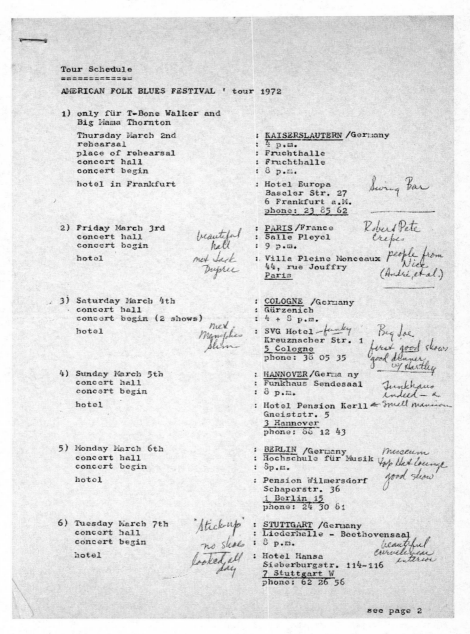

Tour Schedule
=============
AMERICAN FOLK BLUES FESTIVAL ' tour 1972

1) only für T-Bone Walker and
Big Mama Thornton

Thursday March 2nd	: KAISERSLAUTERN /Germany
rehearsal	: 4 p.m.
place of rehearsal	: Fruchthalle
concert hall	: Fruchthalle
concert begin	: 8 p.m.
hotel in Frankfurt	: Hotel Europa *Swing Bar*
	Baseler Str. 27
	6 Frankfurt a.M.
	phone: 23 85 62

2) Friday March 3rd   : PARIS /France   *Robert Pete*
   concert hall   *beautiful*   : Salle Pleyel   *Crepes*
   concert begin   *hall*   : 9 p.m.
   hotel   *met Jack*   : Villa Pleine Monceaux *people from*
                Dupree   44, rue Jouffry   *Nice*
                                   Paris   *(André, et al.)*

3) Saturday March 4th   : COLOGNE /Germany
   concert hall   : Gürzenich
   concert begin (2 shows)   : 4 + 8 p.m.
   hotel   *met*   : SVG Hotel *—funky*   *Big Joe*
        Memphis   Kreuznacher Str. 1 *first good show*
        Slim   5 Cologne   *good dinner*
                                  phone: 38 05 35   *w/ Hartley*

4) Sunday March 5th   : HANNOVER /Germa ny
   concert hall   : Funkhaus Sendesaal *Funkhaus*
   concert begin   : 8 p.m.   *indeed — a*
   hotel   : Hotel Pension Kerll *← small mansion*
                                  Gneiststr. 5
                                  3 Hannover
                                  phone: 88 12 43

5) Monday March 6th   : BERLIN /Germany   *museum*
   concert hall   : Hochschule für Musik *top that lounge*
   concert begin   : 8p.m.   *good show*
   hotel   : Pension Wilmersdorf
                                  Schaperstr. 36
                                  1 Berlin 15
                                  phone: 24 30 81

6) Tuesday March 7th *"stick-up"* : STUTTGART /Germany
   concert hall   : Liederhalle - Beethovensaal *beautiful*
   concert begin   *no show*   : 8 p.m.   *curvilinear*
   hotel   *looked all*   : Hotel Hansa   *interior*
               day   Sieberburgstr. 114-116
                                     7 Stuttgart W
                                     phone: 62 26 56

see page 2

Tour schedule of the American Folk Blues Festival, 1972 (collection Paul Lenart).

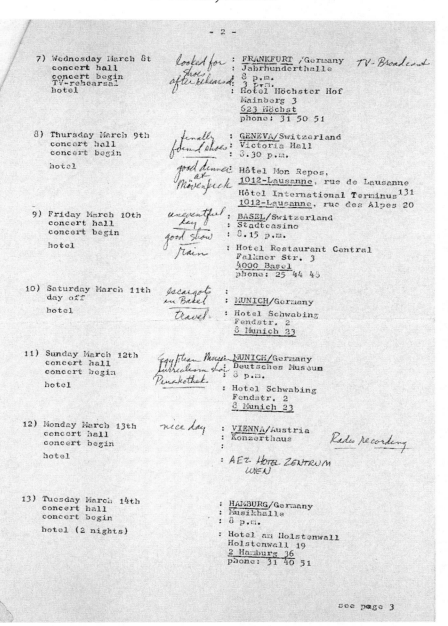

- 2 -

7) Wednesday March 8t — *looked for shoes after rehearsal* : FRANKFURT /Germany — *TV-Broadcast*
   concert hall — : Jahrhunderthalle
   concert begin — : 8 p.m.
   TV-rehearsal — : 3 p.m.
   hotel — : Hotel Höchster Hof
   Mainberg 3
   623 Höchst
   phone: 31 50 51

8) Thursday March 9th — *finally found shoes* : GENEVA/Switzerland
   concert hall — : Victoria Hall
   concert begin — : 8.30 p.m.
   hotel — *good dinner at Mövenpick* : Hôtel Mon Repos,
   1012-Lausanne, rue de Lausanne
   Hôtel International Terminus 131
   1012-Lausanne, rue des Alpes 20

9) Friday March 10th — *uneventful day* : BASEL/Switzerland
   concert hall — : Stadtcasino
   concert begin — *good show* : 8.15 p.m.
   hotel — *train* : Hotel Restaurant Central
   Falkner Str. 3
   4000 Basel
   phone: 25 44 45

10) Saturday March 11th — *escargots in Basel* :
    day off — : MUNICH/Germany
    hotel — *travel* : Hotel Schwabing
    Fendstr. 2
    8 Munich 23

11) Sunday March 12th — *Egyptian Museum Jerusalem shot Pinakothek* : MUNICH/Germany
    concert hall — : Deutsches Museum
    concert begin — : 8 p.m.
    hotel — : Hotel Schwabing
    Fendstr. 2
    8 Munich 23

12) Monday March 13th — *nice day* : VIENNA/Austria
    concert hall — : Konzerthaus — *Radio recording*
    concert begin — :
    hotel — : AEZ HOTEL ZENTRUM WIEN

13) Tuesday March 14th — : HAMBURG/Germany
    concert hall — : Musikhalle
    concert begin — : 8 p.m.
    hotel (2 nights) — : Hotel am Holstenwall
    Holstenwall 19
    2 Hamburg 36
    phone: 31 40 51

see page 3

Tour schedule of the American Folk Blues Festival, 1972 (collection Paul Lenart).

RP "God bless your skin"

— 3 —

14) Wednesday March 15th — *Manfred* — BREMEN/Germany — *museum w/*
    concert hall — *fick* — : Glocke — *art nouveau*
    concert begin — *good dinner* — : 8 p.m. — *+ Germ. Exp.*
    hotel in Hamburg — *St Pauli* — : Hotel am Holstenwall
    Holstenwall 19
    2 Hamburg 36
    phone: 31 40 51

15) Thursday March 16th — : LÜNEN/Germany — *Festival*
    concert hall — : Hilpert Theater — *recorded*
    concert begin — : 7:45 hours p.m. — *poor show*
    hotel in Düsseldorf — *near RR track* — : Hotel Christina
    Gustav Poensgen **Str.** 79
    4 Düsseldorf
    phone: 34 40 91

16) Friday March 17th — *good pasta* — BERGAMO/Italy — *weird show*
    concert hall — : Teatro Donizetti — *Herbie Hancock*
    concert begin — : hours
    hotel — : Moderno Hotel
    Via Papa Giovanni XXIII
    Bergamo
    phone: 23 30 33

17) Saturday March 18th — *great show* — ROTTERDAM/Holland — *Big Joe dancing*
    concert hall — : De Doelen — *w/ Willa Mae*
    concert begin — *the best so far* — : 12.00 p.m. (mid night) — *Rot. Pete dancing*
    hotel — : Hotel Amsvoorde — *along stage*
    Sgravendigkwal 151
    Rotterdam
    phone: 003110 - 23 79 79

18) Sunday March 19th — *small crowd* — COPENHAGEN/Denmark — *Glyptothek*
    concert hall — : Tivolis Koncertsal — *Museum*
    concert begin — : 8.00 p.m. — *etc.*
    hotel — *poor drunken show* — : Hotel Merkur
    Vester Farimagsgad 17
    Copenhagen
    phone: 12 57 11

19) Monday March 20th — *very good show* — MALMÖ/Sweden — *short prop flight*
    concert hall — : Olympen (Lund)
    concert begin — : 7.00 p.m.
    hotel — : Alexandra Hotel Malmö
    Sallerupsveien 5
    Malmö
    phone: 18 09 00

20) Tuesday March 21st — *very tiring night* — GOTHENBURG/Sweden — *prop flight*
    concert hall — : Konserthuset — *weird landing*
    concert begin (2 shows) — : 7 p.m. + 9.30 p.m.
    hotel — : Heden Hotel
    Stensturegatan
    Gothenburg
    phone: 20 02 35

see page 4

Tour schedule of the American Folk Blues Festival, 1972 (collection Paul Lenart).

- 4 -

21) Wednesday March 22nd, 1972, *ellological museum* : OSLO/Norwegen, *by gymnasium*
    concert hall : Nordhallen - *50/50 show*
    concert begin *walked around town* : 7.30 p.m.
    hotel : Hotel Atlas
        Karl Johansgaten 12
        Oslo
        phone: 42 33 78

22) Thursday, March 23rd *walked* : UPPSALA/Sweden *good show*
    concert hall *around town* : University
    concert begin *w/ Hartley* : 8.00 p.m.
    hotel *+ Phil* : Palace Hotel
        St. Eriksgatan 115 *— too exp.*
        Stockholm
        phone: 24 12 20

23) Friday, March 24th : ~~STOCKHOLM~~/Sweden *try to Helsinki*
    d a y   o f f
    hotel : Palace Hotel
        St. Eriksgatan 115
        Stockholm
        phone: 24 12 20

24) Saturday, March 25th : HELSINKI/Finland
    concert hall : Finlandia
    concert begin : 8.00 p.m.
    hotel : Hospits
        Berggatan 17
        Helsinki
        phone: 10 481

25) Sunday March 26th : HELSINKI/Finland
    d a y   o f f
    hotel : Hospits
        Berggatan 17
        Helsinki
        phone: 10 481

26) Monday March 27th : STOCKHOLM/Sweden
    concert hall : Folkhuset
    concert begin (~~2 shows~~) : 7.00 p.m. + 9.30 p.m.
    hotel : Palace Hotel
        St. Eriksgatan 115
        Stockholm
        phone: 24 12 20

Tour schedule of the American Folk Blues Festival, 1972 (collection Paul Lenart).

classics "Oh, Happy Day," "Down By The Riverside," "Glory, Glory Hallelu-jah," "He's Got The Whole World In His Hands," "Lord Save Me," "Swing Low, Sweet Chariot," "One More River" and "Go Down Moses" on this LP. She proved again with this record what a gifted singer she was. On Penta-gram the song "Sing Out for Jesus," written by Kim Carnes, was also issued then. The song as sung by Thornton was part of the soundtrack for the movie *Vanishing Point*.

Two weeks before the release of *Saved*, Thornton had a memorable performance on July 22, 1971, at 7:30 p.m. at the Jazz in the Garden series at the Museum of Modern Art in New York City. Ed Bland, the producer of Jazz in the Garden, recalls, "Through some now forgotten acquaintance I was informed that Big Mama would be in this part of the country and might be interested in performing in my series. I booked her. She showed up a week early for her performance. I put my press aide, Garry George, on her case. Garry babysat her with food and whiskey. She performed and had spent all her performance fee. Luckily I was able to get an infusion of additional funds so that she could return home with a little money in her purse."[16] With the help of Garry George, Thornton also had an appearance on the *Dick Cavett Show* that aired on July 22, 1971.

Garry George says about his meeting with Big Mama Thornton: "She called me when she arrived in Manhattan in her big Cadillac. I took a taxi to the Royal Hotel in Columbus Circle. When I got there, she was in an altercation with the bellboy and had pulled a knife on him when he tried to take her bags from the car. We spent a few days together at press inter-views and at her record label, which was Pentagram distributed by Warner Bros. She got a lot of coverage including a big feature in *Women's Wear Daily*, a fashion newspaper. We visited the Warner Bros. press offices in New York with Bob Merlis. She told me how grateful she was that Janis Joplin had sung 'Ball and Chain.' We talked about Houston, as I had grown up there. I used to sneak into blues clubs in the 5th Ward. On the concert day, I threw a press party for her and she enjoyed the attention. When it came time to perform, she handed me a pint of Old Granddad bourbon that she had in a paper bag. She had already drunk some of it. I assumed or she told me not to let her have it until after the concert. Her concert was spectacular, and when it came time for intermission, she asked me for the paper bag with the pint in it. I refused. She begged. I withheld. She finished the concert without drinking more and I gave her the bottle. I felt that we had bonded and I was sorry to see her go. I admired her struggle and her artistry."[17]

One of the people in the audience that day was jazz legend Charles Mingus. He was living with Susan Graham of *Changes Magazine* at the time and she brought him to a few of the concerts. Thornton's appearance was well documented by photographer Jan van Raay, who recalls, "I had been hired by the Museum of Modern Art to shoot photos of the Jazz in the Garden series that took place in the Sculpture Garden of the museum in July and August of 1971. Also, I had given birth to my son on May 11 of that year. For each of the concerts I had to bring my baby with me and my husband would arrive a half hour or so later and take over watching him. I would put him on the corner of the stage in his little plastic carrier where I could see him and go on with my job taking photos. Well, Big Mama fell in love with him and would give him little kisses and stroke him. Afterwards she was happy to connect with Charlie Mingus. She was very warm and genuine."[18]

After her successful show in New York, Thornton appeared at the Paramount Theatre in Portland, Oregon, on August 1, together with the Paul Butterfield Blues Band. Thornton then went on a tour of the Pacific Northwest. Muddy Waters, Big Joe Turner, George "Harmonica" Smith, Bee Houston and J.B. Hutto were part of this tour package. Organized, filmed and recorded by the crew of the popular TV show *Gunsmoke*, including Thornton's manager Link Wyler, the troupe played venues like the Monroe State Prison in Washington, the University of Washington and the University of Oregon in Eugene. Big Mama Thornton brought along her backing band, The Hound Dogs, with J.D. Nichols (piano), Bill Potter (tenor sax), Steve Wachsman (guitar) and Bruce Sieverson (bass). They would back up all the other acts too.

We would not have live footage from those performances today if not for Richard Chalk from Topcat Records. By chance he met the recording crew of that tour many years later and managed to meet Link Wyler too. Wyler had audio and videotapes from 1971 and had stored the material for twenty-seven years. Chalk made a deal with Wyler shortly before Wyler died of brain cancer. As a result of the deal Topcat records produced a live CD in 2001, featuring Muddy Waters, Big Joe Turner, George "Harmonica" Smith, Bee Houston and J.B. Hutto in their best moments at the Monroe State Prison in Washington, the University of Washington and the University of Oregon in Eugene, along with an interview of Thornton and Big Joe Turner. In 2004 Chalk added the release of the DVD *Gunsmoke Blues* that features Thornton, Smith, Turner and Waters on a live concert in Eugene, Oregon. Thornton is blowing harp as she makes her way dancing to the stage from the back of the venue through the audience to the stage and playing her great harmonica on "Early One Morning." After this harmonica-based song, she goes over to her hit "Ball and Chain," which she performs with an incredible intensity. In the bonus tracks you can hear her again with "Rock Me Baby" and her biggest hit "Hound Dog." Between the concert parts and the DVD bonus tracks, there are different scenes that give us a great impression about what life on tour meant in those days. The filmed scenes show Thornton, Waters and Turner being interviewed and chatting with everyone sitting in a van as they head from out of Portland to Eugene for the show. They are talking about their lives how they all had met many years ago; they are making jokes all around, sharing a bottle of some hard stuff as Thornton tells stories. One is about Elvis Presley, saying that he refused to share the stage with her one time. She repeated this story in another interview nine years later: "Everybody [is entitled] to their own opinion. He was all right. I called him 'Shakin' Hound Dog' because he shook everywhere he went. But ain't but one thing I didn't like about Elvis, when he refused to play on the same bill with me. Right after 'Hound Dog.' When he came out with 'Hound Dog,' they wanted to bill us on the same bill. And he refused, saying nothing that a colored person could do for him but shine shoes. That was a big write-up in the papers. We never did play on the same bill. In fact, it didn't make no difference, because I was just as proud, prouder than he was—because I'm black and he is white. He's making a million, I'm making a zillion nothing, you understand? But I'm still living. Gonne keep living. That light has been shown to me."[19] There is no account or article that proves an event like Thornton describes it, but it shows how bitter she was about some things that happened after "Hound Dog" became such a hit for Elvis Presley. In the same interview she happily says that she always promptly gets her royalties out of "Ball and Chain." In a great scene, Thornton and Turner can be seen and heard singing old songs, and she does a great interpretation of Louis Armstrong's "Wonderful World." Muddy Waters is pretty quiet during the interviews. He just sits there and listens, amused.

In August 1971, Lee Magid Productions, a business run by the manager of singer Della Reese, had packaged a show called Super Heavy Blues Express with Big Mama Thornton, Big Joe Turner, T-Bone Walker, Eddie "Cleanhead" Vinson and others. They started their tour at the Bitter End West Club in Los Angeles. The rest of the year (1971), Thornton played mainly at the Ash Grove. So she did on New Year's Eve, when she joined the show of her dear Johnny Otis.

By now the American blues revival had come to an end. While the original blues acts like Big Mama Thornton mostly played smaller venues, younger people played their versions of blues in massive arenas for big money. Since the blues had seeped into other genres of music, the blues musician no longer needed impoverishment or geography for substantiation; the style was enough. While at home the offers became fewer and smaller, things changed for good in 1972. Again, like seven years before, the reason was a call from Europe. Thornton was asked to rejoin the American Folk Blues Festival tour and, since she always thought of Europe as a very good place for her and given the lack of engagements in the U.S. she agreed happily.

Thus, on March 2, the tour brought Big Mama Thornton to Germany, France, Switzerland, Austria, Italy, Holland, Denmark, Norway, and Finland ending on March 27 in Stockholm. With her on the bill were Eddie Boyd, Big Joe Williams, Robert Pete Williams, T-Bone Walker, Paul Lenart, Hartley Severns, Edward Taylor and Vinton Johnson. As in 1965 they garnered recognition and respect from other great musicians who wanted to see them. One day Herbie Hancock came backstage to meet the blues greats. Also, Memphis Slim visited the tour while they played in Cologne and Jack Dupree joined them in Paris. Memphis Slim had been part of the American Folk Blues Festival in 1962 and since then stayed in Europe.

Some of these concerts must have been magical, such as the one in Rotterdam, on March 18, when Big Joe Turner, Big Mama Thornton and Robert Pete Williams danced along the stage. "I do remember that the show in Rotterdam was one of those rare nights when everybody was having a great time. I remember sitting on the side of the stage [backstage] and watching Robert Pete singing. He did this song about his woman 'doin' him wrong,' and he kept singing 'you wrong' over and over, and building in intensity, until he was almost jumping off of the chair he was sitting on. Man, he was electrifying. And the crowd loved it. The rest of the musicians were all having a great time that night, too. It was almost like the crowd

Big Mama Thornton in Berkeley, California (Jon Sievert).

wasn't there and they were playing at some fish fry at home, yelling at one another and urging them on. A special night for sure," recalled Paul Lenart.[20]

For Thornton, Europe again was a big success, as Lenart recalls. "She just kicked it! We really enjoyed playing with her. She had such a reputation for being hard on her musicians, but she was not that way with us at all. She took a lot of pride in her performances and expected that we keep an eye on her. She was in charge and knew how to deliver a show." Even though they only rehearsed about 30 minutes before their first show, everything went well. Lenart describes the rehearsal process. "She said to us, 'Fellas, just keep your eyes on me! When I pull out this harmonica, we will be in the key of F. Just listen for me to start and then come on in when you feel it.' We played a few bars of each of the songs that we would be playing on the show. The show went without any problems and by about the fourth concert, we were smokin.' She had a great stage presence and it was really easy to be with her on stage. We just followed along in her wake. We had a great band with Vinnie Johnson on drums, Phil Morrison on bass, myself on guitar, and two horn players. Vinnie and Phil drove the beat and the rest of us just floated along on top. She was warm, friendly and a lot of fun to be around. Once, while performing in Copenhagen, while I was playing a guitar solo during 'Ball and Chain' she ran off-stage, got a towel, came out and started fanning me off, much to the crowd's delight. I felt a tap on my shoulder, and while I was still playing she leaned over and kissed me on the cheek. The crowd roared. I will never forget that moment."

Thornton's and other people's drinking sometimes had a negative effect on the performances Paul Lenart recalls: "Usually when a show was not that good, it was because we were either tired, or T-Bone and Big Mama were drunk and not at their best. But they all had their demons. Big Mama and T-Bone would get their bottles of Wild Turkey and Courvoisier every day as we passed through the duty-free at the airport (as we flew almost daily) and by the time we showed up for sound check they were 'half in the bag' (half drunk). Sometimes the shows started out a little rough until they got their feet under them. Once that happened, the band usually cooked right along. Then, after every show, no matter where we were, a local club owner would take us all over to his club for drinks and to show us off to his clientele. It was grueling to do this night after night."

But for Lenart a dream came true with this tour. "I had heard about these people for years and to be actually traveling and performing with them was an absolute dream. The truth was that they were real people, warts and all, and they made no bones about it. They were warm and friendly and fun to be with. Robert Pete told me about how he killed a man in self-defense, when the man mistakenly took him for his wife's lover. Big Joe Williams told me that putting a silver spoon under your pillow at night keeps the ghosts away. Big Mama, once when a waiter had mistaken her for a man, stood up, pulled back her blazer, and said 'Who are you calling sir?' The waiter was mortified and apologized immediately. Looking back on it now, it was a blast and worth every minute of it. We all got pretty friendly and were sad to part at the end of the tour." Thornton certainly enjoyed playing with him and due to the lack of a backing band in the U.S., she asked Lenart if he would like to join her and come with her to Los Angeles. But Lenart, who had a life in Cambridge, wasn't willing to give this up, not knowing how secure Thornton's offer would be.

9

Sassy Mama Still Swings

Back home Big Mama Thornton entered the club scene again. In those days it was very difficult to travel with a larger band. So Big Mama always traveled only with George "Harmonica" Smith. Again, the audience in the U.S. was so different from her experiences in Europe. While she could still fill big concerts halls with the American Folk Blues Festival, she did not draw hundreds or thousands of people in her home country. She mainly played in small clubs. Besides the lack of great opportunities musically, it was also clearly visible now that Thornton was starting to get sick. By now, Thornton had already lost a lot of weight. But that didn't stop her from making music.

To add something to her stage show she developed a style of special comedy. Thornton would bemoan the faults of the band, talking to the audience in humorous asides, often at the expense of the backing band. That wasn't meant seriously, but if you didn't understand her humor it was easy to be hurt by her jokes. When she played a week in Boston with George "Harmonica" Smith, she told the audience every evening how bad the backing band was and that this was all the fault of the club's manager. But when the manager asked her what the problem was, she said that there was no problem and that the boys in the band just play fine, only to start the next day again with punishing the club manager on stage for giving her such a bad backing band. If you took her too seriously about those things—your fault.

Thornton did know what she wanted and when she wanted something, not just on stage but also outside the showroom. If she'd like to cook herself one of her favorite meals, chitterlings and hog maws, for breakfast, she would have a huge kettle cooking on a hot plate, not taking care that she was staying in a hotel room and the smell of her meal may be disturbing for the other hotel guests.

When she played in and around San Francisco, she was now mostly backed by the Luther Tucker Band. Big Walker Derrick, who played saxophone in the band recalls how he got to play with them and Thornton. He also gives a good example of Thornton's bitter sweetness. "Luther Tucker ask me if I could give him a ride to a gig in Oakland. He told me to bring some instruments just in case. On the way to the gig he asked me to stop at a liquor store. He bought two half pints of something. He got back in the car and wrapped one of the bottles tightly in its small brown paper bag. 'Watch this,' he said, hitting the bottom of the bottle with palm of his hand. The seal of the twist top breaks. Then he drinks it down in one breath. 'Dang Luther,' I said. We got to the gig. Luther says, 'I'll introduce you but if you want to play you have to ask her yourself.' Luther says, 'Mama, this boy name be's Derrick.' Mama says, 'Yeah? And la de da.' I said, 'Mama, can I play?' 'I don't know can you?' she answered. I heard laughing in the backroom coming from the band. I stuttered, 'Ye ye yes I'mmm not too bad, Mama.' 'What you play boy?' I said, 'S s s sax and ha Harp.' 'Harp?' she says. 'Well, we don't need no harp. I play the harp!' I said, 'I know.' She said, 'OK well we'll see what you can do.' Mama could sound angry, but she wasn't. It was just her way."[1] Derrick was hired then and played with the band and Big Mama Thornton off and on for some years. "I was hired to play sax and some harp. We did about five fantastic gigs or so with that band, Mark Naftalin, Harvey Brooks, Luther Tucker and myself. I can't remember the drummer's name but as I recall he was playing with Anthony Broxton, and he was great. When I met Big Mama Thornton she was only about 120 pounds and I was also hired to bring Mama her medicine. Mama said 'I'll call you up. Bring my medicine to the stage when you come." What Thornton called her medicine was a mix of 10 percent milk, 90 percent gin in a large glass! She mixed the gin together with the milk because she thought this way it would be better for her stomach.

Big Walker Derrick adds: "So Mama calls me to the stage like this 'Well, come on if you're coming.' And says, 'Did you bring my medicine son?' 'Yes, Mama,' I said. Most people in the audiences believed that she was my mama and I her henpecked son. Mama talked me through a solo on a slow blues, and I mean every note. 'Now go up high, take it easy now, not that high, now go down, play it strong now, like you mad at it.' The crowd loved it. Man, I was in!"

In a package with other blues greats Thornton could still fill larger venues, as she did following her European tour on April 29, in the Pepperland in San Rafael, CA, and on April 30 at the Berkeley Community Theatre. Both shows included B.B. King as the second act.

Thornton toured again in Canada, as she had done before and as many other blues giants did in those years, as Canadian guitarist James Anthony recalls: "There were famous clubs in Toronto where all of these famous blues guys played in. There were two or three different places where you could always have blues. It was an amazing city because being so close to Buffalo. A lot of blues artists came up to Canada. They were received quite well. Toronto was, in the sixties and seventies, a very blues and R&B city. I saw Big Mama Thornton in Toronto when I was around 17 years old, when she playing with George 'Harmonica' Smith. I remember going over to them. I sat down and I talked to George and Big Mama Thornton came over. I just wanted to meet them and talk to them. They had not had good experiences with white people in the U.S.A. so the only way to be able to talk to them was when you gave them a little present. Then they sat down with you for five minutes and they give the time. I thought it was just absolutely wonderful that these blues legend guys would actually sit down and talk to us. That's how I first met Big Mama Thornton."

On the Memorial Day weekend 1973, Thornton performed in the Ozark Mountain Folk Fair in Eureka Springs, Arkansas. Performers included Thornton, Leo Kottke, Clifton Chenier and the Red Hot Cajun Band, Michael Murphy, and the Earl Scruggs Revue. The concert was filmed and later released under the name "Gettin' Back."

Thornton's tour through the smaller-club scene was shortly interrupted on June 29, 1973, by a big event. B.B. King had organized and hosted two shows called the "Blues Summit." The show was presented by George Wein at the Lincoln Center for the Performing Arts in the Philharmonic Hall in New York as part of the Newport Jazz Festival. Beside Thornton, there were Gatemouth Brown, Arthur Crudup, Lloyd Glenn, Jay McShann Trio, Big Joe Turner, Eddie "Cleanhead" Vinson and the Muddy Waters Blues Band performing. The electrified violin was played by Clarence "Gatemouth" Brown, who backed other performers as well as taking the lead on two tunes. The show was recorded and released under Buddah Records in 1973. Again, Thornton proved that she was still the great show stopper. And the *New York Times* even wrote on July 1, 1973, that Thornton "who received some informal riffing from King's backing group, came close to stealing the show" from Muddy Waters. According to the *New York Times*, the two shows sold out one time and "four-fifths of the audience was made up of young people from the jeans-and-sandals set."[2]

Thornton came back to New York on November 16, 1973 and played with Hound Dog Taylor and others at the Academy of Music. She later had an engagement at the Shaboo Inn in the little town of Willimantic in Northeastern Connecticut. For major artists, the Shaboo Inn was the stop between New York and Boston and was called the hottest spot in New England. Though only 15-foot by 30-foot wide, one foot high and 1 foot away from the audience, the club's stage was a place where many of the blues greats played over the years: Muddy Waters, James Cotton, Howlin' Wolf, John Lee Hooker, T-Bone Walker, Buddy Guy and Junior Wells, B.B. King, Freddie King, Willie Dixon, Hound Dog Taylor and Big Mamma Thornton. At the Shaboo Inn, the bass player Perry Yeldham was part of her backing band. He recalls: "I played a lot of blues and she was doing a tour of colleges and small venues in New England. I got hired to play bass for her. I played five or six concerts with her. She drank a full bottle of Johnny Walker for every gig. In a certain way she was difficult to work with because she was very demanding. But you wouldn't know that she was drinking so much. She didn't look drunk. If you played the way she liked than she was very friendly. There were some other musicians that weren't that good and she was pretty horrible to them."[3] During this week Thornton had an opening act before her show started. The opening act was a locally known piano player named Paul Winer, who called himself Sweet Pie. His specialty was to perform almost naked. Winer recalled, "They hired two acts a week, a big feature act and a regional act. I was regionally well-known and the opening act for Big Mama that week. The audience loved her."[4]

For the next year, very little is known about her tour schedule. Thornton played another show at the Brooklyn Academy of Music in January and February and she took part in the *Midnight Special* on NBC-TV on August 30, hosted by B.B. King, with John Lee Hooker, Big Joe Williams, Bobby Bland and Jimmy Witherspoon. After this show Thornton appeared at the American Theatre in Washington, DC.

Thornton wasn't doing too good and sometimes she stayed in her halfsister's home in Buffalo. Mattie Fields would also help Thornton from now on with all the financial dealing and managing. In those days, jazz and blues musician Jeannie Cheatham met Thornton for the first time. Cheatham had met Fields and she told her that Thornton got stranded at her home. Finally, Fields introduced Cheatham and her husband into her house. The Cheathams felt shocked to see Thornton's physical condition. She ate very little. And was no longer the rounded, well-padded woman of her earlier years and began to show a raw-boned figure that forecast the shadow of things to come. The doctor told Thornton if she didn't stop touring and drinking she wouldn't last much longer. But you don't tell a woman like Thornton what she should do. The only things she changed was to stop drinking pure gin (but she still drank her "medical mix" of gin and milk). As the years went on, Jeannie Cheatham and Big Mama Thornton would work together on and off.

Nineteen seventy-five brought Big Mama Thornton another great recording possibility, after a four-year span without any new recording. Ed Bland, who Thornton knew since 1971 when he had produced the Jazz in the Garden series at the Museum of Modern Art, was now Vanguards' A&R Manager. He signed Thornton for the release of some of her live recordings from the 1971 Pacific Northwest Tour with Muddy Waters, Big Joe Turner, George "Harmonica" Smith, Bee Houston and J.B. Hutto. "Big Mama introduced me to her manager Link Wyler and her sister Mattie Fields. I was doing some recording and producing for GWP Records (Jerry Purcell). I introduced Big Mama, Link and Mattie to Jerry. Jerry had a small soul/R&B label and production company at that time. Link played me some cuts from the album. A few weeks later I was asked by Vanguard Records to become head of A&R for them. Among my first acquisitions for Vanguard was this recording. I oversaw the contractual arrangements between Vanguard and GWP Records (including Jerry Purcell, Link Wyler and Big Mama) concerning the purchase of the master of the live recording," he recalls.[5] The live performance from the shows at the Monroe State Prison in Monroe, Washington, and the Oregon State Reformatory, in Eugene, Oregon, was released 1975 under the name *Jail*, but with little change in the sound. The live atmosphere that we now hear on the *Jail* album doesn't show the reality at the venues, says engineer John Kilgore: "The audience were not widely enthusiastic and we had taken some of their bigger cheers and distribute them through the album in order to make to crowd sound more excited. At the end of each of the songs there come some similarities."[6]

After the *Jail* album, Thornton also recorded new songs in the Vanguard studio. Some of them were released the same year under the title

Sassy Mama, while other songs from the recording session were only found and released in 2000, under the name *Big Mama Swings*. Ed Bland recalls the recording: "I was in charge of the booking of the musicians for the *Sassy Mama*, and *Big Mama Swings* albums and studio and instrumental rentals if any. I was also in charge of the musician's union contracts, and the publishing company info. Needless to say I was in charge of the album concept, the artwork, and the determination of the musical qualities and the sonic qualities of the recordings." Thornton was accompanied by her sister Mattie Fields during the recording sessions. There were at least four sessions. "As long as Big Mama was happy with the performance of the musicians (and she was sober) she was easy to work with. As long as one was straight with her money, she was easy. She was happy with me because I had gotten her performances at the Museum of Modern Art (NYC), the Brooklyn Academy of Music and national TV before. Also she liked the musicians I selected to play with her. And she got her money promptly," Bland says. The engineer for the session was John Kilgore. He was just a brand new hire for Vanguard Records. "I just graduated college. I was 26 years old. I had been hired in the late summer of 1974. I was responsible for setting the session, deciding how to record, what microphones to use and managing the recording. We recorded at Vanguard Recording Studio. It was an old former ballroom in a hotel which was on 2004 Street in Manhattan," Kilgore says.

The session musicians were Paul Griffin (keyboards), Jimmy Johnson (drums), Buddy Lucas (tenor sax), Wilbur Bascomb (bass), Cornell Dupree (guitar), Ronnie Miller (guitar) and Ernie Heyes (piano). "I have a very clear memory of Jimmy Johnson. He always used to wear a little yardsman cap when he played. He was a cool laid back guy. Who was very easy to work with and had a very solid beat. He knew how to get a great sound out of his drums. I remember Cornell Dupree. He was a very easy guy to work with too," Kilgore recalls.

The sessions began in the morning and stretched into the afternoon. Of course, the morning was not Big Mama's best recording time and before she could work she needed her breakfast drink. "She would come to the sessions and said, 'Mattie, give me my grapefruit juice.' The juice was a big glass that you use for cold water in the refrigerator. It was like half grapefruit juice and the rest was Gin," Kilgore recalls. It was not an easy recording situation, he adds: "If she didn't liked the way you were acting she let you know. I managed to get along with her all right. Although I think she tested me. I think she was like, let's see what's he is made out of. So she kind of needled me but when I responded with humor, she warmed up eventually and stopped bothering me so much. And she also could see that Ed Bland trusted me. She liked Bland all right."

The songs she recorded, were mostly made up by her. The only songs not written by Thornton were Muddy Waters' "Rolling Stone" and "Everybody's Happy (But Me)," written by Jeannie Cheatham and Mattie Fields. Thornton often had only some fragments of lyrics in her head and she would just put them together. But she knew exactly what she wanted during the sessions, as Kilgore recalls: "She would direct the band and say, 'I want this to be a shuffle,' and gives the tempo. And she maybe sings a line or two and they picked it up. Then they came into the control room and listen back to it."

There were a couple of occasions where nothing was working, Kilgore recalls: "Big Mama was in the room with the rest of the band. She would sit there and they tried to follow her. That was the hard part in the sessions and one of the reasons why *Big Mama Swings* was later released. Because it was felt that the band was sort of scrambling to keep up with her. Because Big Mama Thornton didn't follow regular blues forms, sort of like Lightning Hopkins. She made her changes when she felt like it. And you just better go along with her. If you weren't fast enough to keep up with her, then too bad. So there were a lot of takes that would have otherwise been good but the band didn't make the change when she did. The songs would break down because nobody could figure out what she really meant. She would stop things because she was frustrated because they weren't following her correctly. I think we had a morning session where nothing was going right." Wilbur Bascomb, the bass player, recalls that it was all very loose: "That wasn't a very tight recording session, because there was no real rehearsal. We had no previous knowledge what we are gonna do before we got there. I remember Big Mama didn't wanna record one day because Paul Griffin wasn't gonna be there. She liked him very much. She called him 'Little Brother.' Big Mama was very quiet but she knew what she wanted. It was very informal. I don't remember any music that was written, that we had to stick to. Back in those days it was like working in a factory. It was a very low budget and we had to work fast. We had to sit in that chair, make it happen real quick and got out of there. There wasn't that much time to socialize. On the other hand musicians in those days had a lot of input as far as what they played instead of someone looking over your shoulder and telling you what to play."[7]

There weren't really many conversations between the musicians and Thornton, Kilgore says: "I think the only interaction that I remember her barking at people when it was like 'Hi, you didn't make my change.' Cornell was used to being in the right most of the time. He didn't like being wrong. So when it wasn't working, he was blaming Big Mama. And Big Mama was like: 'Well, I gonna make my change when I feel like it and you better follow me.'" Although the record sounds great Thornton was in a terrible condition at that time. The alcohol was taking his toll. "She was kind of shapeless. It looked like she was getting skinny arms and so on. She depended on Mattie and Mattie was looking out for her and was trying to keep her together in body and soul. There was a deep caring between both of them. Mattie was as sweet as Big Mama was sour," says Kilgore. Three years later Vanguard would reissue the sessions and release a compilation from some of the songs from *Jail* and *Sassy Mama* under the name *Mama's Pride*.

Besides the recording for Vanguard, and although her health was not the best, Big Mama Thornton never stopped touring. She played in New Hampshire backed up by the so-called John Wardwell Blues Band and performing in her now more and more typical way, as former band member piano player Anthony Geraci says: "I was attending the Berklee College of Music in Boston. I had befriended a great blues band from New Hampshire called the John Wardwell Blues Band, and I would frequently hop the bus to New Hampshire to play some great blues with them. They were offered a gig to do their own set of music and then back up Big Mama. Sounded like great fun! We did our set and then called Big Mama up to do a set with us. She enjoyed her gin, and was in a feisty mood. We did the first number and she threw everyone off the bandstand except me. She said: 'You all leave except for that piano picker.' She proceeded to sit behind the drums, grabbed a microphone and pulled out a harmonica. The harmonica was an F sharp, so I think I had to play in B or C sharp the entire set—not really the best keys for playing blues on the piano, especially at that early stage of my career. We careened around her usual hits 'Hound Dog' and the like, but I just remember it as being put into the fire and holding on for dear life. We played about an hour or so and I didn't get kicked off the bandstand. It was a night to be remembered."[8]

Michael "Mudcat" Ward recalls another of those show nights in 1975.

Big Mama Thornton publicity photo for Vanguard Records in 1975, personally signed by Thornton for guitarist Tom Principato (© collection Tom Principato).

This time Big Mama Thornton played in Cambridge, Massachusetts: "There was a dark brown, one story, wooden building that housed a club called The Speakeasy ("Home of the Blues") on Norfolk Street, a small one-way street leading into Central Square, in Cambridge, Massachusetts. The club presented blues artists in its small, tight confines, artists including pianist

Roosevelt Sykes, harmonica player Big Walter Horton, guitarist J.B. Hutto, and Big Mama Thornton. Sometimes the appearing artists would be hired to play and bring their own bands, and at other times, they would come alone without sidemen and require a provided back-up band, the job of the 'house' band, local musicians hired by the club to be the band for the headliner on any given night. I played Fender bass at that time with guitarist Ronnie Horvath (who had yet to become known as Ronnie Earl). Earl had just left Johnny Nicholas's band, the Rhythm Rockers, who had served as house band at the Speakeasy until John Nicholas took up an offer to live and play in Texas, joining the established western swing band, Asleep at the Wheel. Now on his own as leader rather than sideman, Earl quickly assembled a blues group to his liking, comprised of local black drummer Charles Robinson, singer/harmonica player Mark Cedrone, and me on bass, and we assumed the house band position at the Speakeasy. We called ourselves The Hounddogs. Big Mama Thornton, once describable as 'big' physically, showed up astonishingly slender, nearly skeletal, but by no means frail. And, as the evening progressed, she became exceedingly feisty and fiery. She led the band and sang with great spirit and emotion, and, though her still-large and earthy voice became increasingly raspy as the night unfolded, she stormed through her musical legacy: 'Ball and Chain,' 'You Ain't Nothing But A Hound Dog,' and her version of Robert Nighthawk's 'Sweet Little Angel,' slaying the audience, that is, 'taking no prisoners.' All the while, the band had all eight eyes like lasers tightly focused in her direction; it was all we could do just to stay with her and provide the steady backup. She warmly indicated that she was highly pleased with our level of musicianship and how we did our jobs behind her. Mama Thornton may have misunderstood that The Hounddogs was our band name, with only a serendipitous connection to the song she introduced to the world. It seemed she thought Ronnie's name was Hound Dog, for she would sing a few verses of vocals, and then she would implore Ronnie, shouting, 'Play that guitar, Hound Dog.' Ronnie would respond to her with searing guitar work that made all of us reach for greater musical heights and dig deeper into the heartfelt blues. By the end of the first of the two sets, the audience and the musicians, streaming with perspiration, were nearly exhausted but evidently satisfied, having been transported by Mama's blues. The break between sets offered an opportunity for all to re-fuel, which meant, for the most part, drink. Mama spent the break sitting at a table speaking to a girlfriend and profusely consuming gin. After nearly an hour (much beyond the normal break time allotted between sets at the Speakeasy), Pete, the proprietor, deflected his own duty and 'appointed' me to tell Big Mama it was time to get the final set started. I approached her table gingerly but she and her friend continued their conversation. When there was the semblance of a lull, I jumped in to ask if she was ready for the next set. Now, showing a previously concealed irascible side (revealed thanks to all that gin), 'Hell no' was her reply. 'Okay then,' I muttered as I turned and made my way back to the band. Pete instructed us to get started, which we did, and after

three or four instrumentals, Big Mama Thornton made her way to the bandstand and joined in on a long, slow hushed blues. She finished the night singing and talking to those audience members that were fortunate enough to endure the long intermission and remain for the second set."[9]

While on tour, alcohol was an ongoing topic not just for Thornton but for many musicians around her, as Al Copley from the Roomful of Blues recalls from a show in Rhode Island: "I played with Roomful of Blues from 1968 through 1984. We backed up many blues singers, and it was in the mid–1970s that we backed up Big Mama and George 'Harmonica' Smith at an outdoor concert in Rhode Island. The seventies were a hard-drinking time

Big Mama Thornton performing at The Sweetwater, Mill Valley, California, 1978 (© Mush Emmons).

120

```
SUM CONCERTS THIRD ANNUAL JUNETEENTH BLUES FESTIVAL 1979
PRESENTED IN COOPERATION WITH THE NAACP
HOUSTON, TEXAS

MONDAY, JUNE 18
* 5:00 PM  SHOW I
  Arnett Cobb and the Mobb with Milton Larkin
  Sherman Robertson and The Crosstown Blues Band
  Peppermint Harris
  Lou Ann Barton and Double Trouble
  John Lee Hooker
  Mighty Joe Young

  TUESDAY, JUNE 19
* 10:00 AM  SHOW II
  Arnett Cobb and the Mobb with Milton Larkin
  Samuel Blue
  NAACP Special Program:
                    Introduction, Johnny Johnson, SE President
                    Mayor Jim McConn
                    Mrs. Benjamin Hooks, Guest Speaker
  Special Presentation to Sam Lightnin' Hopkins by Mayor McConn
  Albert Collins

* 2:00 PM  SHOW III
  Lowell Fulson
  Roosevelt Sykes
  The Fabulous Thunderbirds

* 6:00 PM SHOW IV
  Junior Wells
  Professor Longhair and the Blues Scholars
  Big Mama Thornton and The Fabulous Thunderbirds
  Albert Collins
```

THE BLUES

Concert flyer for the 3rd annual Juneteenth Blues Festival in Houston, 1979 (author's collection).

for a lot of us, and I was no exception. We had a ball with those two—they drank a quart of Four Roses onstage, and before we'd started a couple of songs, George looks at Big Mama and asked, 'Whiskey are we playing in?' (Translation: 'Which key are we playing in?') We all had a ball in spite of a barbeque fire which enveloped the stage in smoke. She was the real deal,

121

man. What you saw, was what you got."[10] Roy Book Binder recalls another story from that time that shows how alcohol became more and more important in Thornton's life and how much her sister tried to prevent her from drinking. "I did meet Big Mama Thornton in Washington, DC. I had been working a two night gig at The Child Herald, on Connecticut Avenue. There was a blues show that weekend at a local theatre featuring Big Mama Thornton, along with local acts, including Archie Edwards and Flora Molton. I was invited to the show. Before the sound check, Big Mama and Mattie Fields were brought to The Child Herald for lunch by a concert promoter. I was asked to join and we were seated at an outside table. It was a beautiful spring day and we enjoyed the meal and the conversation. We were getting ready to leave when Big Mama asked Mattie if she had gotten a bottle of whiskey, to carry her through the evening. It was a Sunday show and when her manager said that she hadn't, all hell broke loose! They were going at it with verbal profanities when I blurted out that I knew the bartender upstairs, and although it was illegal to sell a bottle on Sunday, that I would see what I could do! She started emptying her handbag to get me money for the bottle, pulling out all kinds of stuff, including a .38 snub-nosed pistol which she flopped onto the table! Finally, she found a $20 bill and handed it to me. I told the bartender what's going on and he handed me a quart of Wild Turkey and said it's on the house for Big Mama! I gave the bottle and the money back to Mama. She thanked me and said, while glaring at Mattie who was her 'manager,' 'Now that boy knows something about being a manager!'"[11]

Big Mama Thornton was now visibly sick. In fact she had developed cancer. As a result she was no longer the big woman she used to be. Her stomach was huge but the rest of her body became more and more frail. She received treatment for the cancer, but it never stopped her from performing. Sometimes she mixed her Granddad with sugar-free cola and joked about it, saying that she was now on a diet. She saw no problem with her drinking but she really hated drugs and had no problem telling that to her audience, recalls Big Walker Derrick. "Mama hated pot. Her first song [at a particular concert]: 'Don't Smoke That Stuff Around Me.' Looking angry with all the pot smokers. And for her next number, a slow minor blues: 'That Evil Weed.' Mama was glaring and pointing at anyone smoking anything. I never heard these songs before or after. I suspect she made them up on the spot." Thornton herself said once about drinking and drugs: "I don't use dope. I just stick with my Old Granddaddy 100 proof and my old moonshine corn liquor. Weeds, pills, needles—I don't need nothing like that jive to get out on the stage and sing. I drink, yeah. It makes me happy. But as for getting drunk, falling around on the street—never! When some jive bum comes on and asks me, 'Would you like to be lit up?' I tell him, 'Yeah. I got a match. You want to be on fire? I got a little gas around here. I'll burn you up.' I'm working at this one club. Here comes a cat. Comes up with a handful of weeds. Says, 'Take your choice.' You know what I told him? 'Best thing you can do is put those things in your pocket and get out of my face. Not only out of my face, but out of the place.' The owner come up and asked me why I insulted that man. I said, 'If you think I insulted him, call him in your office and search his pockets.' When I saw him next, he had this jive cat up in his hand, man, carrying him to the door. I don't know why, they always think I ... they always come to me."[12] And in a later interview, Thornton adds: "Me, I'm an alcoholic. I'm just tell the world that. I don't need no needles in my arm. I don't need no smoking, I don't need no coke, just give me my good old Seagram's Gin, which I switched from hundred Old Granddad."[13]

In 1976, Thornton met the musician and manager Lee Ashford. Even though they would not work together immediately, because of her bad shape, the meeting would prove important some time later. Thornton played that year mostly in L.A. at The Rubaiyat Room, a small R&B club on the south side of Wilshire Boulevard in the black part of the city. Eddie "Clean-head" Vinson played there with Dan Papaila, and Thornton used to stop by regularly, as it was a jam session atmosphere. Typically she would come on stage and sing "Hound Dog." "By that time she was quite frail, but she had a great impact on the audience," Papaila recalls.[14]

Additionally to her drinking-related health problems, for which she needed to receive treatment at the hospital, she was also involved in a serious car accident and had to spend six months in the hospital.[15] The treatment at the hospital helped her get some strength back but she had to stay in a wheelchair for a while and never got back her full-body strength.

10

Life Goes On

Feeling better now, Big Mama Thornton did what she always did: she went her own way. When Elvis Presley died on August 16, 1977, in his home in Memphis, Thornton thought: "Look at all that he had, and he's dead and gone and I'm still here." And she adds: "Last time I was in Memphis they told me, 'Well we lost so-and-so.' I said, 'Did you find him?' That's blues humor in a nutshell—laughing to keep from crying."[1]

In 1977, Thornton got back in touch with Lee Ashford. Although Thornton and Ashford never signed a contract, they had a deal where Ashford would manage her from now on. Thornton didn't need to approve their deal because in her opinion her strong right hand was her contract. Ashford would now stay as her manager for the next eight years, until she died. He did put together a 25-date tour all through the U.S. and Canada and, of course, she played San Francisco; that was always a big market for her.

But Lee Ashford, along with her half-sister Mattie could not help Thornton to stop drinking. One could not really tell her what to do. Thornton was now widely known for her medicine mix of gin with milk that she drank every day, and she ate very little. But her strength was sufficient to be able to tour the U.S. from coast to coast and play clubs, hotels, universities and festivals. She even toured on different occasions through Canada. One of her Canadian concerts from these days had been recorded and released in 2003. It's a recording from her appearances at The Rising Sun Celebrity Jazz Club, owned by her long-time friend Doudou Boicel. His Rising Sun club was located on the first and second floor of a building not far from the main location of the Montreal Jazz Festival. Thornton was backed up on April 12, 1977, by a fine band with Buddy Guy's brother, Phil Guy, and John Primer on guitar, J.W. Williams on bass, Burt Robertson on drums and Big Moose Walker on piano. She played her hits and the songs she had recorded earlier on Vanguard Records.

Big Mama Thornton sitting on stage while performing at the Buffalo Tavern in Seattle, Washington, November 1979. Harmonica player Kim Field is on the left (Jonathan Ezekiel).

The same year, Thornton had the chance to perform at George Washington University in Washington, DC. There she was backed up by the Powerhouse Band: "I received a call from Elliot Ryan, who was then publisher of the arts paper *Unicorn Times* asking me if I could put together a band on short notice to back up Big Mama Thornton for a show that night at Lisner Auditorium at George Washington University. Powerhouse was a 7-piece group, but I knew all we needed was a rhythm section to back up Big Mama Thornton, so after calling our rhythm section—Steve Jacobs on bass, and Steve Brown on drums—we quickly headed down to Lisner Auditorium to do the show. When we arrived at Lisner Auditorium, Big Mama Thornton was already in the dressing room, and I remember her as being quite a colorful character, and a little outspoken. She seemed to take a liking to me and we sat and talked for a while," recalls former band member Tom Prin-

Thornton performing at the Buffalo Tavern in Seattle, Washington, November 1979 (Jonathan Ezekiel).

cipato.[2] As usual, she played her comedian role and took over the drums. As Principato recalls, "From what I remember, for most of the evening the show went really well. It was only at the end when Big Mama called for us to do her most famous song which was a huge hit for Elvis Presley—'Hound Dog'—that things got a little weird. As soon as the band launched into the song, Big Mama turned around and glared at Steve Brown the drummer, proclaiming, 'This ain't no Elvis Presley song, son,' and proceeded to go back behind the drum kit, stand next to the drummer and motioned for him to stand up and to give her the drum sticks. She then proceeded to play drums and instruct the drummer as to just exactly what was the correct way to play 'Hound Dog' the 'Big Mama way!' All of this was done to the astonishment of the band and the embarrassment of the drummer who had to stand there and watch Big Mama give him a drum lesson in front of the audience. Really something! I did have the impression though, that this was not the first time this had happened between Big Mama and a drummer, and that Big Mama used it as part of her show. Quite a grand finale. Big Mama was a pretty good drummer, too."

In the summer of 1978, Thornton went back to her musical roots and took part in the Juneteenth Blues Fest in Houston, which also featured Lightnin' Hopkins and many others. Then the band Wooden Teeth with Michael Pickett (harmonica/vocal), Omar Tunnoch (bass), Vitto Rezza (drums), Dave Tyson (keys) and John Tilden (guitar) backed her up for a show where she shared the bill with John Lee Hooker on September 3,

Thornton performing at the Buffalo Tavern in Seattle, Washington, November 1979 (Jonathan Ezekiel).

1978, at the Massey Hall in Toronto, Canada. Michael Pickett could tell that rehearsal was not what Thornton liked or needed: "My band (Wooden Teeth) was scheduled to play Massey Hall in Toronto. We would perform one set, back up Big Mama Thornton, and then John Lee Hooker. I found out where Thornton was staying, went down and met her at her Park Plaza Hotel room. I introduced myself and asked her if and when she wanted a rehearsal. She said, 'You know "Hound Dog," don't you?' I said yes. 'You know "Ball and Chain?"' I said yeah. 'You know how to play in the key of C?' I said yeah. She said, 'Rehearsal's over. Wanna drink?'"[3] It was clear for everybody that Thornton was past her prime but still a major force. "We had enormous respect for these icons and it was a privilege sharing that prestigious stage with them. Both Thornton and Hooker told the promoter that they had a great time with Wooden Teeth. I had seen Hooker a number of times and watched as bands steamrolled all over him ... no fun for the man. But that night at Massey Hall, Hooker had the time of his life because the band did what it was supposed to do ... back him up. The boys didn't make a move until Hooker or Thornton did," Pickett says.

Thornton was sick and too often drunk, but she could sing as if nothing had changed, and she could, with all of her gruff and rough behavior, be very sweet, as Doug MacLeod remembers: "I met her through George Harmonica Smith. George said, 'Doug I got you a gig with Big Mama Thornton and you got to be careful with her, cause she is rough. I said 'OK' and we had the first set and I thought it was pretty well. I was playing electric guitar at that time. I just played very tasteful, very simple, just a couple of notes, B.B. King-style. It sounded good to me. On the break I was sitting down on this table and she was doing something on stage and then she walked over to me. I was like, oh she coming to me, oh, God. She was just an inch from my nose. And she said, 'You like me?' and I said, 'Yes I like you.' She said, 'What do you like about me?' And the first thing that came out of my mind was: 'I like your eyes.' And she [said] 'WHAT.' I said that I didn't mean any disrespect. And then, she turned on to George Smith and he just worried and thought I got in trouble. And she said, 'You

Thornton at the Buffalo Tavern in Seattle, Washington, November 1979 (Jonathan Ezekiel).

know what this little Doug said to me? He likes my eyes.' George said, 'He do?' I could do no wrong with that woman after that."[4]

Between 1978 and 1979, Thornton played in the Los Angeles club scene and along the West Coast, with people like Kenny Blue Ray, Ben "King" Perkoff or Ron Thompson, who noted, "It was an honor to play with her. I couldn't believe I even had the chance to play with her. I really learnt the stuff right and I was very concerned with her having the right backing. She was my boss and I did what she wanted me to do. I played a lot of shows with her. We played the L.A. area, in Eugene, Oregon, and at the San Francisco Blues Festival."[5] Sax player Ben "King" Perkoff was asked to form a backing band for her to do shows in and around San Francisco; he recalls, "We used to play at this club called The Palms Café on Polk Street in San Francisco and played there with many different bands. The manager of the club asked me if I would put together a band to back up Big Mama Thornton. I said: 'Yeah sure.' The manager liked the way I played and I ended up backing up some other people too. But that was the first time I played at The Palm under my name with the band that I put together. We backed Big Mama for a weekend there and then she flew back to L.A. And then I had a manager at the time and he put together some other gigs for Big Mama Thornton at the Sweetwater in Mill Valley, California. We also played in this television program called *Good Morning San Francisco*. We had talked with her sister Mattie and had arranged everything and the first day she came in we picked her and Mattie up from the airport and brought her to her hotel. Mattie was like her road manager and I think she even did the money. *Good Morning San Francisco* was a very early morning show that was taped live at 7 o'clock in the morning. So the next day we picked her up at the hotel at 6 o'clock in the morning and before the show Big Mama Thornton had her orange juice-gin mix for breakfast. During the show we played two or three songs and then the TV host interviewed Big Mama Thornton. It was very funny. The host asked Big Mama, 'Where did you find this great Band, the King Perkoff Band?' And she answered, 'Right here in L.A.' Then the host said, 'Oh, but this is San Francisco here.' Then we did a couple of nights gigs at the Sweetwater, which went off very well and then she flew back to L.A. Big Mama Thornton was very gracious and nice to be around."[6]

Thornton also toured on the East Coast. So on April 10, 1979, when Thornton joined Clifton Chenier with whom she been on stage before a few times, on a memorable Tuesday evening at New York's Carnegie Hall as part of a Boogie 'n' Blues show. It was Chenier's first show in town since 1956, and in the package with Chenier again Thornton "simply stole the show. The body may be frail but the voice isn't, and she retains a fine good humor and a dazzling smile," as the *New York Times* reported.[7]

In June 1979, Thornton was again part of the Juneteenth Blues Festival in Houston. On the same bill were some others of the last original blues greats like Junior Wells, Albert Collins, John Lee Hooker, Roosevelt Sykes and Lowell Fulson. And on August 11–12, she appeared at the San Francisco Blues Festival backed up by Ron Thompson and his band including Mark Naftalin. She gave a great concert, and as the *New York Times* remembered a year later, "she sang the blues with conviction and with the exceptional control of dynamics, inflection and pitch that separates the very best blues vocalists from the rest of the pack."[8] Or as her piano accompanist, Mark Naftalin, put it shortly after the show: "There was a lot of really deep feeling coming off that woman."[9] Tom Mazzolini, the festival organizer recalls: "I booked Big Mama Thornton on the 1979 San Francisco Blues Festival. Other performers that year included Stevie Ray Vaughan, Robert Cray, Jimmy Rogers, Louis Myers, Roy Brown, Luther Tucker, Big Joe Duskin, Mel Brown, HiTide Harris and many more. Big Mama was living in Los Angeles at the time and I had seen her in a concert in the late '60s with George Smith and others. She was quite well known on the West Coast at the time, largely due in part to Janis Joplin, who covered her hit 'Ball and Chain.' Big Mama traveled to the San Francisco Blues Festival with her sister, Mattie Fields. I was quite shocked upon seeing her because she had become so thin and fragile. She was always a large, healthy-looking woman, but seeing her at the festival, it was quite noticeable that she was not well. She wore a cowboy hat and a man's suit jacket, brown with thin white stripes. Her stomach was quite distended on an otherwise thin frame and it was obvious that she was suffering from either liver disease or cancer. I remember Sonny Rhodes helped her to the stage and she had difficulty walking."[10] But let's not forget that Thornton was a comedian until the end of her life, and even though she had serious health problems, she still played this role. "She was a big put on. I played with her once at the Santa Barbara Blues Society. And when she got there she had the people to help her on stage. She played this whole role, that everything was just so down and out. She was sitting down singing. Then she grabbed the microphone and started walking across the stage and when she left the stage, she was dancing," recalls Nat Dove, who adds, "I remember one time at the jazz workshop some guy walked over to Big Mama and said: 'Big Mama you are out-of-sight.' And Big Mama answered: 'You mean, you can't see me?'"[11]

While performing at the San Francisco Blues Festival, Thornton sat on a chair for her performance and was backed by the superb Ron Thompson band with Mark Naftalin. She greeted the crowd saying, 'Hello, folks,' and then the band kicked off their first number, and Big Mama gave an incredible performance, covering all her hits and playing some wonderful harmonica. She got a rousing reaction from the audience, who were with her from the beginning. "I believe most of them recognized how fragile she was and they were deeply on her side. The respect for Big Mama that afternoon was deep and she really acknowledged it between songs. It was one of the most memorable moments in the history of the San Francisco Blues Festival and if memory serves me correct, I believe portions of her performance were filmed on 16mm by a local filmmaker. Roy Brown, the great shouter, was also on that show and he was in the midst of a comeback. Brown suffered a fatal heart attack a few month later. Big Mama's performance was taped and few years later was issued as part of a three-volume set on Solid Smoke Records. Her performance was powerful on the record and was one of the best I've ever heard. Given the fact she died not too long after made it all the more poignant. I was quite proud to have her be part of the Festival and for those fortunate enough to have witnessed it that afternoon, it will remain forever a part of blues history," Tom Mazzolini recalls.[12]

And in September 1979, Thornton crossed paths with the old counterculture community that had brought her new fame in the sixties. She took part in the Tribal Stomp at Monterey Fairgrounds, September 8 and 9, 1979, with The Clash, The Blues Project with Al Kooper, Dan Hicks, The Chambers Bros., Nick Gravenites, Peter Tosh and many more. That same month, she played with Sugar Pie de Santo, Eddie "Cleanhead" Vinson, Charles Brown, Roy Brown, Robert Cray, John Heartsman, Charley Baty and Rick Estrin and many others the Third Annual Sacramento Blues Festival at the William Land Park Amphitheatre on September 22–23, 1979. Thornton would now sit for at least parts of the show, but that was the only change in her stage program.

In November 1979, Thornton gave a concert at the Buffalo Tavern in

Seattle, Washington. The harmonica player, Kim Field, was booked for backing her up that night, but soon he found out that Thornton normally didn't like a harmonica player in her backing band. Field didn't give up and tried to talk with Thornton about the issue—with success. "Big Mama then arrived for the sound check and I told her, 'I'm a harmonica player that was hired for the show and I understand that you are not very happy on having a harmonica player playing with you. But I'm a good player and I really respect your music. You can trust me.' She looked at me and said, 'Well that's ok. We go ahead and give it a chance.' We did two sets that night," Kim Fields recalls.[13] It all worked out very well. Finally, Fields and Thornton ended up doing a harmonica duet on the song "Watermelon Man." "That was completely thrilling for me. One of the most memorable gigs I have ever done for sure," Fields said.

The rest of the year Thornton played in her hometown Los Angeles in a club called the Parisian Room. There she met again Tommy Brown, who had first met Thornton back in the late 1940s. They played a session together, as Brown recalls: "By that time she lost a lot of weight, but she was still singing very well. It was obvious that she was or had been sick. But everybody in the club loved her very much."[14]

11

Swing It On Home

The eighties started for Big Mama Thornton as the seventies had ended: with touring all over in the club scene. She said that she felt "better than I have in a long time."[1] One highlight of her live touring program was on July 2, 1980, when Thornton was part of the famous Kool Newport Jazz Festival. The festival had organized a special program called "Blues is a Woman" at Avery Fisher Hall in Manhattan, with blues veterans Koko Taylor, Linda Hopkins, Sippie Wallace, Beulah Bryant, Nell Carter and many others. Before the show Big Mama Thornton gave an interview, attended by Mattie Fields, in her hotel room to the *New York Times*, while a selection of her Hoehner Marine Band Harmonicas were scattered across the bed. She said: "I just started back to walking six month ago. I had to be in a wheelchair."[2]

Steve Ditzell who toured at that time with Koko Taylor, also played with Thornton in the program. She was backed by the famous Jay McShann, with his Kansas City Jazz Orchestra. Ditzell was aware of Willie Mae's sometimes brittle mood on stage, but he wanted to have this great opportunity to play with her. And when Thornton needed a guitarist, he jumped at the chance, although some of the musicians told him before she could be very ornery and might cuss him out in front of everybody and embarrass him. But it worked out very well. According to the *New York Times*, the producer of the Blues is a Woman program, Rosetta Reitz, wanted to "bring what she feels is long overdue acknowledgement to the women whose contribution to the history of jazz is 'enormous.'"[3] Thornton gave her utmost to fulfill this goal. The *New York Times* reviewed the concert and celebrated Big Mama, who had proved that she could still be a class-act despite the fact that she still had difficulties walking after her automobile accident three years ago; she "gradually built the mood and energy of her singing and her harmonica-playing ('Gimme some beat back there!' she shouted to the classic jazz band), moaning gently through 'Rock Me, Baby' and asserting her definitive right to "Hound Dog"—'a song I got robbed of,' she said, referring to the fact that Elvis Presley made his celebrated record of the song three years after she made hers. And she managed to loosen up her hips enough to dance her way across the stage with a slow, deliberate strut."[4] *Ebony* magazine wrote about the event: "She shuffled across the stage, a frail woman in a man's suit. She didn't need to stand. Big Mama wailed from her chair and made it tap dance as she belted her gut-bucket sound. The audience wouldn't let her go. They stood and embraced her with their applause. Big Mama smiled sweetly and looked thunderstruck."[5]

Right after the Kool Newport Jazz Festival, on July 4 and 5, 1980, she played a two-night show in New York with the Robert Ross Blues Band at Tramps on 125 East Fifteenth and this time it would be one of the hardest and also best nights for the band. Terry Dunne, the owner of the club, used to hire the band to back up blues performers like Lightnin' Hopkins, Otis Rush, Louisiana Red, and Wilbert Harrison, among others. Thornton had sent a practice tape to Terry Dunne, which he passed on to the band. It was from a live show, but there was no song list, or date, or any other information included with the tape. "I already knew many of the songs, but enjoyed listening to the tape and studying the arrangements. Everything was very standard and straight ahead. It was just great Chicago blues, the music I loved and had been listening to and playing since I was a kid. This was not going to be a problem at all," thought Robert Ross.[6] Thornton had to be helped onto the stage at Tramps (although it was only about 6 inches high), but that was not just because of her bad health; it was also part of a show. Tramps was a hot spot for real blues fans, people for whom blues was a way of life. The crowd was always very hip and very demonstrative in their appreciation of the music, but not on this particular night, according to Ross. "The place was crawling with blues tourists attracted by a sensational piece in the *New York Times* that came out earlier that day entitled, 'The Last of the Red Hot Bitchin' Babes,' or something like that. The article focused more on Willa Mae's erratic personality then her music and voice. We opened up the show like always, but the reaction of the crowd was disappointing. The tourists didn't know us and didn't want to know us. To them, I guess we were just some nice, young white guys who weren't going to cause a spectacle, and this crowd was looking for a spectacle. I could feel that they were only interested in seeing this cantankerous old blues singer

Canadian musician Plume Latraverse and Big Mama Thornton performing together in Quebec in 1980 (collection Plume Latraverse).

they had just read about. They didn't know what to make of me and my band. They just didn't seem very interested in hearing me sing. I don't think they were even interested in hearing Big Mama sing either, because, hey, they weren't a blues crowd. They were tourists slumming in blues world. I think the crowd was mostly made up of curious thrill seekers like the kind you might see at a carney show in the Midwest or someplace. It was like, 'Hey, maybe this crazy old bitch is gonna knife somebody or something like that.' Big Mama Thornton didn't deserve that, she was a great and unique artist, revered all over the world, not a two headed pig in some sleazy freak show. I do admit though that the *New York Times* article sold a lot of tickets. The power of the *New York Times* is awesome. If another person had tried to get into the club, I think the rear wall would have collapsed," Ross recalls, and adds, "Big Mama was helped up to the stage by a friend of hers and myself. With brown paper bag in hand, she just plopped down hard in her chair, took a big belt from the bottle, and started singing into a hand held mic without so much as a hello to the band. By some miracle of nature, the voice that had rocked the world was exactly the same heat sensing, guided missile of the early fifties. What a voice, whew! But, she was completely bombed. She was blitzed. She was a blindfolded kamikaze pilot coming in for a landing. Look out below!"

But the band wasn't aware of her comedic way of bashing the backing band. "About 30 seconds into the show, she stopped singing and ordered the band to stop playing. 'Wait a minute! Wait just a damn minute!' She started complaining about the drumming of George Morales. For no reason at all, she was picking on one of my best friends and loyal drummer. George looked so guilty and embarrassed being bawled out like that in front of a packed house. In the next song Big Mama stopped us again and complained about the sax player, Jeff Sheloff. The song after that she complained about George again. This time she got up from her stool and got him off of his! She sat down behind his drum set to 'Show that white boy how to play them drums.' George had to stand there in the bright stage lights with egg on his face and allow this to happen." The band was shocked but the crowd was nevertheless impressed with her outburst and gave her an ovation. "She got up from behind the drums and handed the sticks to George and said, 'You got that son?' George looked very relieved that the drum lesson and embarrassment were finally over—at least for the moment. He was able to crawl out from behind the eight ball with his tail between his legs, and sit back down behind the drums again where he was safe. After the first show I jumped on Terry Dunne like a line-backer on a loose ball, imploring him to do something to straighten Big Mama out. I told Terry, 'If you don't do something about this, then I'm gonna do something about it myself.' Lord knows what, if anything, I had in mind. Terry scoffed and waved his hand at me. 'It's a joke, man. You gotta laugh it off. Don't be so serious. That's her act. She's an old lady and she's half in the bag. Just roll with the punches. Make a show out of it. But all right, I'll speak with her.' Whatever Terry said to Big Mama fell on deaf ears. We got more of the same crap from her in the second show. At one point Big Mama asked me to kick off a slow blues like B.B. King. So I started to play B.B.'s incredibly powerful introduction to 'Night Life,' a tune that Willie Nelson wrote. She stopped me only six beats into the song and insisted I start again. 'Play it like B.B. King, and turn down that treble, baby,' her speech slurred by the whiskey. I turned down the treble a little and started again only to be stopped in the same place. 'Play it like B.B. King, baby, and turn down that damn treble,' she growled. By now I am very embarrassed, everyone in the room was staring at me. I am feeling very uncomfortable. It was a struggle to keep control of myself. I felt like an emotional outburst right about now would feel soooo good. I started the song once again only to be stopped a third time. She growled, 'Turn down *all* the treble and play it like B.B. King *God damn it!*' Well, this time I turned the treble completely off, and turned the bass all the way up, and played the lick an octave lower. My guitar sounded like a damn tuba being played under water, from the deck of the Titanic. This time she didn't stop me. Thank you, Lord. By now the audience was starting to get into the act, following her example. They started to heckle the band. Things were getting ugly. After yet another of her complaints about the band, some ignorant yahoo, trying to impress his girlfriend with his cool, yelled out, 'Well, that's what you get when you hire amateurs, Big Mama.' After that all hell broke loose. My sax player and old friend Jeff Sheloff, a very serious jazz musician, had had it up to his eyeballs with Big Mama, and this yahoo crowd. He pointed his finger in the moron's face and yelled right back at him. 'You don't know what the hell you're talking about, she's drunk as hell and so are you.' The next night was Saturday night, and we were told that the *Eyewitness News* team [ABC] was going to send down a crew to film the show for airing on the eleven o'clock news that night. The band was aghast at the idea. We grabbed Terry before he got too busy. 'Terry you gotta speak to Big Mama man, please. We ain't gonna be her whipping boys in front of 20 million people!' We were desperate, even panicky. We were ready to walk. Mutiny was in the air. Terry talked to Big Mama Thornton again and begged her, even pleaded with her to leave the band alone and just go up there and sing her tunes. Good job, Terry. She was on her best behavior that night. No problem at all. Not a one. The show went without a hitch. Big Mama belted out her wicked, evil blues right from the pit of her tortured soul. She stood on her feet all night, and made no excuses or complaints. She didn't touch a drop of whiskey as far as I could tell. Big Mama treated the band with respect. She had words of appreciation and encouragement during a good solo. She'd say, 'I hear ya, son' or 'Tell the story boy.' She would scream and holler at a poignant moment. It was like being in blues heaven. I lowered my hat and hid behind my shades trying like hell to avoid the lights and cameras because of my chicken pox, and played my little heart out. The band was well received by the crowd that night, as there were very few blues tourists in attendance, mostly the regular crowd. The band was very happy and very, very proud. It was one of the best nights of our lives."

Thornton still played a lot, including in Canada. She had a week-long show at the Club Isabella in Toronto. The Isabella was a very famous, small smoky little blues bar. There she met Kenny, Raful Jr., Larry and Ronnie Neal, known as the Neal Brothers Band, with whom she would play a lot from now on. The brothers were still very young so their dad had to agree that his sons could play with Thornton. To make sure everything went OK, Thornton even called their dad to confirm that his sons could really play. After hanging up the phone she laughed and told the Neal brothers that her dad said she could whip 'em if they got out of hand. Among the band at the Club Isabella was guitar player James Anthony, who had met Big Mama Thornton backstage as a fan around eight years earlier. Now he had finally the chance to play with her. He recalls: "They used to have matinees from 3 o'clock in the afternoon until about 6. We used to get a call from the agent, and he says, 'Look it, Big Mama or somebody is coming up from the states and they need a band to back them up for a week.' We would put together a four piece band or whatever they needed. And they would come over the border, we would learn their material as fast as we can. Sometimes we didn't even rehearse. We just went up and played. The guys that I played with all knew the old blues stuff so well, they could pretty much trust us. So we played the whole week and they also had a matinee Saturday afternoon."[7]

Even though Thornton is often described as a tough woman, there was always a lot of sweetness and a great sense of feeling in her personality and in her music. James Anthony had one experience with Thornton that proves that. "We were all sitting at the dressing room at the Isabella. We already played the set. She was drinking gin. Mattie was with her. Mattie was sitting in the corner. And one by one all of them got up out of the room and they all kind of left. I was sitting and playing guitar and I looked around and there was nobody there, but me and Big Mama. Big Mama had a great suit on and was drinking her gin and I just started playing some old Robert Johnson kind of style. And she started singing for about twenty minutes. It was amazing! I just sit there playing guitar and she sang with me. She was smiling and playing her harmonica. Just a wonderful thing to remember." Anthony also recalls the comedic part of her show, which she had since her days in the Hot Harlem Revue and that she would use now more and more: "The two [George Smith and her] were almost like a comedy act. They just joked around a lot. It depended on the mood they were in." George "Harmonica" Smith was a tremendous harmonica player. He described his style: "Be very sensitive to your surrounding when you playing. Listen to what the singer is singing. And play the song. Don't just play, play, and play. Play the lyrics, play the words. If it's a sad song, make it sad, is it a happy song, make it happy." It worked out well between the band and her, and so the Neal brothers joined Thornton on tour with Muddy Waters, James Cotton and Brownie McGhee through Canada and would play with her off and on for the next two years.

On her tour through Canada, she met and deeply impressed another Canadian musician, the prolific singer, musician, songwriter and author from Quebec, Plume Latraverse. They were on the same bill on a show in Quebec, as Latraverse fondly recalls: "They told me: 'Don't try to meet her before the show 'cause she's got a special "Hound Dog" temper.' So I did not. Then I was relaxing with the band in our dressing room when she came in. 'So, you're the white cat who sings the blues?' she asked. Her set went on, finished, and then, out of nowhere she got back on stage while we were playing and joined us ... singing in English, myself improvising crazily in French. Magic, simultaneous moment! We really met each other in the middle somewhere."[8]

Thornton also played a week-long show in St. John, on the island of Newfoundland, accompanied by her sister. St. John was not an unusual place for a blues concert and the circumstances were unusual too, as guitar player Sandy Morris recalls: "St. John's has always had a blues scene partially because of the American servicemen stationed here and in nearby

Argentina during and after the Second World War. But it was distinctly not a bastion of blues fans. The wiring in the club was bad—really bad—and there was no heat. None except for a huge device called a Salamander—a kerosene-powered industrial heater meant to be used for heating construction sites. It stank of kerosene fumes and exhaust and was completely illegal to use indoors. It also roared like a jet engine when it was turned on. Generally he would fire it up on the band's breaks and turn it off when we played—but sometimes freezing cold customers forced him to fire it up while we were onstage. I had done a number of gigs there with local musicians before Big Mama showed up. The club never drew very many people because of both the bad heating situation and the fact the blues didn't have a dedicated enough following in St. John's to get people up a flight of stairs to pay the cover charge."[9]

The band consisted of Sandy Morris on guitar, Rocky Wiseman, drums, Rick Hollett, piano, and Nelson Giles, bass. As Morris says, they were "typical white Newfoundlanders with little real experience playing the blues." Only the drummer and Morris himself were keenly aware of who Big Mama was and of her stature in blues and R&B history. The others guys in the band had never heard of her before, as Nelson Giles recalls: "When I arrived I was introduced to a lady … Big Mama Thornton from the U.S. We rehearsed and as the week rolled on she told me of her work with T-Bone Walker, Louis Armstrong, Howlin' Wolf and John Lee Hooker. She was a great blues singer and berated the musicians if they ventured into any jazz phrasings during their solos. She was all blues. For the record, I did not believe she was who she said she was. Weeks later I am returning home from another weekend gig and I turned on my TV to see a special for Aretha Franklin and who is her special guest? … Yes … Big Mama Thornton … I fell off my chair. We played for a week together and I now realize that I had a chance to play with [one of the] blues giants on this planet. I have been truly blessed."

It's an understatement to say that this wasn't the best atmosphere for a show with a tough woman like Big Mama Thornton. And indeed it didn't start well, as Morris recalls: "She was an imposing and impressive woman, Big Mama, and she wasn't happy. By then her health had deteriorated and she moved slowly and painfully. She was bummed out by the venue which, although the building itself was beautiful, was cold and hard with a high ceiling and stone walls making the sound bounce around. As soon as we started to rehearse it became obvious that she was also not very pleased with the band. There were also very few customers and the manager insisted that, since he was a blues fan and was paying for us all to be there, that we play the customary three sets a night. Doing three shows a night with a band she could barely relate to in a cold empty hall in a place where she knew nobody and didn't seem to have a single fan didn't help Willie Mae's mood much at all. Overall I found the whole experience exhilarating but frustrating. I really wanted people to come out and see her—she was such a legend and she sang so well. Of course, there were probably no more than ten or fifteen people in the place counting the band and the bar staff. I hope she got her money. The situation was impossibly bad but when Big Mama Thornton started to sing everything changed. She sang like a bird. I had never really heard an authentic blues singer live and I was completely blown away. Despite the fact that she would often stop songs in the middle to berate the band for not being at the proper tempo or groove when she opened her mouth to sing it was pure heaven. She could shout and testify. She improvised constantly, never singing a song the same way twice but always lifting whatever she sang to heights of soul and feeling. I couldn't believe what I was hearing." Thornton loved to shift sometimes into a spiritual, running roughshod over the sacred-secular divide, as Morris recalls: "My favorite memory—though vague—was one night late in the week when she told the Christmas story over a slow blues by the band. We just sat there and quietly jammed through while she spoke—and occasionally sang—the whole story of Jesus and Joseph and the Christ child and the whole works, but in her own language and vernacular and it lasted for twenty minutes or half an hour. Some of the band were baffled and thought it was self-indulgent but I was moved practically to tears. It's something I will never forget." His bandmate, Nelson Giles, adds that Thornton's personality impressed him very much: "The thing that I took away from the gig about her was that even though she lived a very hard life, she had the most beautiful smile that seemed to indicate she wasn't bitter about the path her life took. She was frail, but her great white teeth made you melt for the great human being that she was. She was still an optimist and her voice was still strong even though she loved her gin."[10]

Although a heavy drinker herself, Thornton was always aware of the dangers connected with alcohol abuse, as Giles recalls: "One night when we were on stage, I remember one time I asked her for a swig from her juice jar (thinking it was water), and she said, 'Sonny, I don't think you can't handle what's in that jar. You are not old enough to drink from that bottle.' She was right. It was pure gin! My Newfoundland tonsils would not have received that gin positively."

In addition to those shows, Thornton played mostly around her home area in California. She played a few times at the Belly Up Tavern at Solana Beach in San Diego. She had changing backing bands, as always, since the club always had musicians available from the different bands around town. Mark Lessman recalls one of these shows, when he was part of her band: "I played with Big Mama when I was very young. I co-led a band with another sax player named Johnny Almond and we were asked to back a lot of artists who came to the Belly Up Tavern. Also on the stage when I played with her was Lee Allen, tenor player from James Brown's band, and trumpeter Luis Gasca. She was pretty frail, or so it seemed. She wouldn't start the first song until a guy who was sitting on the floor partially under the front table moved to a proper seat and was very feisty about it. She was also somewhat of a practical joker. At one point she looked at me and said 'solo.' When I stepped up to the mike and started to blow she said in a drawn out and loud voice 'not now.' When she saw my face turn red she got a big smile and let me know she was just kidding."[11]

Dave Camp recalls another night with Thornton at the Belly Up Tavern and how he was instructed before the show to follow her comedic act: "She brought her bass player with her. I was part of the house band at the Belly Up Tavern. They just picked me out to play keyboards for her. She wanted a keyboard player, so they hired me as sideman. All she wanted was a piano, she just wanted those honky tonk pianos. During the second set when she did 'Rock Me Baby,' the bass player came over to me and he whispered, 'No matter what she says, you keep playing!' And so one by one she started picking on the musicians in the band, the saxophone player, the guitar player, the drummer until they stopped playing. I was like, what in the world is going on, 'cause I didn't know what she was doing. So she ended up doing the song with just me and the bass player. And it was kind of funny, 'cause I was the only one included by the bass player. But I guess that was one of her little showbiz tricks that she got on the road. I don't know if she did it in all of her shows, but she did it in my show. She was excellent. That was one of my favorite nights of playing. She was a wonderful act."[12]

On September 10, 1980, Thornton performed at the Los Angeles Bicentennial Blues with B.B. King and Muddy Waters, and in December 1980 she sang on *Omnibus*, an ABC-TV special hosted by actor Hal Holbrook. Jeannie and Jimmy Cheatham were asked by Mattie Fields to back up Thornton for the TV special. They had not seen Big Mama Thornton since her meeting in Buffalo, and what they saw now was Thornton thin as a rail, even thinner than she had been in Buffalo. But Thornton had obviously not lost her strong will and still didn't like other female singers in her show. She didn't want to share the stage with Aretha Franklin so she stomped up and down the dressing room. In fact, Thornton was just jealous of Franklin—and insecure. But she was professional enough to do the show anyway. She broke hearts with her rendition of "Ball and Chain." Franklin came on to sing "Trouble in Mind," and together they then sang "Nobody Knows You When You Down and Out."

Big Mama Thornton in a photograph taken while visiting her family in the eighties (Big Mama Thornton Family Estate).

In 1981, Thornton played on the East Coast on June 29 at the Lone Star Café in New York City, with Koko Taylor on the bill. Photographer Joe Rosen saw her: "She was cranky and cantankerous. She was also prone to chewing out band members for no apparent reason. But every so often she would throw her head back and wail and it all seemed to go away. She sang all the barnyard sounds, chickens, dogs, like sound effects during 'Little

Red Rooster.'"[13] One month later, on July 29, Thornton was again part of the "The Blues is a Woman" program at the Newport Jazz Festival with Linda Hopkins, Vi Redd, Sammy Price and others. She still performed also off and on in Canada with the Neal brothers and others, but when Thornton played in Montreal and at her Canadian friend Doudou Boicel's Rising Sun Club, she mostly had the same backing band, with bassist Stephen Barry, guitarist Andy Cowan, pianist Big Moose Walker, drummer Paul Paquette or Paul Jankowski and guitarist John Reisner plus Gordon Adamson. One time, after Stevie Ray Vaughan had quit David Bowie's band, Vaughan played Montreal at the Spectrum and that club was almost next door to the Rising Sun. He must have had 1,000 people to see him play, and next door Big Mama Thornton had about 30. When Vaughan heard Thornton was playing at a club next door, he asked her if he could sit in and so it happened that they got to play together.

When Thornton was in her hometown of Los Angeles, she played at clubs like the El Rey, at the newly opened Solari Theatre in Beverly Hills, or she performed with the band The Gun Club at the Los Angeles club Lingerie, as she did on October 3, 1981. When she performed in the San Francisco Bay-area, she was now often backed by a black band called The Eddie Ray Rhythm and Blues Band. She played with them on New Year's Eve 1981 at the club The Continental in Oakland: "I was with the Eddie Ray Rhythm and Blues Band. We backed a lot of artists from out of town and in the area. Eddie Ray himself was a very talented and charismatic guitar player singer/songwriter from Bastrop, Louisiana. He used to play with Ernie K-Doe and Little Milton. The Continental was a very famous club in West Oakland on Twelfth and Campbell. The night with Big Mama was very special ... she wore a gown! I remember it was turquoise and white, very regal— like the Queen of the Blues that she was. Percy Mayfield was on the bill too," recalls Carlos Zialcita. But after a while, according to Big Walker Derrick, who played saxophone in the band, it stopped going well: "We usually backed Big Mama when she played in the black areas. Eddy was a long, good-looking, smooth singer-guitar player. When we played in black clubs the girls would have competitions just to see who could scream the loudest, cry, or faint and make the biggest scene. Then a crew of the winner's friends would carry her out of the venue. Eddy Ray's band was Big Mama's band then. She still was taking her medicine."[14] But, as Derrick says, "the money got funny and the band often sounded bad, and I don't mean good. So I quit just in time to miss the worst reviews Mama maybe received in her life."

When she didn't have any shows to play, Big Mama Thornton kept to herself at home and loved to watch reruns of seventies TV series, or to hang around with friends, play cards or have a drink with her buddies.

In 1983, she was a special guest at a B.B. King concert in Montreal's Theatre Maisonneuve. Thornton was playing across the street at the Rising Sun nightclub. After the show, King and his band came across to the Rising Sun, where they jammed until four in the morning with Thornton and James Cotton. And in March 1983, Thornton was a part of the award-winning PBS television special *Three Generations of the Blues*, with Wallace and Jeannie Cheatham. The first hour featured ninety-two-year-old vocalist Sippie Wallace with her accompanist. The second hour showcased Thornton with Jack Pollack on piano, Patty Padden on drums, Guy Gonzales on guitar; Thornton brought her own bass player. The third hour was Jeannie Cheatham's part playing with her husband and her band.

The show had a finale planned with everyone together on stage, but Wallace and Thornton didn't know that, and for good reason. Wallace and Thornton had, according to Cheatham, disliked each other on sight. Everybody around wasn't sure if the finale would work out without trouble. After the third set, Cheatham called out: "Now, ladies and gentlemen, we gonna have a really great treat! We gonna have a good old-fashioned finale! Ladies, come on up on this stage and show all these good people how to perform a finale!" And the ninety-two-year-old vocalist Wallace, and the almost thirty-five years younger Thornton, started trading verse after verse of made-up-on-the-spot lyrics—insulting each other and each other's man and their mamas.

On April 30, 1983, Muddy Waters, Thornton's long-time friend, died, and another important chapter in the history of blues was closed. On August 18, Thornton performed at the Lone Star Café in New York City, and on October 7, 1983, she played at Gerte's Folk City in New York City, where she again met Diamond Teeth Mary, who had helped her to join the Hot Harlem Revue over forty years before. Meeting the woman that had once helped her to start her way in the music business appeared to be a sign that the circle of her life in music was closing.

In her last years Thornton had to sometimes play with backing bands, which she didn't like. She was often not paid well and the circumstances weren't always good, as Lloyd Jones, who met her in the winter 1983 recalls: "When I went to see her for the last time it was in a club in Portland called Key Largo. I went to visit her back stage and she was drinking brandy and cream. She said it was doctor's orders. There was no heat in the back room where she was waiting to start the show (it was winter). She was freezing and said the club wouldn't spring for a hotel so they would have to start driving back to California after the show. I thought that was the ultimate disrespect."[15] Thornton's health would cause her more and more problems, but she didn't stop doing what she loved to do. In March 1984, Thornton was part of an R&B concert at the Variety Arts Theatre in downtown Los Angeles. The veteran DJ Huggy Boy was hosting the show, and the lineup featured, many top stars from the '40s and '50s, including Big Jay McNeely, Lowell Fulson, Joe Liggins and His Honeydrippers and Lloyd Glenn. The show was filmed by Channel 4 (UK). Thornton still played the California club scene, for instance at the Belly Up Tavern at Solana Beach in San Diego where she frequently played in her last years. The singer Jimmy Whitherspoon saw her there and recalled that even if she could hardly walk on stage, "her voice was still so powerful it made me weak to listen."[16] In July 1984, Thornton went on a little tour in Canada and played a gig at the Commodore Ballroom in Vancouver. It would be her last tour. She was accompanied by a backing band she used off and on, led by the left-handed guitarist Carl "Good Rockin'" Robinson. They were joined by harmonica player David Hoerl, who recalls, "In July 1984 I get a call from Carl Robinson that the Big Mama Revue Band was to play at the Commodore Ballroom in Vancouver and he asked if I could come down and sit in, since I was an honorary member. So I did come down and sit in and finally got to meet and play with Big Mama. She took a sip of her whisky and milk backstage and said she liked my playing."[17] After the gig, she did something that was very unusual for her. Normally she drove her way back home alone in her car. But this time she drove back together with the band and stayed in San Francisco, where she performed at the I Beam before she went back home to Los Angeles.

The newspapers, for the most part, wrote that she was found dead, alone in a boarding house, but her friends say that this is not the truth. It seems more realistic that she had gathered together her old buddies one last time on July 25, 1984. Around six in the evening, rumor has it, she phoned her sister Mattie. She sang for her, her favorite song "That Lucky

Old Sun." Then she went to the sofa, drank some gin and milk, fell to sleep and never got up. In a slightly different version, Thornton died suddenly while playing cards with friends and sipping gin and milk.

Thornton was now part of the great orchestra of legendary blues artists playing in heaven. "Big Mama lived well. She lived as she wanted to live. She wasn't a millionaire and I don't think she was trying to be one. But I do think that she was very successful in doing what she wanted to do, the way she wanted to do it," said Nat Dove.[18] Or, as Thornton, explained in her own words: "What would I want with diamonds and things like that? You can't take 'em with you when you go. You can't eat 'em."[19] A few years before she died, she said: "What did they do with the millions, the billions, whatever they made? They ain't here to even tell about it. That's why I hold this hand up to God that I'm here."[20]

Two hundred of her friends came to her funeral. Three years earlier, Thornton had asked Johnny Otis, who was also a preacher now, to preside over her funeral if she died before him. Otis followed the last wish of his long-time friend and conducted her funeral services at the Conner Johnson Mortuary on Avalon Boulevard in central Los Angeles. The pallbearers were Big Terry DeRouen, Jeremiah Wright, Eldridge Hall and O.B. Wright. Blues singer Jimmy Witherspoon and Margie Evans sang at the funeral. Tina Mayfield, the wife of composer Percy Mayfield, read a short obituary.

Johnny Otis told the guests: "She told me to make it short and make 'em smile. So smile and rejoice." He added: "Mama always told me that the blues were more important than having money. She told me: Artists are artists and businessmen are businessmen. But the trouble is the artist's money stays in the businessmen's hands." Mourners nodded their heads in agreement. "Tell 'em, Otis," several called out. "That's the truth."[21] Christine Hooks, who lived in the same house as Thornton, said that the singer was like her sister and that she was "filled with love."[22] Otis added at the end of the ceremony: "Don't waste your sorrow on Big Mama. She's free. Don't feel sorry for Big Mama. There's no more pain. No more suffering in a society where the color of skin was more important than the quality of your talent. Thank God, she's free in the arms of the Savior."[23] In addition to the money that was gathered at the funeral, friends held a benefit concert on August 12 at the Music Machine in West Los Angeles to celebrate her for one last time. Big Mama Thornton was laid to rest in the famous Inglewood Park Cemetery in a grave marked by a simple headstone engraved with her name and the names of two other people who share her burial place.

The little girl from Ariton, Alabama, had made her dream come true and became the famous Big Mama Thornton. She had lived her life to the fullest and managed to make a living with her music for over forty years. To be successful in the music business was, and maybe still is, especially for a black woman, not the easiest task. Big Mama Thornton made it her own way without many compromises, keeping her self-respect and humor. Above all, she was as real as it gets, and if you cannot feel the blues when you hear her sing then you've got a hole in your soul. Or, as Big Mama Thornton would have said, "You ain't nothing but a Hound Dog."

Epilogue

Big Mama Thornton's Legacy

In the year of her death, 1984, Big Mama Thornton was inducted into the Blues Hall of Fame. The Blues Hall of Fame is a historical record of those who have made the blues timeless through performance, documentation, and recording. Since its inception in 1980, The Blues Foundation has inducted new members annually into the Blues Hall of Fame for their historical contribution, impact and overall influence on the blues. Without doubt, this is the right place for a person like Big Mama Thornton, as she had been nominated six times as Best Contemporary Blues Female Artist, Best Female Artist and Best Traditional Blues Female Artist by the National Blues Music Awards, known as Handys, after blues composer W.C. Handy, presented under the banner of The Blues Foundation.

Big Mama Thornton's songs "Ball and Chain" and "Hound Dog" are included in the Rock 'n' roll Hall of Fame's list of the "500 Songs that Shaped Rock 'n' roll."

Thornton never made big money with her music during her lifetime, and this continued with her heir, her half-sister Mattie Fields. For years after Thornton's death, Fields didn't receive anything more than a $100 check per year from the royalties of Thornton's records. In the late nineties, Fields could, with the help of a lawyer, finally receive more royalties. With her first royalties, she bought a wheelchair to get around better, since her health wasn't very good anymore. Fields stayed in touch with Jeannie Cheatham for a long time, but she didn't have too much time to benefit from the royalties. Fields is described by everybody who knew her as a generous, loving, caring person, and one can say without a doubt that the care and help Fields gave her was the reason Thornton stayed alive as long as she did. Fields died after a long illness at the age of 76 on September 13, 2008. She is survived by two daughters, three sons and one sister.

The Big Mama Thornton legacy is still honored in many ways. In 2004, the Willie Mae Rock Camp for Girls was founded by a group of female New York City musicians as a grassroots effort. This nonprofit organization has offered girls from ages eight to eighteen musical mentoring. During two one-week day-camp sessions each summer, girls learn to play musical instruments, write lyrics and music for songs, and perform a concert at a local rock club. The inaugural camp session took place in 2005 at the New York Society for Ethical Culture in Manhattan with sixty-six girls attending. In 2006 2006 camp season took place at Brooklyn Friends School. The program expanded to include two sessions, and a total of 160 girls attended. Since 2007, the Rock Camp has been hosted by the Urban Assembly School for Music and Art in Downtown Brooklyn. The camp is named after Willie Mae "Big Mama" Thornton in honor of her musical legacy.

In 2007 a coming-of-age drama film written, directed, and produced by Deborah Kampmeier and starring Dakota Fanning, Isabelle Fuhrman, Robin Wright Penn, and Piper Laurie, among others, with the title *Hounddog* was released. The movie takes place in the late 1950s American South, and the film story is about a troubled twelve-year-old girl who finds solace from an abusive life through music. Not only is the movie named after Thornton's biggest hit, but she is also part of the movie script: the role of Big Mama Thornton is played by Jill Scott.

Also the Canadian jazz icon Jackie Richardson plays the larger-than-life performer in the musical *Big Mama! The Willie Mae Thornton Story*, written by Audrei-Kairen. Richardson, dressed in a man's hat and checked shirt, performs in a ninety-minute show that's more a revue than a musical, and more storytelling than theatre.

Appendix A: Timeline

1926

December 11, 1926: Willie Mae "Big Mama" Thornton is born in Ariton, a small town near Montgomery, Alabama.

Her mother died early, and Thornton left school and got a job washing and cleaning spittoons in the local tavern.

1940

Willie Mae Thornton left home and joined Sammy Green's Hot Harlem Revue and was soon billed as the "New Bessie Smith."

1948

After a show in Houston, Willie Mae Thornton left the Hot Harlem Revue and stayed in Texas.

1950

She makes her first record "All Right Baby" and "Bad Luck Got My Man" for the E&W label in Houston. On the records she appears as the "The Harlem Stars."

Bandleader Joe "Papoose" Fritz hires her as a singer at the Eldorado Ballroom in Houston.

Don Robey, owner of Peacock Records, heard Willie Mae at the Eldorado Ballroom and signed her to an exclusive five-year contract and had her play in his Bronze Peacock Club in Houston. Thornton now toured the so-called Chitlin' Circuit, and she and Marie Adams became the female heavyweights at Peacock Records.

1951

In January she recorded for Peacock Records the single "I'm All Fed Up/Partnership Blues." The third song of this first session, "Mischievous Boogie," appeared in the summer of 1952.

The next recording session for Peacock Records took place in December 1951 with the Bill Harvey Band accompanying. The songs "No Jody For Me" and "Let Your Tears Fall Baby" appeared as a further Peacock single.

Willie Mae became now part of a two-week show at the Bronze Peacock Club. With her were Billy Wright with Marie Adams and Jimmy McCracklin and the Blues Blasters were the headliners.

Then she recorded the "Cotton Picking Blues" and "Everytime I Think of You" with the Bill Harvey Orchestra.

1952

Willie Mae Thornton meets Johnny Otis with his Rhythm and Blues Caravan and goes on tour with him. Soon she is the show-stopper of the Johnny Otis Revue.

On August 13, 1952, Johnny Otis and his orchestra recorded several songs with Willie Mae at Radio Recorder Studio on Santa Monica Boulevard in Los Angeles. Pete Lewis was on guitar, James Von Streeter and Fred Ford played horns, and Devonia Williams played keys. One of the songs recorded that day was "Hound Dog," which became Big Mama's biggest hit.

In October, Willie Mae toured with Johnny Otis on the West Coast and they prepared a Texas tour over the holidays.

From November 28 until December 5, 1952, the Johnny Otis Orchestra with Little Esther, Mel Walker and Willie Mae Thornton played at the Apollo Theatre in New York's Harlem. Here they minted the nickname "Big Mama" for her after the audience applauded so much that they had to pull the curtain down to move on with the show.

Thornton opened a show at the Bronze Peacock Club in Houston and was also celebrated in her newly adopted home town.

1953

The single "Hound Dog/ Nightmare" is released. "Hound Dog" takes off immediately and begins to look like a national hit.

With the chart success of "Hound Dog," Thornton was added to the Peacock Blues Consolidated Tour Package Show, which featured Johnny Ace, Junior Parker and Bobby "Blue" Bland.

In April, "Hound Dog" was the nation's top-selling blues record and ranked first in sales in New York, Chicago, New Orleans, San Francisco, Newark, Memphis, Dallas, Cincinnati, Los Angeles and St. Louis. By midsummer, it is obvious that "Hound Dog" will be the biggest seller in the history of Peacock Records.

In August, Thornton appears with Johnny Ace and his band at the Shrine Auditorium in Los Angeles at the Fourth Annual Rhythm and Blues Jubilee.

In late September, Thornton's second signature tune, "They Call Me Big Mama" is released.

In late October, Thornton and Johnny Ace appeared at New York's Apollo Theater in their first eastern show. They then played at the Howard Theater in Washington and at the Royal Theater in Baltimore.

On Thanksgiving night in Houston, B.B. King joined the Ace-Thornton-Parker show.

At the end of the year, Peacock released Thornton's next single "The Big Change" and "I Ain't No Fool Either" (#1626).

On December 5, 1953, the new record from Johnny Ace called "Yes Baby" was released with Thornton singing duet with him.

1954

Big Mama Thornton tours the Southeast with Johnny Ace and the orchestra of drummer C.C. Pinkston. They played one-nighters in the Alabama-Georgia area throughout January and February.

In March, Thornton and Ace did a week at Pep's in Philadelphia backed by the Johnny Board band.

Then they played a series of one-nighters in Michigan and Ohio followed by a week at the Apollo Theatre in New York beginning April 23.

The same month Thornton's new singles "I Smell A Rat" and "I've Searched The World Over" is released.

In July, Thornton and Johnny Ace were touring through Texas, Louisiana, and New Mexico.

In August, Peacock Records released Thornton's next singles "Stop Hopping On Me" and "Story Of My Blues."

In October, Peacock released Big Mama's singles "Rock a Bye Baby" and "Walking Blues."

Added to the Ace-Thornton package for a West Coast swing were now Memphis Slim and Faye Adams.

Johnny Ace and Thornton played December 25 at the City Auditorium in Houston for a Negro Christmas dance. After the show Johnny Ace shoots himself in the head and dies.

1955

Thornton's whole career unraveled after the death of Johnny Ace.

In March, "Laugh Laugh Laugh" and "The Fish" come out as Peacock Record singles, and later in the year Willie Mae recorded "How Come" and "Tarzan and The Dignified Monkey" with Elroy Peace on vocal for Peacock.

Thornton now played the clubs on her own and toured often with Junior Parker and Bobby "Blue" Bland.

1956

In early 1956 she performed sometimes at the Club Matinee in Houston in the show hosted by DJ King Bee.

In 1956, as Elvis Presley recorded "Hound Dog" to international acclaim, Peacock rereleased Thornton's original version.

Thornton left Houston, set off with Gatemouth Brown on a tour of the West Coast and settled in the San Francisco Bay Area where she mostly played local blues clubs.

Appendix A

1957–1963

After she had left Houston, "Just Like A Dog" and "My Man Called Me" (Peacock # 1681) were released as her last productions for Robey's label.

On February 9, 1957, Thornton joined up again with Johnny Otis and his band. She was part of a two-day show in San Francisco and Oakland where Otis presented his rock 'n' roll concert, featuring forty top recording artists including Julie Stevens, The Youngsters, Mel Williams, Don and Dewey, Little Arthur Mathews, The Premiers, Arthur Jee Mays, Marie Adams and The Three Tons of Joy, Little Julian Herrera, Jackie Kelso and Abe Moore.

"Hound Dog" had a spurt of airplay during the summer of 1958 which led to another rerelease of the original by Peacock Records.

Thornton played at many California clubs such as the Rhumboogie in Oakland, the Gateway, the Beachcomber Club in Santa Cruz, and Basin Street West in San Francisco.

Meanwhile, Thornton met Carroll Peery in Los Angeles; Peery would later help her a bit to find her way back into the business.

In 1961, Thornton accompanied by Jimmie Mamou and Billy Dunn played some gigs in Russell City, an unincorporated area of Hayward, California.

Thornton recorded her first 45 since leaving Peacock Records for the Baytone Label in Oakland owned by Bradley Taylor. It included "You Did Me Wrong" and "Big Mama's Blues."

1964

In 1964, Thornton performed often at the Savoy Hotel in Richmond and meets her new manager Jimmy Moore.

Thornton plays with great success at the Monterey Jazz Festival.

She had moved to Los Angeles, where she lived with her relatives. She played at the Jazz Workshop in Boston with Muddy Waters, a double show with Miles Davis, and another one with Louie Jordan.

1965

On February 27, 1965, Thornton was one of the performers at the blues festival in the Berkeley Community Centre.

In September 1965, Thornton joins the American Folk Blues Festival for a tour through Europe. The first live show took place on October 1 in Bern, Switzerland followed by appearances in Switzerland (Lausanne, Zürich, Luzern, Basel, Genf), Germany (Mannheim, Bremen, Hamburg, Berlin, Düsseldorf, Iserlohn, Munich, Frankfurt), Denmark (Copenhagen), Sweden (Stockholm), England (London, Manchester, Newcastle, Glasgow, Birmingham, Bristol), Belgium (Brussels), Netherlands (Amsterdam, The Hague), Ireland (Belfast, Dublin), France (Strasbourg, Paris) and Spain (Barcelona). In addition to Big Mama Thornton, the lineup for the American Folk Blues Festival in 1965 consisted of J. B. Lenoir, Buddy Guy, Eddie Boyd, Lonesome Jimmy, Lee Robinson, Fred Below, John Lee

Hooker, Roosevelt Sykes, Big Walter, Shaky Horton, Fred McDowell and Dr. Ross. She was the highlight of the show.

On October 20, 1965, Thornton recorded "Big Mama in Europe" in London. The backing band for Thornton included Buddy Guy (guitar), Eddie Boyd (piano or organ), Walter "Shakey" Horton (harmonica), Fred Below (drums) and Jimmy Lee Robinson (bass).

Back home in Los Angeles from her European tour, Big Mama Thornton recorded "Summertime" and "Truth Comes To The Light," "Tomcat" and "Yes I Cried/ Mercy" for Sotoplay Records, her first singles since 1961.

1966

Thornton recorded for Kent Records, with the Johnny Talbot Band, "Before Day" and "Me And My Chauffeur." Besides singing and playing the harmonica, Thornton also played drums.

On April 25, 1966, Thornton made her next recordings. For Galaxy, she recorded "Because It's Love" and "Life Goes On."

For Arhoolie Records, Thornton recorded her second LP. *Big Mama Thornton Vol. 2: The Queen At Monterey with the Chicago Blues Band* was recorded at the Coast Recorders in San Francisco. The Muddy Waters outfit consisted of Muddy Waters (guitar), Sammy Lawhorn (guitar), James Cotton (harmonica), Otis Spann (piano), Luther Johnson (bass guitar), and Francis Clay (drums).

Besides recording, Thornton continued to play the Bay Area club scene the whole year of 1966. On May 22, Thornton performed at the Both/And Club on Divisadero Street in San Francisco. Here, she met Janis Joplin and members of Big Brother & the Holding Company. After Thornton's set at the Both/And Club they asked her if they could do "Ball and Chain."

Thornton played a benefit for the Both/And at the Fillmore Auditorium in San Francisco with Garry Goodrow, Jon Hendricks, Elvin Jones, The Joe Henderson Quartet, Denny Zeitlin Trio, Jefferson Airplane, Great Society, Wildflower and Bill Ham.

On September 17, 1966, Thornton appeared again at the Monterey Jazz Festival on Saturday afternoon in a program titled "Nothing But the Blues," an appendage by Jon Hendricks to his play *Evolution of the Blues*.

Big Mama would from now on also appear regularly at the legendary blues showcase, the Ash Grove Club, in Los Angeles.

On October 8, 1966, Thornton played at the Pacific Jazz Festival in Costa Mesa, CA, along with Jon Hendricks, Jimmy Rushing, Shakey Horton, Memphis Slim, Jefferson Airplane, Muddy Waters and the Paul Butterfield Blues Band on the same bill.

From October 14–16, 1966, Big Mama and her band were on the same bill with the Paul Butterfield Blues Band and Jefferson Airplane for a run of six shows at the Fillmore Auditorium.

On November 1, 1966, Thornton and her band were also part of a giant fundraiser for California gubernatorial candidate Pat Brown at the Winterland Auditorium in San Francisco.

From November 10 until November 20 of that year, Thornton played again the Both/And Club in San Francisco.

From December 9–11, 1966, Thornton played to a sold-out Fillmore Auditorium on the same bill as the Grateful Dead and Tim Rose.

The year 1966 ended for Thornton with a weekend at the Ash Grove from December 16 to 18, 1966.

1967

Thornton began the year on the same bill as the Grateful Dead on January 6, 1967, in the Freeborn Hall, UC-Davis, and continued with two concerts on January 7 at the Jazz '67 on the Berkeley Campus.

On January 15, 1967, Thornton performed at the Spirituals to Swing Show in Carnegie Hall, New York, with the Count Basie Orchestra.

In February 1967, boxer Archie Moore took over management for Big Mama Thornton.

In April, Thornton performed at the Bear's Lair of the Student Union in Berkeley, and on April 8 she played the Jazz Festival 1967 at the Berkeley Hearst Greek Theatre on the UC Campus.

On April 22, Thornton played the UCLA "Chamber Jazz."

On April 28 and 29, Thornton played the California Hall in San Francisco with Big Brother & the Holding Company, with The Weeds and a light show by Aurora Glory Alice on the same bill.

On May 9, Thornton began a week's engagement at the Jazz Workshop backed by a group that included saxophonist Jules Broussard, pianist Nat Dove, guitarist Jay Hodge, drummer Linton Jacquet and George Smith, harmonica.

On May 12, Thornton was, along with Quicksilver Messenger Service, the Bobby Hutcherson–Harold Land Quintet, the Majesties from East Palo Alto and special guest performer Mike Bloomfield, part of the "Pops Festival" organized by students at the College of San Mateo, California.

On September 19 to 24, 1967, Thornton had daily shows at the Golden Bear Club, Huntington Beach, California, along with Big Brother & the Holding Company.

Big Mama Thornton played now often together with Muddy Waters around Chicago, Detroit, and Cleveland and Muddy Waters' manager at that time, Bob Messinger, would help her with the management.

The year ended for Thornton with an appearance at the New York's Apollo with Odetta, T-Bone Walker, Jimmy Witherspoon, Big Joe Turner and the Chambers Brothers on the bill.

1968

The year 1968 started with shows at the Ash Grove in Los Angeles with Edward Bee Houston on guitar, Curtis Tillman on bass, Everett Minor on tenor sax, Nathaniel Dove on piano, and Gus Wright on the drums.

On August 3, 1968, Big Mama played at the Shrine Exposition Hall, Los Angeles, along with the Jeff Beck Group, Blue Cheer, and the Steve Miller Band.

On August 30, 1968, she appeared at the Palace of Fine Arts, San Francisco, with Big Brother & the Holding Company, John Stewart and Buffy Ford. On this show Janis Joplin announced that she would leave Big Brother at the end of 1968.

On September 2, 1968, Thornton played with James Cotton at the first Sky River Rock Festival. On the last day, the Grateful Dead arrived unscheduled. Thornton played with James Cotton on mouth harp, Ron "Pigpen" McKernan from the Grateful Dead on organ, and a drummer and guitarist from the Dead.

In 1968, Big Brother & the Holding Company recorded the Thornton song "Ball and Chain" on their album *Cheap Thrills*. The album entered the charts on August 31, 1968, stayed in the number one spot for eight weeks and went gold in three days. This success would bring Thornton even more recognition.

On September 13–15, 1968, Thornton played the Avalon Ballroom featuring George "Harmonica" Smith on Harmonica with the British blues legend John Mayall on the same bill, followed by her third appearance at the Monterey Jazz Festival in the same month.

In October she played two shows in Torrance, California. A show on October 18, 1968, with the Grateful Dead on the same bill was followed by a show on October 19, 1968, with the Cleveland Wrecking Company.

November 6–10, 1968 saw her at the Whisky a Go Go with Taj Mahal.

Following the success of Janis Joplin with Thornton's song "Ball and Chain," Arhoolie Records now released a new album with the same title. The *Ball and Chain* LP by Arhoolie Records contains three songs from a 1968 session recorded on January 25, 1968, in Hollywood, California with Edward Bee Houston on guitar, Curtis Tillman on bass, Everett Minor on tenor sax, Nathaniel Dove on piano, and Gus Wright on the drums, along with titles by *Lightnin' Hopkins* and *Larry Williams*.

From November 22 to 24 1968, Thornton played at Mandrake's on 1048 University Avenue in Berkeley.

1969

Big Mama Thornton started the year with an eleven-day-long appearance at The Hungry I in Ghirardelli Square in San Francisco.

From February 12–14, Thornton played at the Keystone Korner Club in North Beach, San Francisco, and on February 14–16, with It's a Beautiful Day and Country Weather, at the Avalon Ballroom in San Francisco.

On March 21, 1969, Thornton performed at the Vulcan Gas Company in Austin.

From April 15 to 20, she played at the Boston Tea Party with Ten Years After and Albert King. From April 28 to May 4, Thornton performed at the Ungano's Club in New York City.

On May 21, Thornton was part of the First Generation Blues Festival organized by

Will Ashwood Kavana at the Electric Circus on St. Marks Place in Greenwich Village, New York.

On June 29, she played the Denver Pop Festival, and on July 4, 1969, the Saugatuck Pop Festival in Michigan.

On July 18, 1969, Thornton played at the Newport Folk Festival.

On August 3, 1969 Thornton was one of the headliners for the last day of the Ann Arbor Blues Festival.

On August 30, Thornton performed at the Sky River Rock Festival II and a Labor Day Weekend festival in Grant Park hosted by Willie Dixon.

In September, she appeared with Muddy Waters at The Plugged Nickel in Chicago.

In October 1969, Thornton played a few times with Sunnyland Slim, vocals, piano; Shakey Jake, harmonica; and herself on drums at the Ash Grove.

From October 16 to 18, Thornton and Smith played at Thee Experience in Los Angeles, California.

In the fall of 1969, Thornton performed at the Jazz Workshop in Boston.

At the end of 1969, Thornton released her new record *Stronger than Dirt* from Mercury Records. The LP brought Thornton back onto the *Billboard* charts.

1970

From January 5 to January 11, 1970, Big Mama Thornton played at The Jazz Workshop in San Francisco.

Her second album on the Mercury label, *The Way It Is*, which contained the performance at the club Thee Experience in Los Angeles (October 1968), is released.

Thornton continued to play in the clubs around the Bay Area. Thornton now toured mostly with George "Harmonica" Smith. He would always open the show with a few songs and then played together with Thornton.

From March 27 to April 1, backed up by The Eastside Blues Band, they played at The Twelfth Gate Coffeehouse in Atlanta.

On April 3, Thornton performed at the Blues Festival at U.C. Berkeley.

On May 2, 1970, Thornton was part of the lineup for B.B. King's first all-blues show in New York's famed Carnegie Hall.

From May 15–16, 1970, Thornton played at the Great Highway in San Francisco with Sandy Bull, Mendelbaum, and Doug McKechnie.

The show at the Great Highway was followed again by a concert at the Jazz Workshop in San Francisco. She was then backed by some new instrumentalists, led by bassist Dale A. Renee, including guitarist Lloyd Howe, tenor Sleepy Carothers, and drummer Ken Kenny.

In August 1970, Big Mama appeared again at the Ann Arbor Blues Festival.

In October 1970, Thornton performed at the Berkeley Folk Festival Open-Air Jubilee Concert.

On December 9–16, 1970, she appeared with B.B. King, Junior Parker and Bobby "Blue" Bland at the New York Apollo.

At the end of 1970 and the beginning of 1971, Thornton acquired new management from Link Wyler.

1971

Big Mama Thornton had an appearance on the *Dick Cavett Show* that aired on July 22, 1971.

Thornton performed on July 22, 1971, at the Jazz in the Garden series at the Museum of Modern Art, New York City.

Thornton signed a contract with Pentagram Records and recorded a gospel record called *Saved*.

On August 1, Thornton appeared at the Paramount Theatre in Portland, Oregon, on August 1, together with the Paul Butterfield Blues Band.

Thornton then went on a tour of the Pacific Northwest. Muddy Waters, Big Joe Turner, George "Harmonica" Smith, Bee Houston and J.B. Hutto were part of this tour.

In August 1971, Thornton was part of the Super Heavy Blues Express with Big Joe Turner, T-Bone Walker, Eddie "Cleanhead" Vinson and others.

The rest of the year, Big Mama played mainly at the Ash Grove.

1972

From March 2 to March 27, Big Mama Thornton toured again with the American Folk Blues Festival through Europe.

March 2: Frankfurt, Germany with rehearsals and concert.

March 3: Paris, France.

March 4: Cologne, Germany.

March 5: Hanover, Germany.

March 6: Berlin, Germany.

March 7: Stuttgart, Germany.

March 8: Frankfurt, Germany.

March 9: Geneva, Switzerland.

March 10: Basel, Switzerland.

March 11: Munich, Germany with a day off.

March 12: Munich, Germany.

March 13: Vienna, Austria.

March 14: Hamburg, Germany.

March 15: Bremen, Germany.

March 16: Lünen, Germany.

March 17: Bergamo, Italy.

March 18: Rotterdam, Holland.

March 19: Copenhagen, Denmark.

March 20: Malmö, Sweden.

March 21: Gothenburg, Sweden.

March 22: Oslo, Norway.

March 23: Uppsala, Sweden.

March 24: Helsinki, Finland with a day off.

March 25: Helsinki, Finland.

March 26: Helsinki, Finland with a day off.

March 27: Stockholm, Sweden.

Back in the U.S., she played in and around San Francisco with the Luther Tucker Band in small clubs.

On April 29, in the Pepperland, San Rafael, California, and on April 30 at the Berkeley Community Theatre she performed with B.B. King as second act.

1973

On June 29, 1973, Big Mama Thornton played at two shows at the Blues Barn organized and hosted by B.B. King in the Philharmonic Hall New York as part of the Newport Jazz Festival.

On November 16, 1973, Thornton played with Hound Dog Taylor and others at the Academy of Music, New York.

For the rest of the year, she had an engagement at the Shaboo Inn in of Willimantic in northeastern Connecticut.

1974

In January and February, Big Mama Thornton played a show at the Brooklyn Academy of Music, New York.

On August 30, she took part in the *Midnight Special* on NBC, hosted by B.B. King. After the show Thornton appeared at the American Theatre in Washington, DC.

1975

She recorded for Vanguards Music the LP *Sassy Mama*. Other songs from the recording session were released in the 2000 under the name *Big Mama Swings*.

Big Mama Thornton played in New Hampshire, Cambridge, Massachusetts, Rhode Island and Washington, DC.

1976

Thornton meets musician and manager Lee Ashford.

Thornton played mostly in Los Angeles at The Rubaiyat Room on Wilshire Blvd.

Thornton had a car accident and had to spend six months in the hospital.

1977

Big Mama Thornton started with working with Lee Ashford's management.

Ashford put together a 25-date tour through the U.S. and Canada. During the tour Thornton plays The Rising Sun Celebrity Jazz Club in Montreal and performs at George Washington University in Washington, DC.

1978–1979

In the summer, Big Mama Thornton took part in the Juneteenth Blues Fest in Houston.

On September 3, 1978, she shared the bill with John Lee Hooker at the Massey Hall, Toronto, Canada.

Between 1978 and 1979, Thornton played the Los Angeles club scene and along the West Coast.

In June 1979, Thornton was again part of the Juneteenth Blues Festival in Houston.

On August 11–12, she appeared at the San Francisco Blues Festival.

On September 8 and 9, Thornton took part in the Tribal Stomp at Monterey Fairgrounds.

On September 22–23, she played the Third Annual Sacramento Blues Festival at the William Land Park Amphitheatre.

From now on Thornton always sat for at least part of the show, but that was the only change.

In November 1979, Thornton gave a concert at the Buffalo Tavern in Seattle, Washington.

The rest of the year, Thornton played in Los Angeles in the Parisian Room.

1980

The eighties started for Willie Mae Thornton as the seventies had ended: with touring all over in the club scene.

On July 2, 1980, she was part of the famous Kool Newport Jazz Festival special program called "Blues Is a Woman" at Avery Fisher Hall in Manhattan.

On July 4 and 5, 1980, Thornton played a two-night show in New York with the Robert Ross Blues Band at Tramps.

Thornton played a lot in Canada. She performed at the Club Isabella in Toronto and toured with Muddy Waters, James Cotton and Brownie McGhee through Canada.

Thornton also played a week-long show in St. John, Newfoundland, and at the Belly Up Tavern at Solana Beach in San Diego.

On September 10, 1980, Thornton performed at the Los Angeles Bicentennial Blues with B.B. King and Muddy Waters.

On December 1980, she sang on *Omnibus*, an ABC special hosted by actor Hal Holbrook, and joined by Aretha Franklin.

1981–1984

June 29, 1981, she played a show at the Lone Star Café, New York City, with Koko Taylor on the bill.

On July 29, 1981, Thornton was again part of the "Blues Is a Woman" program at the Newport Jazz Festival.

She now played off and on, performing in Canada at the Los Angeles clubs El Rey and the Solari Theatre in Beverly Hills.

On October 3, 1981, Thornton performed with the band The Gun Club at the Los Angeles club Lingerie.

On New Year's Eve 1981, she performed at the club The Continental in Oakland, together with the Eddie Ray Rhythm and Blues Band.

In 1983, Thornton played Canada and was also a special guest at a B.B. King concert in Montreal's Theatre Maisonneuve.

Appendix A

In March, Thornton was a part of the award-winning PBS television special *Three Generations of the Blues*, with Sippie Wallace and Jeannie Cheatham.

On August 18, Thornton performed at the Lone Star Café in New York City.

On October 7, 1983 she played at Gerte's Folk City in New York City.

In the winter 1983, she played the Key Largo Club in Portland.

In July 1984, she went for a last little tour in Canada and played a gig in Vancouver.

On July 25, 1984, Willie Mae "Big Mama" Thornton died of a heart attack.

Appendix B:
Selected Discography

Singles

1950

"All Right Baby"/ "Bad Luck Got My Man" by the Harlem Stars (vocals by Willie Mae Thornton, unknown band, possibly with Odie Turner on piano). E&W 100.

1951

"I'm All Fed Up"/ "Partnership Blues" by Willie Mae Thornton with the Joe Scott Orchestra: Joe Scott (trumpet), unknown (piano, sax, guitar, bass, drums). Recorded in Houston. ACA 1861, ACA 1864, Peacock 1567.

"No Jody for Me"/"Let Your Tears Fall Baby" by Willie Mae Thornton with the Bill Harvey Band/Bill Harvey Orchestra: Bill Harvey (tenor sax), unknown (trumpet, sax, piano, guitar, bass, drums). Recorded in Houston. ACA 2070, ACA 2071, Peacock 1587.

"Everytime I Think of You" by Willie Mae Thornton with the Bill Harvey Band/Bill Harvey Orchestra: Bill Harvey (tenor sax), unknown (trumpet, sax, piano, guitar, bass, drums). Recorded in Houston / **"Mischievous Boogie"** by Willie Mae Thornton with the Joe Scott Orchestra: Joe Scott (trumpet), unknown (piano, sax, guitar, bass, drums). Recorded in Houston. ACA 1862, ACA 2069, Peacock 1603.

1953

"Hound Dog" by Willie Mae Thornton with members of the Johnny Otis Orchestra: Pete Lewis (guitar), Albert Winston (bass), Johnny Otis (drums) / **"Nightmare"** by Willie Mae Thornton with members of the Johnny Otis Orchestra: Johnny Otis (vibes), Don Johnson (trumpet), George Washington (trombone), James von Streeter (tenor sax), Fred Ford (baritone sax), Devonia Williams (piano), Pete Lewis (guitar), Albert Winston (bass), Leard Bell (drums). Recorded in Los Angeles August 13, 1952. ACA 2258, ACA 2260, Peacock 1612.

Appendix B

"Hound Dog" by Willie Mae Thornton with members of the Johnny Otis Orchestra:
Pete Lewis (guitar), Albert Winston (bass), Johnny Otis (drums) / **"Rock A Bye
Baby"** by Willie Mae Thornton with members of the Johnny Otis Orchestra:
Johnny Otis (vibes), Don Johnson (trumpet), George Washington (trombone),
James von Streeter (tenor sax), Fred Ford (baritone sax), Devonia Williams
(piano), Pete Lewis (guitar), Albert Winston (bass), Leard Bell (drums). Recorded
in Los Angeles August 13, 1952. ACA 2258, ACA 2261, Peacock 1612.

"Cotton Pickin' Blues" by Willie Mae Thornton with the Bill Harvey Band: Bill
Harvey (tenor sax), unknown (trumpet, sax, piano, guitar, bass, drums).
Recorded in Houston 1951 / **"They Call Me Big Mama"** Willie Mae Thornton
with members of the Johnny Otis Orchestra: Johnny Otis (vibes), Don Johnson
(trumpet), George Washington (trombone), James von Streeter (tenor), Fred
Ford (baritone sax), Devonia Williams (piano), Pete Lewis (guitar), Albert Winston (bass), Leard Bell (drums). Recorded in Los Angeles August 13, 1952. ACA
2068, ACA 2256, Peacock 1621.

"I Ain't No Fool Either" / **"Big Change"** by Willie Mae Thornton with members
of the Johnny Otis Orchestra: Johnny Otis (vibes), Don Johnson (trumpet),
George Washington (trombone), James von Streeter (tenor), Fred Ford (baritone
sax), Devonia Williams (piano), Pete Lewis (guitar), Albert Winston (bass), Leard
Bell (drums). Recorded in Los Angeles, August 1953. R 105–5, and R 107–9, Peacock 1626 .

"Yes Baby" by Johnny Ace, duet vocals with Willie Mae Thornton with the Johnny
Otis Band: Johnny Ace (v, org, piano), Johnny Otis (vibes), Don Johnson (trumpet), George Washington (trombone), James von Streeter (tenor), Fred Ford
(baritone sax), Pete Lewis (guitar), Albert Winston (bass), Leard Bell (drums).
Recorded in Los Angeles, 1953 / **"Saving My Love for You"** by Johnny Ace. Duke
118.

1954

"I Smell a Rat" / **"I've Searched the Whole World"** by Willie Mae Thornton with
members of the Johnny Otis Orchestra: Johnny Otis (vibes), Don Johnson (trumpet), George Washington (trombone), James von Streeter (tenor), Fred Ford
(baritone sax), Devonia Williams (piano), Pete Lewis (guitar), Albert Winston
(bass), Leard Bell (drums). Recorded in Los Angeles, 1953. RR 108–9, ACA 2263,
Peacock 1632.

"Stop Hoppin' on Me" / **"Story of My Blues"** by Willie Mae Thornton with Burt
Kendricks and His Orchestra.: Burt Kendricks (guitra), unknown (trumpet, sax,
bass, drums Recorded in Houston, 1954. ACA 2834, ACA 2835, Peacock 1642.

1955

"Rock-a-Bye Baby" / **"Walking Blues"** by Willie Mae Thornton with members of
the Johnny Otis Orchestra: Johnny Otis (vibes), Don Johnson (trumpet), George
Washington (trombone), James von Streeter (tenor), Fred Ford (baritone sax),
Devonia Williams (piano), Pete Lewis (guitar), Albert Winston (bass), Leard Bell

(drums). Recorded in Los Angeles on August 13, 1952. ACA 2261, ACA 2251, Peacock 1647.

"The Fish" / "Laugh, Laugh, Laugh" by Willie Mae Thornton with Bill Harvey's Orchestra: Joe Scott (trumpet), Pluma Davis (trombone), Bill Harvey (tenor sax), Roy Gaines (guitar), unknown (sax, piano, bass, drums). Recorded in Houston, 1955. ACA 3086, ACA 3088, Peacock 1650.

"Tarzan and the Dignified Monkey" by Willie Mae Thornton and Elroy Peace (Willie Mae "Big Mama" Thornton [vocals], Elroy Peace [vocals], Burt Kendricks [guitar], unknown [trumpet, sax, bass, drums] / **"How Come"** by Willie Mae Thornton with Bill Harvey's Orchestra: Joe Scott (trumpet), Pluma Davis (trombone), Bill Harvey (tenor sax), Roy Gaines (guitar), unknown (sax, piano, bass, drums). Recorded in Houston, 1955. ACA 2832, ACA 3089, Peacock 1654 .

1957

"Just Like a Dog (Barking Up the Wrong Tree)" / "My Man Called Me" by Willie Mae Thornton and the Johnny Otis Orchestra: Pete Lewis (guitar), unknown (trumpet, sax, piano, bass, drums, vocals). Recorded in Houston, 1957. FR 1034, FR 1035, Peacock 1681.

1961

"Big Mama's Coming Home" / "Don't Talk Back" by Willie Mae Thornton with The Hi-Tones. Recorded in Oakland, CA, 1961. IR 13XX, Irma 13.

"You Did Me Wrong" / "Big Mama's Blues" by Willie Mae Thornton, band unknown. Recorded in Oakland, CA, 1961. Bay Tone #107. Also recorded during that session but not released was "Ball and Chain."

1965

"Summertime" / "Truth Comes to the Light" by Willie Mae Thornton, band unknown. Recorded in Los Angeles. Sotoplay 0033, 0034.

"Tomcat" by Willie Mae Thornton, band unknown. Recorded in Los Angeles. Sotoplay 0039.

"Yes I Cried" / "Mercy" by Willie Mae Thornton, band unknown. Recorded in Los Angeles. Sotoplay 0050.

1966

"Mercy" / "Yes I Cried" by Willie Mae Thornton, band unknown. Recorded in Los Angeles. Carolyn 006.

"Before Day" / "Me and My Chauffeur" by Willie Mae Thornton with the Johnny Talbot Band, Johnny Talbot (guitar). Recorded in Berkeley, CA. Kent 424.

"Because It's Love" by Willie Mae Thornton, band unknown. Recorded in Los Angeles. Galaxy 749, released April 25.

"Life Goes On" by Willie Mae Thornton, band unknown. Recorded in Los Angeles. Galaxy 746, released April 25.

1967

"There Ain't Nothin' You Can Do / Hear" by Willie Mae Thornton with Curtis Tillman and Band. Movin 144.

"Don't Do Me This Way/ Let's Go Get Stoned" by Willie Mae Thornton with Curtis Tillman and Band. Movin 145.

1968

"Ball and Chain" / **"Wade in the Water"** by Big Mama Thornton with Everett Minor (tenor sax), Nat Dove (piano), Bee Houston (guitar), Curtis Tillman (bass), Gus Wright (drums). Recorded in Los Angeles. Arhoolie 45–520.

"Swing It On Home" / **"My Heavy Load."** Both cuts taken from *In Europe* LP. Arhoolie 45–512.

1992

"You Don't Move Me No More" by Willie Mae Thornton with the Bill Harvey Band: Joe Scott (trumpet), Pluma Davis (trombone), Bill Harvey (tenor sax), Roy Gaines (guitar), unknown (sax, piano, bass, drums, claves, maracas). Recorded in Houston, 1955 / **"Hard Times"** by Willie Mae Thornton with members of the Johnny Otis Orchestra: Johnny Otis (vibes), Don Johnson (trumpet), George Washington (trombone), James von Streeter (tenor), Fred Ford (baritone sax), Devonia Williams (piano), Pete Lewis (guitar), Albert Winston (bass), Leard Bill (drums). Recorded in Los Angeles, August 13, 1952. MCAD 10668 (CD).

Albums

All U.S. releases unless noted.

In Europe. Arhoolie Records F 1028. Released 1966. "Swing It on Home," "Sweet Little Angel," "The Place," "Little Red Rooster," "Unlucky Girl," "Hound Dog," "My Heavy Load," "School Boy," "Down-Home Shake-Down," "Your Love Is Where It Ought to Be," "Session Blues." Recorded October 20, 1965, at Wessex Studio, London. Band: Buddy Guy (guitar), Eddie Boyd (piano or organ), Walter "Shakey" Horton (harmonica), Fred Below (drums), Jimmy Lee Robinson (bass) and Fred McDowell (slide guitar on "Your Love Is Where It Ought to Be," "Session Blues" and "Chauffeur Blues").

Big Mama Thornton Vol. 2: The Queen at Monterey with the Chicago Blues Band. Arhoolie Records F 1032 / AR 19017 (U.S.). Released 1967. "I'm Feeling Alright," "Sometimes I Have a Heartache," "Black Rat," "Life Goes On," "Everything Gonna Be Alright," "Bumble Bee," "Gimme a Penny," "Looking the World Over," "I Feel the Way I Feel," "Big Mama's Blues (My Love)." Recorded April 25, 1966, at Coast Recorders in San Francisco. Band: Muddy Waters (guitar), Sammy Lawhorn (guitar), James Cotton (harmonica), Otis Spann (piano), Luther Johnson (bass guitar), and Francis Clay (drums). On "Everything Gonna Be Alright": Big Mama Thornton (drums).

Stronger Than Dirt. Mercury 45223 SR 61225 (U.S.), Mercury 134.234 MCY (France), Mercury 134 234 MCY (Netherlands). Released 1969. "Born Under a Bad Sign," "Hound Dog," "Ball and Chain," "Summertime," "Rollin' Stone," "Let's Go Get Stoned," "Funky Broadway," "That Lucky Old Sun,""Ain't Nothin' You Can Do,""I Shall Be Released." Band: Big Terry DeRouen (guitar), Everett Minor (sax), Nat Dove (piano) and Curtis Tillman (bass).

The Way It Is. Mercury–SR 61249 (U.S., UK.) Released 1969. "Little Red Rooster," "One Black Rat," "Rock Me Baby," "Wade in the Water," "Sweet Little Angel," "Baby Please Don't Go / Got My Mojo Workin'," "Watermelon Man," " Don't Need No Doctor." Live at the Thee Experience, Los Angeles, October 1969. Band: George Smith (harmonica), Jay Hodges (tenor sax), J.D. Nicholson (piano), Bee Houston (guitar), Flip Graham (bass), Unknown (drums).

Saved. Pentagram–PE 10005. Released 1971. "Oh, Happy Day," Down by the Riverside," "Glory, Glory Hallelujah," "He's Got the Whole World in His Hands," "Lord Save Me," "Swing Low, Sweet Chariot," "One More River," "Go Down Moses." Unknown backing band.

Jail. Vanguard VSD 79351 (U.S.), Vanguard VSD 23023 (France). Released 1975. "Little Red Rooster," "Ball and Chain," "Jail," "Hound Dog," "Rock Me Baby," "Sheriff O.E. & Me," "Oh Happy Day." Recorded live at Monroe State Prison, Monroe, Washington, and Oregon State Reformatory, Eugene. Band: J.G. Nichols (piano), George "Harmonica" Smith (harmonica), Bill Potter (tenor sax), B. Huston and Steve Wachsman (guitar), Bruce Steverson (bass), Todd Nelson (drums).

Sassy Mama! Vanguard VSD 79354(U.S.), Vanguard VSD 23014 (France). Released 1975. "Rolling Stone," "Lost City," "Mr. Cool," "Big Mama's New Love," "Private Number," "Sassy Mama," "Everybody's Happy (but Me)." Recorded 1975 at Vanguard Recording Studio, New York. Band: Paul Griffin (keyboards), Jimmy Johnson (drums), Buddy Lucas (tenor sax), Wilbur Bascomb (bass), Cornell Dupree (guitar), Ronnie Miller (guitar) and Ernie Heyes (piano).

Mama's Pride. Vanguard VPC 40001 (U.K.) Released 1978. "Big Mama's New Love," "Rolling Stone," "Mr. Cool," "Lost City," "Private Number"(from *Sassy Mama!*) "Little Red Rooster," "Ball and Chain," "Hound Dog," "Rock Me Baby," "Jail" (from *Jail.*)

Sherman & Friends. Lunar 20016. Released 1981. "Ball and Chain," "Hound Dog," "Rock Me Baby," "Rooster Blues (Early One Morning)." Recorded live in Houston. With Sherman Robertson (guitar) and the Crosstown Blues Band.

Sassy Mama. Justin-Time Just A Memory Records RSCD 0002 (Canada), CD. Released 2005. "Tell Me Pretty Baby," "Rock Me Baby," "Ball and Chain," "Watermelon Man," "Summertime," "Medley: Hound Dog/Walkin' the Dog," "Medley: Sweet Little Angel/ Three O'Clock Blues," "Sassy Mama." Recorded live at Rising Sun Celebrity Jazz Club, Montreal, Canada, April 12, 1977. Band: Phil Guy and John Primer (guitar), Johnny "Big Moose" Walker (piano), J.W. Williams (bass), Burt Robertson (drums), Big Mama Thornton (harmonica).

Big Mama Thornton & Clifton Chenier Live & Together! Crazy Cajun 1104. Release date unknown. "Two Steppin'," "Night Time," "Little Red Rooster," "Let's Do the Mess Around," "Crawfish for Soul." Recorded live at Liberty Hall, Houston.

Compilations and Reissues

She's Back. Backbeat Records–BLP 68. Released 1968. "Cotton Picking Blues," "Willie Mae's Blues," "Big Change," "Walking Blues," "Just Can't Help Myself," "Hound Dog," "They Call Me Big Mama," "Tarzan and the Dignified Monkey," "My Man Called Me," "I Smell a Rat." Compilation of Peacock singles.

Ball and Chain: Big Mama Thornton, Lightning Hopkins, Larry Williams. Arhoolie 1039, Arhoolie AR 19022. Released 1968. Arhoolie 1039 (1974 repressing). Features "Ball and Chain," "Wade in the Water," "My Love."

Vanishing Point (**Original Motion Picture Soundtrack**). Amos Records–AAS8002. Released 1971. Features "Sing Out For Jesus."

John Hammond's Spirituals to Swing 30th Anniversary Concert, 1967. Columbia G 30776. Released 1972. Features "Backdoor Blues," "Sweet Little Angel," "Hound Dog." Willie Mae (Big Mama) Thornton, vocals, with Cafe Society All-Stars (Buck Clayton, Edmond Hall, clarinet; Buddy Tate, tenor saxophone; Ray Bryant, piano; Milt Hinton, bass; Jo Jones, drums, Count Basie, pianist).

The 10th American Folk Blues Festival (Blues Giants—Rock Creators). Atlantic–ATL 60036, Stern Musik–ATL 60036 (Germany, Austria, and Switzerland). Released 1973. "Tell Me Baby" and "Ball and Chain" by Big Mama Thornton & the Blues Band: Phillip Morrison (bass), Vinton Johnson (drums), Paul Lenart (electric guitar); T-Bone Walker (piano); Edward Taylor (tenor saxophone), Hartley Severns tenor saxophone, baritone saxophone, soprano saxophone, violin); blues harp (Big Mama Thornton. Also features songs by Bukka White, Big Joe Williams, Robert Pete Williams, Roosevelt Sykes, Memphis Slim, Johnny Young, T-Bone Walker and the Blues Band, Jimmy Rogers, Lightnin' Slim and Jimmy Dawkins Chicago Blues Band. Recorded live, March 16, 1972, in Lünen, Hilpert Theatre, and October 26, 1972, in Munich, Circus-Krone-Bau. This double LP has been edited for later L+R reissues on CD, and some selections are missing. Other versions: *American Folk Blues Festival '72*, L+R Records LS 42018(CD) Germany; *American Folk Blues Festival '72*, Optimism Incorporated, L+R Records LR CD-2018 (CD) North America.

The Blues: A Real Summit Meeting. Buddah BDS 5144–2. Released 1973. Features "Little Red Rooster," "Ball and Chain." Re-releases: 1992, Sutra 2007 (CD); 1994, Kama Sutra 2007 (CD); 1994, Unidisc 2007 (CD); 2000, Universe 10 (CD); 2001,Sutra AGEK2–2007 (CD); 2003, Unidisc 22007 (CD); 2013, Goodfellas/Klimt MJJ 356DLP (LP).

San Francisco Blues Festival 1979, Vol. 3. Solid Smoke Records. Released 1981. Features "Fo' Day Blues," "Ball and Chain" and "You Don't Have to Go." Band: Mark Naftalin (piano), Ron Thompson (guitar), Melvin Davis (flute), Walter Savage (bass), Harold Banks (drums), Mike Lewis (bass).

B.B. King & Big Mama Thornton & Muddy Waters–Live At Newport. Blue Moon BMM 002 (U.K.), Tobacco Road B 2635 (Germany) Astan 20039 (Germany), released 1984; Famous Music FM 14506 (Greece), released 1985. "Little Red Roos-ter," and "Ball and Chain" by Big Mama Thornton, with songs by B.B. King and Muddy Waters. Recorded live June 29, 1973, at the Blues Barn, Newport Jazz Festival in Philharmonic Hall, New York.

The Original Hound Dog. Ace CDCHD 940. Released 1986. "Hound Dog," "Walking Blues," "My Man Called Me," "Cotton Picking Blues," "Willie Mae's Blues," "The Big Change," "I Smell a Rat," "I Just Can't Help Myself," "They Call Me Big Mama," "Hard Times," "I Ain't No Fool Either," "You Don't Move Me No More," "Let Your Tears Fall Baby," "I've Searched the World Over," "Rockabye Baby," "How Come," "Nightmare," "Stop A-Hoppin' on Me," "Laugh, Laugh, Laugh," "Just Like a Dog," "The Fish," "Mischievous Boogie." Peacock singles.

Stronger Than Dirt/The Way It Is. Charly (two LPs, CDX 24), and Charly R&B (two tapes, TC-CDX 24), UK. Released 1988. *The Way It Is.* Mercury (CD) 314 558 550-2 U.S. Released 1998. Refer to 1969 LP listings for tracks.

Ball and Chain. Arhoolie CD 305. Released 1989. "Sweet Little Angel," "Unlucky Girl," "Swing It on Home," "Little Red Rooster," "Hound Dog," "Your Love Is Where It Ought to Be," "School Boy," "My Heavy Load" (all from *In Europe* LP), "I'm Feeling Alright," "Sometimes I Have a Heartache," "Black Rat," "Life Goes On," "Bumble Bee," "Gimme A Penny" (all from *Big Mama Thornton Vol. 2: The Queen at Monterey with the Chicago Blues Band* LP), "Wade in the Water," "Ball and Chain" (from *Ball and Chain* LP). Arhoolie tracks.

You Ole Houn' Dawg. Ace–CHAD 277. Germany. Released 1989. "Hound Dog," "Walking Blues," "My Man Called Me," "Cotton Picking Blues," "Willie Mae's Blues," "The Big Change," "Partnership Blues," "I'm All Fed Up," "I Smell a Rat," "I Just Can't Help Myself," "Yes Baby," "Tarzan and the Dignified Monkey," "They Call Me Big Mama," "Before Day (Big Mama's Blues)," "Me and My Chauffeur." Singles.

Hound Dog—The Peacock Recordings. MCA MCAD 10668. Released 1992. "Hound Dog," "My Man Called Me," "I Smell a Rat," "They Call Me Big Mama," "You Don't Move Me No More," "Let Your Tears Fall Baby," "Rock-A-Bye Baby," "Yes, Baby," "How Come," "Nightmare," "Stop A-Hoppin' On Me," "Just Like a Dog," "Walking Blues," "The Big Change," "Hard Times," "Laugh, Laugh, Laugh," "The Fish," "I've Searched The Whole World Over." Peacock singles.

The Baytone Records Story. Gold Dust GDR-CD-200. Released 1994. Features "You Did Me Wrong," "Big Mama's Blues."

The Hustler, **by Bee Houston & His High Steppers.** Arhoolie CD 9008. Released 1997. Features "Woke Up This Morning." Band: Bee Houston (guitar), Curtis Tillman (bass), Nat Dove (piano), Gus Wright (drums) and Everett Minor (tenor sax). Recorded in Hollywood, January 25, 1968.

The Complete Vanguard Recordings. Vanguard–175/77-2. Released 2000. "Little Red Rooster," "Ball and Chain," "Jail," "Hound Dog," "Rock Me Baby," "Sheriff O.E. & Me," "Oh Happy Day." Recorded live at Monroe State Prison, Monroe, Washington, and Oregon State Reformatory, Eugene. Band: J.G. Nichols (piano), George "Harmonica" Smith (harmonica), Bill Potter (tenor sax), B. Huston and

Steve Wachsman (guitar), Bruce Steverson (bass), Todd Nelson (drums). "Rolling Stone," "Lost City," "Mr. Cool," "Big Mama's New Love," "Private Number," "Sassy Mama," "Everybody's Happy (But Me)." Recorded 1975 at Vanguard Recording Studio, New York. Band: Paul Griffin (keyboards), Jimmy Johnson (drums), Buddy Lucas (tenor sax), Wilbur Bascomb (bass), Cornell Dupree (guitar), Ronnie Miller (guitar) and Ernie Heyes (piano). Plus *Big Mama Swings*, an unreleased album: "Good-Bye Baby," "Gonna Leave You," "Mixed Up Feeling," "Special," "Going Fishing," "Big Mama Swings," "Happy Me."

Sassy Mama! Vanguard VMD 79354–2 (Germany). Released 2000. Refer to LP listing for tracks.

Blues Review of the 20th Century. TopCat Records. Released 2001. Features "Interview with Muddy Waters, Big Mama Thornton and Big Joe Turner," "Introduction for Big Mama Thornton," "Ball and Chain," "Hound Dog," "Oh Happy Day." From a 1971 tour that played universities and prisons in Washington and Oregon. Band: J.G. Nichols (piano), George "Harmonica" Smith (harmonica), Bill Potter (tenor sax), B. Huston and Steve Wachsman (guitar), Bruce Steverson (bass), Todd Nelson (drums).

The Chronological Big Mama Thornton: 1950–1953. Classics 5088. France. Released 2004. "All Right Baby," "Bad Luck Got My Man," "Partnership Blues," "Mischievous Boogie," "I'm All Fed Up," "Cotton Picking Blues," "Everytime I Think of You," "No Jody for Me," "Let Your Tears Fall Baby," "They Call Me Big Mama," "Walking Blues," "Hound Dog," "Just Can't Help Myself," "Nightmare," "Rock-a-bye Baby," "Hard Times," "I've Searched the World Over," "I Ain't No Fool Either," "The Big Change," "I Smell a Rat," "Yes, Baby," "Willie Mae's Blues." Singles from Peacock.

Big Mama Thornton with the Muddy Waters Blues Band. Arhoolie CD 9043. Released 2004. Reissue of *Big Mama Thornton Vol. 2: The Queen at Monterey with the Chicago Blues Band.* This CD adds seven previously unissued tracks: "Black Rat" (take 2), "Wrapped Tight," "Gimme a Penny," "Big Mama's Shuffle," "Since I Fell for You," "I'm Feeling Alright" (fast version), "Big Mama's Blues (My Love)." Refer to 1967 LP for other tracks.

In Europe. Arhoolie 9056. CD reissue 2005. Adds six bonus tracks from the original session: "I Need Your Love," "Good Times in London," "Chauffeur Blues," "Swing In on Home" (take 2), "Hound Dog" (take 2), "Big Mama Talks with Chris Strachwitz." Fred McDowell (slide guitar) on "Chauffeur Blues." Refer to 1966 LP for other tracks.

Hear Me Howling. Arhoolie 518. Released 2011. Features "'Fore Day in the Mornin'" (recorded at the Fillmore Auditorium in San Francisco, October 15, 1966), "Ball and Chain," "Hound Dog" (recorded at the Berkeley Blues Festival, Pauley Ballroom, April 3, 1970, with an unknown band). Previously unreleased.

Appendix C:
Selection of TV Appearances, Films, DVDs and Videos

Black, White and Blue (PBS, 1967).

Della (WOR, New York, episode 97, October 21, 1969): Host Della Reese and side-kick Sandy Baron with Big Mama Thornton, Woody Woodbury and the Four Freshmen.

Rock 1 (CBC-TV, Toronto, January 11, 1970): Big Mama Thornton plays with Toronto-based blues band Whiskey Howl, who also played their own set. The November 5, 1969, concert was taped for music producer David Acomba's special.

The Dick Cavett Show (ABC-TV, episode 213, July 22, 1971: Guests are Big Mama Thornton, actor Roger Moore, and writer-organizer Saul David Alinsky.

Gunsmoke Blues (DVD): Features "Early One Morning," "Ball and Chain," "Hound Dog," "Rock Me Baby," an interview, plus "So Long" by George "Harmonica" Smith, Big Mama Thornton, Big Joe Turner and Muddy Waters. Taped by MCA studios at the University of Oregon, Eugene.

Muddy Waters in Concert 1971(Vestapol videotape): West Coast tour of 1971, with Big Mama Thornton and Big Joe Turner.

Gettin' Back (documentary film): Performing are Big Mama Thornton, Leo Kottke, Clifton Chenier and the Red Hot Cajun Band, Michael Murphy, and the Earl Scruggs Revue. Live at Ozark Mountain Folk Fair, Eureka Springs, Arkansas, in 1973.

Midnight Special (television, episode 48, August 30, 1974): "Ball and Chain." Host: B.B. King.

Omnibus (television, December 28, 1980): Big Mama Thornton and Aretha Franklin. Host: Hal Holbrook.

Appendix C

Three Generations of Blues (PBS-TV): Big Mama Thornton, Sippie Wallace and Jeannie Cheatham, filmed at Belly Up Tavern in Solana Beach, San Diego, California, 1983.

American Folk Blues Festival, vol. 2 (DVD, 2003): Features "Down Home Shakedown."

American Folk Blues Festival, vol. 3 (DVD, 2004): Features "Hound Dog."

Chapter Notes

Preface

1. Jimmy McCracklin, interview with author, July 10, 2009. All further quotations from Jimmy McCracklin in the preface come from this interview.
2. Mahon, Listening for Thornton's Voice, 15.
3. Quoted in Neff and Connor, 51.
4. Big Mama Thornton in an interview with Roy Greenberg on July 3, 1980 (Roy Greenberg Collection [MUM00208] in the Blues Archive, The Department of Archives and Special Collections, J.D. Williams Library, University of Mississippi).
5. Chris Strachwitz, liner notes for the CD Ball 'n' Chain, Arhoolie Production, Inc., CD 305.
6. Mahon, Listening for Thornton's Voice, 14.
7. Thornton quoted in Arnold Shaw, The World of Soul: Black America's Contribution to the Pop Music Scene (New York: Cowles Book Company, 1970), 108.
8. Ron Thompson, interview with author, November 28, 2009. All further quotations from Ron Thompson in the preface come from this interview.

Chapter 1

1. As written in her birth certificate (number 1926–130–64618) from March 8, 1927. Confirmed by an affidavit to amend record of birth, July 31, 1965.
2. Her birth certificate says that her parents had six children, but this figure includes Willie Mae Thornton. The 1930 U.S. Census lists all family members, including Willie Mae.
3. Interview with Big Mama Thornton conducted by Chris Strachwitz, October 20, 1965, included on the CD Big Mama Thornton in Europe, Arhoolie 9056.
4. Interview with Big Mama Thornton conducted by Ralph J. Gleason, San Francisco Chronicle, April 6, 1970.
5. New York Times, July 4, 1980.
6. Peter Gallagher, interview with author, February 17, 2010. All further quotations from Peter Gallagher in this chapter come from this interview.
7. Quoted in Salem, 79.
8. Quoted in White, 25.
9. Interview with Big Mama Thornton conducted by Chris Strachwitz, October 20, 1965, included on the CD Big Mama Thornton in Europe, Arhoolie 9056.
10. Quoted in Neff and Connor, 50.
11. Jimmy Scott, interview with author, March 6, 2009. All further quotations from Jimmy Scott in this chapter come from this interview.
12. Tommy Brown, interview with author, July 5, 2009. All further quotations from Tommy Brown in this chapter come from this interview.
13. Quoted in Neff and Connor, 57.

Chapter 2

1. Texas Johnny Brown, interview with author, March 6, 2012. All further quotations from Texas Johnny Brown in this chapter come from this interview.
2. Roger Wood, "Eldorado Ballroom,"

Handbook of Texas Online (http://www.tshaonline.org/handbook/online/articles/xde02), accessed January 20, 2012. Published by the Texas State Historical Association.

3. Texas Johnny Brown, interview with author, March 6, 2012.

4. Milton Hopkins, interview with author, February 19, 2010. Unless otherwise noted all further quotations from Milton Hopkins in this chapter come from this interview.

5. Interview with Big Mama Thornton conducted by Chris Strachwitz, October 20, 1965, included on the CD Big Mama Thornton in Europe, Arhoolie 9056.

6. Ray Topping, liner notes for Big Mama Thornton: The Original Hound Dog, Ace Records CDCHD 940, 1990.

7. Quoted in Govenar, 7.

8. Quoted in Salem, 126.

9. Tommy Brown, interview with author, July 5, 2009. All further quotations from Tommy Brown in this chapter come from this interview.

10. Grady Gaines, interview with author, March 2, 2012. All further quotations from Grady Gaines in this chapter come from this interview.

11. Quoted in White, 37–38.

12. Quoted in Salem, 79–80.

13. Billboard, December 29, 1951, 23.

14. Jimmy McCracklin, interview with author, July 10, 2009. All further quotations from Jimmy McCracklin in this chapter come from this interview.

15. New York Times, July 4, 1980.

16. Chicago Defender, August 2, 1952, 22.

17. Quoted in Gart and Ames, 51.

18. Story told in Lipsitz, 34.

19. Interview Big Mama Thornton with Ralph J. Gleason, San Francisco Chronicle, April 6, 1970.

20. From Johnny Otis's speech at Big Mama Thornton's funeral, as quoted in Los Angeles Times, December 1984.

21. New York Times, July 4, 1980.

22. Quoted in Rolling Stone, April 19, 1990.

23. Audio70, no. 7–12: 56.

24. Charles Fairchild, Pop Idols and Pi-

rates: Mechanisms of Consumption and the Global Circulation of Popular Music, 45.

25. Quoted in Orr, "Johnny Otis' R&B Caravan keeps on rolling. A talk with one of the great champions of music" (http://triviana.com/BLUES/sfb00/otis.htm), accessed January 20, 2012.

26. "Big Mama Talks." The sacred-music album is Saved, Pentagram, PE 10,005, 1971, 331/3 rpm.

27. Billboard, display ad, March 7, 1953, 49.

28. Billboard, March 14, 1953, 32.

29. "Cash Box" column, reprinted in Moonooogian, 6

30. "Down Beat' Best Bets: Rhythm and Blues," 13-S.

31. Quoted in Neff and Connor, 50.

32. Billboard, September 26, 1953, 34.

33. Billboard, December 19, 1953, 40.

34. "Cash Box," March 29, 1954; April 1954. In Galen Gart, ed., First Pressing: The History of Rhythm & Blues 4: 40–41,43.

35. New York Age Defender, April 24, 1954, 6.

36. Variety, April 28, 1954, 53.

37. Billboard, May 8, 1954, 38.

38. Quoted in Travis, 216.

39. Quoted in Salem, 129; and Milton Hopkins, interview with author, February 19, 2010.

40. Quoted in Salem, 131.

41. Big Mama Thornton, deposition, State of Texas, County of Harris, December 26, 1954.

42. Scotty Moore, interview with author via email, July 2010.

43. Nat Dove, interview with author, July 10, 2009.

44. Quoted in Orr, "Johnny Otis' R&B Caravan keeps on rolling. A talk with one of the great champions of music" (http://triviana.com/BLUES/sfb00/otis.htm), accessed January 23, 2012.

45. Quoted in Neff and Connor, 51.

Chapter 3

1. Chas McDevitt, interview with author, July 2, 2012. All further quotations

from Chas McDevitt in this chapter come from this interview.

2. *El Paso Herald Post*, December 8, 1956.

3. Quoted in Otis, 63.

4. Michael Erlewine, interview with author, May 3, 2009. All further quotations from Michael Erlewine in this chapter come from this interview.

5. *Billboard*, May 15, 1961.

Chapter 4

1. Jimmy Moore, interview with author, March 5, 2009. All further quotations from Jimmy Moore in this chapter come from this interview.

2. Minor, 66.

3. Ralph J. Gleason, "Big Mama Sings the Blues She Likes," liner notes for the CD *Big Mama Thornton and the Chicago Blues Band*, Arhoolie Records, F 1032, 1967, 331/3 rpm.

4. Chris Strachwitz, liner notes for the CD *Big Mama Thornton. In Europe*, 2005 Arhoolie Production. Inc., CD 9056.

5. Quoted in Ed Vulliamy, *Observer*, January 30, 2011 (http://www.guardian.co.uk/music/2011/jan/30/robert-plant-band-joy-interview), accessed February 10, 2012.

6. Quoted in Ray Coleman, *Melody Maker*, May 23, 1964, 9.

7. Chris Huston, interview with author, May 5, 2012. All further quotations from Chris Huston in this chapter come from this interview.

Chapter 5

1. *Oakland Tribune*, June 27, 1965.

2. *Billboard*, November 20, 1965, 26.

3. Jimmy Moore, interview with author, March 5, 2009. All further quotations from Jimmy Moore in this chapter come from this interview.

4. Buddy Guy in *When I Left Home: My Story*.

5. Chris Strachwitz, liner notes for the CD *Big Mama Thornton "Ball 'N' Chain,"* Arhoolie Production, Inc., CD 305.

6. Ibid.

7. Chris Strachwitz, liner notes for the CD *Big Mama Thornton. In Europe*, 2005 Arhoolie Production. Inc., CD 9056.

8. *Jazz Journal* 18, no. 11 (November 1965), 40

Chapter 6

1. Michael Erlewine, interview with author, May 3, 2009. All further quotations from Michael Erlewine in this chapter come from this interview.

2. Quoted in Wyman, *Rolling with the Stones*, 370

3. Quoted in Steve Propes, "Nate McCoy and Sotoplay Records," *B&R*, 193, 19.

4. Chris Strachwitz, liner notes for the CD *Big Mama Thornton "Ball 'n' Chain,"* Arhoolie Production, Inc., CD 305.

5. *Billboard*, October 1, 1966, 10.

6. Bernie Pearl, interview with author, November 5, 2010. All further quotations from Bernie Pearl in this chapter come from this interview.

7. Nat Dove, interview with author, July 10, 2009. All further quotations from Nat Dove in this chapter come from this interview.

8. *Oakland Tribune*, November 11, 1966, 26.

Chapter 7

1. James Gurley, interview with author, May 1, 2008. All further quotations from James Gurley in this chapter come from this interview.

2. Toney Burkhart, interview with author, August 5, 2011. All further quotations from Toney Burkhart in this chapter come from this interview.

3. Thornton quoted in Tam Fiofori, "The Blues," *Melody Maker*, April 29, 1972, 44.

4. Big Mama Thornton in an inter-

view with Roy Greenberg on July 3, 1980 (Roy Greenberg Collection [MUM00208] in the Blues Archive, The Department of Archives and Special Collections, J.D. Williams Library, University of Mississippi).

5. Jimmy Moore, interview with author, March 5, 2009. All further quotations from Jimmy Moore in this chapter come from this interview.

6. *Oakland Tribune*, January 10, 1967, 40.

7. *San Mateo Times*, May 10, 1968, 14.

8. Mac Arnold, interview with author, July 24, 2010. All further quotations from Mac Arnold in this chapter come from this interview.

9. Terry DeRouen, interview with author, July 1, 2010. All further quotations from Terry DeRouen in this chapter come from this interview.

10. Roy Bookbinder, interview with author, August 8, 2008. All further quotations from Roy Bookbinder in this chapter come from this interview.

11. *New York Times*, July 20, 1969.

12. Ibid.

13. *Billboard*, August 9, 1969, 32.

14. Quoted in Robert Gordon, *Can't Be Satisfied. The Life and Times of Muddy Waters*, 352.

15. Michael Erlewine, interview with author, May 3, 2009. All further quotations from Michael Erlewine in this chapter come from this interview.

16. Big Mama Thornton, interview with Michael Erlewine, August 3, 1969.

17. Willa Davis, interview with author, August 21, 2012. All further quotations from Willa Davis in this chapter come from this interview.

18. Quoted in Segrest and Hoffman, *Moanin' at Midnight*, 258.

19. *Los Angeles Times*, October 18, 1969.

20. Peter Malick, interview with author, June 10, 2004. All further quotations from Peter Malick in this chapter come from this interview.

21. *The News (Van Nuys)*, November 21, 1969.

22. *New York Times*, January 4, 1970.

Chapter 8

1. *Charleston Gazette*, February 28, 1970, 4.

2. *Star News*, March 7, 1970, 6.

3. Carlos Zialcita, interview with author, May 1, 2008. All further quotations from Carlos Zialcita in this chapter come from this interview.

4. Bill Sheffield, interview with author, February 7, 2009. All further quotations from Bill Sheffield in this chapter come from this interview.

5. Lloyd Jones, interview with author, March 15, 2010. All further quotations from Lloyd Jones in this chapter come from this interview.

6. *Oakland Tribune*, April 6, 1970, 35.

7. *New York Times*, April 19, 1970.

8. Ibid.

9. Doug McKechnie, interview with author, May, 29, 2012. All further quotations from Doug McKechnie in this chapter come from this interview.

10. Michael Erlewine, interview with author, May 3, 2009. All further quotations from Michael Erlewine in this chapter come from this interview.

11. *New York Times*, August 9, 1970.

12. *New York Times*, January 10, 1971; quoted in Arnold Shaw, *Honkers and Shouters: The Golden Years of Rhythm and Blues*, 483.

13. Ibid.

14. *New York Times*, January 10, 1971.

15. "Big Mama Talks." The sacred-music album is *Saved*, Pentagram, PE 10,005, 1971, 331/3 rpm.

16. Ed Bland, interview with author, March 17, 2012. All further quotations from Ed Bland in this chapter come from this interview.

17. Garry George, interview with author, March 22, 2012. All further quotations from Garry George in this chapter come from this interview.

18. Jan van Ray, interview with author, March 17, 2012. All further quotations from Jan van Ray in this chapter come from this interview.

19. Big Mama Thornton in an interview

with Roy Greenberg on July 3, 1980 (Roy Greenberg Collection [MUM00208] in the Blues Archive, The Department of Archives and Special Collections, J.D. Williams Library, University of Mississippi).

20. Paul Lenart, interview with author, August 4, 2009. All further quotations from Paul Lenart in this chapter come from this interview.

Chapter 9

1. Big Walker Derrick, interview with author, October 3, 2009. All further quotations from Big Walker Derrick in this chapter come from this interview.

2. *New York Times*, July 1, 1973.

3. Perry Yeldham, interview with author, October 10, 2009. All further quotations from Perry Yeldham in this chapter come from this interview.

4. Paul Winer, interview with author, October 11, 2012. All further quotations from Paul Winer in this chapter come from this interview.

5. Ed Bland, interview with author, March 17, 2012. All further quotations from Ed Bland in this chapter come from this interview.

6. John Kilgore, interview with author, June 10, 2010. All further quotations from John Kilgore in this chapter come from this interview.

7. Wilbur Bascomb, interview with author, August 21, 2010. All further quotations from Wilbur Bascomb in this chapter come from this interview.

8. Anthony Geraci, interview with author, August 5, 2010. All further quotations from Anthony Geraci in this chapter come from this interview.

9. Michael "Mudcat" Ward, interview with author, August 6, 2010. All further quotations from Michael "Mudcat" Ward in this chapter come from this interview.

10. Al Copley, interview with author, August 10, 2010. All further quotations from Al Copley in this chapter come from this interview.

11. Roy Book Binder, interview with author, August 12, 2010. All further quotations from Roy Book Binder in this chapter come from this interview.

12. Quoted in Neff and Connor, 113.

13. Big Mama Thornton in an interview with Roy Greenberg on July 3, 1980 (Roy Greenberg Collection [MUM00208] in the Blues Archive. The Department of Archives and Special Collections, J.D. Williams Library, University of Mississippi).

14. Dan Papaila, interview with author, April 10, 2009. All further quotations from Dan Papaila in this chapter come from this interview.

15. Big Mama Thornton talks about the accident in an interview with Roy Greenberg on July 3, 1980 (Roy Greenberg Collection [MUM00208] in the Blues Archive. The Department of Archives and Special Collections, J.D. Williams Library, University of Mississippi).

Chapter 10

1. *New York Times* , July 4, 1970.

2. Tom Principato, interview with author, October 14, 2009. All further quotations from Tom Principato in this chapter come from this interview.

3. Michael Pickett, interview with author, October 20, 2009. All further quotations from Michael Pickett in this chapter come from this interview.

4. Doug Mac Leod, interview with author, November 15, 2009. All further quotations from Doug Mac Leod in this chapter come from this interview.

5. Ron Thompson, interview with author, November 28, 2009. All further quotations from Ron Thompson in this chapter come from this interview.

6. Benjamin Perkoff, interview with author, March 23, 2012. All further quotations from Benjamin Perkoff in this chapter come from this interview.

7. *New York Times*, April 12, 1979.

8. *New York Times*, July 4, 1980.

9. Ibid.

10. Tom Mazzolini, interview with author, August 10, 2004. All further quotations from Tom Mazzolini in this chapter come from this interview.

11. Nat Dove, interview with author, July 10, 2009. All further quotations from Nat Dove in this chapter come from this interview.

12. Tom Mazzolini, interview with author, August 10, 2004. All further quotations from Tom Mazzolini in this chapter come from this interview.

13. Kim Field, interview with author, February 2, 2012. All further quotations from Kim Field in this chapter come from this interview.

14. Tommy Brown, interview with author, July 5, 2009. All further quotations from Tommy Brown in this chapter come from this interview.

Chapter 11

1. *New York Times*, July 4, 1980.

2. Big Mama Thornton in an Interiew with Roy Greenberg on July 3, 1980 (Roy Greenberg Collection [MUM00208] in the Blues Archive. The Department of Archives and Special Collections, J.D. Williams Library, University of Mississippi).

3. *New York Times*, July 2, 1980.

4. *New York Times*, July 4, 1980.

5. *Ebony* 35, no. 11, September 1980, 98.

6. Robert Ross, interview with author, August 10, 2009. All further quotations from Robert Ross in this chapter come from this interview.

7. James Anthony, interview with author, August 30, 2009. All further quotations from James Anthony in this chapter come from this interview.

8. Plume Latraverse, interview with author, November 16, 2009. All further quotations from Plume Latraverse in this chapter come from this interview.

9. Sandy Morris, interview with author, October 25, 2009. All further quotations from Sandy Morris in this chapter come from this interview.

10. Nelson Giles, interview with author, October 30, 2009. All further quotations from Nelson Giles in this chapter come from this interview.

11. Mark Lessman, interview with author, November 20, 2009. All further quotations from Mark Lessman in this chapter come from this interview.

12. Dave Camp, interview with author, December 10, 2009. All further quotations from Dave Camp in this chapter come from this interview.

13. Quoted in http://www.bluesaccess.com/No_27/rosen.html, accessed January 20, 2012.

14. Big Walker Derrick, interview with author, October 3, 2009. All further quotations from Big Walker Derrick in this chapter come from this interview.

15. Lloyd Jones, interview with author, June 5, 2010. All further quotations from Lloyd Jones in this chapter come from this interview.

16. Quoted in *Los Angeles Times*, July 1984.

17. David Hoerl, interview with author, August 15, 2010. All further quotations from David Hoerl in this chapter come from this interview.

18. Nat Dove, interview with author, July 10, 2009. All further quotations from Nat Dove in this chapter come from this interview.

19. *New York Times*, July 4, 1970.

20. Big Mama Thornton in an Interview with Roy Greenberg on July 3, 1980 (Roy Greenberg Collection [MUM00208] in the Blues Archive, The Department of Archives and Special Collections, J.D. Williams Library, University of Mississippi).

21. Quoted in *Los Angeles Times*, July 1984.

22. Ibid.

23. Ibid.

Bibliography

Books

Fairchild, Charles. *Pop Idols and Pirates: Mechanisms of Consumption and the Global Circulation of Popular Music.* Burlington: Ashgate Publishing Company, 2008.

Gart, Galen, and Roy C. Ames. *Duke /Peacock Records: An Illustrated History with Discography.* Milford, N.H.: Big Nickel Publications, 1990.

Gordon, Robert. *Can't Be Satisfied. The Life and Times of Muddy Waters.* New York: Back Bay Books, 2002.

Govenar, Alan. *The Early Years of Rhythm & Blues. Focus on Houston.* Houston: Rice University Press, 1990.

Guy, Buddy, with David Ritz. *When I Left Home: My Story.* Boston: Da Capo Press, 2012.

Lipsitz, George. "Land of Thousand Dances: Youth, Minorities and the Rise of Rock and Roll." In *Recasting America: Culture and Politics in the Age of Cold War,* ed. Lary May, 267–84. Chicago: University of Chicago Press, 1989.

Mahon, Maureen. "Listening for Willie Mae 'Big Mama' Thornton's Voice: The Sound of Race and Gender Transgressions in Rock and Roll." *Women and Music: A Journal of Gender and Culture,* Volume 15, 2011, 1–17.

Minor, William. *Monterey Jazz Festival: Forty Legendary Years.* Santa Monica: Angel City Press, 1997.

Moonoogian, George A. "Ain't Nothin' But a Hound Dog." *Whiskey, Woman, and...,* June 1984, 4–10.

Neff, Robert, and Anthony Connor. *Blues.* New York: David R Godine, 1975.

Otis, Johnny. *Red Beans and Rice and Other Rock 'n' Roll Recipes.* San Francisco: Pomegranate Books, 1997.

Salem, James M. *The Late, Great Johnny Ace and the Transition from R&B to Rock 'n' Roll.* Urbana and New York: University of Illinois Press, 1999.

Segrest, James, and Mark Hoffman. *Moanin'at Midnight.* New York: Thunder's Mouth Press, 2004.

Shaw, Arnold. Honkers and Shouters: *The Golden Years of Rhythm and Blues.* New York: Macmillan, 1978.

Travis, Dempsey J. *An Autobiography of Black Jazz.* Chicago: Urban Research Institute, 1983.

White, Charles. *The Life and Times of Little Richard.* New York: Harmony Books, 1984.

Wyman, Bill. *Rolling with the Stones.* New York: DK ADULT, 2002.

Newspapers and Magazines

Audio 70, no. 7–12, 56.

Billboard, December 29, 1951; March 7, 1953; March 14, 1953; September 26, 1953; December 19, 1953; May 8, 1954; November 20, 1965; October 1, 1966; August 9, 1969.

Cash Box, March 29, 1954; April 1954.

Charleston Gazette, February 28, 1970.

Chicago Defender, August 2, 1952, 22.

Ebony, 35/11, September 1980.

Gleason, Ralph J. "Interview: Big Mama Thornton." *San Francisco Chronicle.*

Jazz Journal 18, no. 11 (November 1965).

Los Angeles Times, July 1984; December 1984.

Melody Maker, May 23, 1964, 9.

New York Age Defender, April 24, 1954.

New York Times, July 1, 1973; July 2, 1980; July 4, 1980.

Oakland Tribune, November 11, 1966; January 10, 1967; April 6, 1970.

Propes, Steve. "Nate Mc Coy and Sotoplay Records." *B&R* 193 (2004), 18–19.

Rolling Stone, April 19, 1990.

San Mateo Times, May 10, 1968.

Star News, March 7, 1970.

The News (Van Nuys), November 21, 1969.

Variety, April 28, 1954.

Vulliamy, Ed. "Robert Plant: The Showman Must Go On." *Observer*, January 30, 2011. (http://www.guardian.co.uk/music/2011/jan/30/robert-plant-band-joy-interview), accessed February 10, 2012.

Other Cited Material

Erlewine, Michael. Interview with Big Mama Thornton, August 3, 1969. Tape, Private Collection, Michael Erlewine.

Greenberg, Roy. Interview with Big Mama Thornton, July 3, 1980. Roy Greenberg Collection (MUM00208) in the Blues Archive, The Department of Archives and Special Collections, J.D. Williams Library, The University of Mississippi.

Orr, John. "Johnny Otis' R&B Caravan keeps on rolling. A talk with one of the great champions of music," 2000. (http://triviana.com/BLUES/sfb00/otis.htm), accessed January 20, 2012.

Rosen, Joe. "Big Mama Thornton." (http://www.bluesaccess.com/No_27/rosen.html), accessed January 20, 2012.

Strachwitz, Chris. "Interview with Big Mama Thornton," October 20, 1965. Big Mama Thornton in Europe, CD, Arhoolie 9056.

_____. Liner notes, 2005. Big Mama Thornton in Europe. Arhoolie Production. Inc., CD 9056.

_____. Liner notes. Big Mama Thornton

"Ball 'n' Chain." Arhoolie Production, Inc., CD 305.

Topping, Ray. Liner notes. Big Mama Thornton: The Original Hound Dog. Ace Records CDCHD 940, 1990.

Wood, Roger. "Eldorado Ballroom." Handbook of Texas Online. (http://www.tshaonline.org/handbook/online/articles/xde02), accessed January 20, 2012. Published by the Texas State Historical Association.

Interviews Conducted by the Author

Except where noted the following were telephone interviews.

Anthony, James, August 30, 2009.

Arnold, Mac, July 24, 2010.

Bascomb, Wilbur, August 21, 2010.

Big Walker, Derrick, October 3, 2009.

Bland, Edward, March 17, 2012. Interview via email.

Book Binder, Roy, August 8, 2008. Interview via email.

Brown, Texas Johnny, March 6, 2012.

Brown, Tommy, July 5, 2009

Burkhart, Toney, August 5, 2011. Interview via email.

Camp, Dave, December 10, 2009.

Copley, Al, August 10, 2010. Interview via email.

Davis, Willa, August 21, 2012. Interview via email.

DeRouen, Terry, July 1, 2010.

Dove, Nat, July 10, 2009.

Erlewine, Michael, May 3, 2009. Interview via email.

Field, Kim, February 2, 2012.

Gaines, Grady, March 2, 2012.

Gallagher, Peter, February 17, 2010

George, Garry, March 22, 2012. Interview via email.

Geraci, Anthony, August 5, 2010. Interview via email.

Giles, Nelson, October 30, 2009. Interview via email.

Gurley, James, May 1, 2008.

Hoerl, David, August 15, 2010. Interview via email.

Bibliography

Hopkins, Milton, February 19, 2010.

Huston, Chris, May 5, 2012. Interview via email.

Jones, Lloyd, March 15, 2010.

Kilgore, John, June 10, 2010.

Latraverse, Plume, November 16, 2009. Interview via email.

Lenart, Paul, August 4, 2009.

Lessman, Mark, November 20, 2009. Interview via email.

Mac Leod, Doug, November 15, 2009.

Malick, Peter, June 10, 2004.

Mazzolini, Tom, August 10, 2004. Interview via email.

McCracklin, Jimmy, July 10, 2009.

McDevitt, Chas, July 2, 2012. Interview via email.

McKechnie, Doug, May 29, 2012. Interview via email.

Moore, Jimmy, March 5, 2009.

Moore, Scotty, July 2010. Interview via email.

Morris, Sandy, October 25, 2009. Interview via email.

Papaila, Dan, April 10, 2009. Interview via email.

Pearl, Bernie, November 5, 2010. Interview via email.

Perkoff, Benjamin, March 23, 2012.

Pickett, Michael, October 20, 2009.

Principato, Tom, October 14, 2009.

Rau, Fritz, January 10, 2010.

Ross, Robert, August 10, 2009.

Scott, Jimmy, March 6, 2009. Interview via email.

Sheffield, Bill, February 7, 2009. Interview via email.

Thompson, Ron, November 28, 2009.

van Ray, Jan, March 17, 2012. Interview via email.

Ward, Michael "Mudcat," August 6, 2010. Interview via email.

Winer, Paul, October 11, 2012.

Yeldham, Perry, October 10, 2009.

Zialcita, Carlos, May 1, 2008.

Index

Index

Index

Index

Index

ALPH

R 080123151

ALPHARETTA
Atlanta-Fulton Public Library